Back to Mandalay

An inside view of Burma

Gerry Abbott

Back to Mandalay

An inside view of Burma

Gerry Abbott

Impact Books

First published in Great Britain 1990
by Impact Books, 26 Market Square, Bromley, Kent BR1 1NA

© Gerry Abbott 1990

ISBN: 0-245-60135-X

Typeset by Photoprint, Torquay, Devon

Printed and bound by The Guernsey Press, Guernsey

*For my friend Thant who
like all good teachers taught me
far more than she knew.*

Acknowledgements

I want to thank the University of Manchester for agreeing to my secondment to the University of Mandalay, and The British Council for supporting me in that post. To the many Burmese people who were so kind to me during my two-year stay, I owe a great debt. In an attempt to repay a little of that kindness, I have arranged for my royalties to be credited to a non-political educational trust for the support of Burmese students. If you bought this book, thank you for your contribution; if you would like to make a donation, however small, please make out your cheque to PROSPECT BURMA and send it to: PROSPECT BURMA Educational Trust, 138 Victoria Rise, London SW4 0NW, United Kingdom.

Apologies are due to Liz, whose husband shut himself away for hours on end day after day to hammer at his old typewriter, but who has not suffered any other ill effects.

Finally, I am bound to have made a few mistakes; I apologise for these in advance and would be grateful for any corrections you care to send to me via the publishers.

All photographs were taken by the author.

Front and back covers: Sunset behind Mandalay Palace, and its reflection in the palace moat.

Contents

1. Arrivals   1
2. Appearances   13
3. Face Values   32
4. Golden Land   44
5. Burmese and English   63
6. Twilit Scenes   76
7. Creatures Great and Small   94
8. The Other Woman   106
9. History Ancient and Modern   120
10. Soldiers Old and New   132
11. *Yaddayā-Kyi*   142
12. 8/8/88   157
13. Massacre   171
14. Departures   182
15. Waiting   202

Postscript   213
Appendix: The Sagaing Massacre   216
Bibliography   219

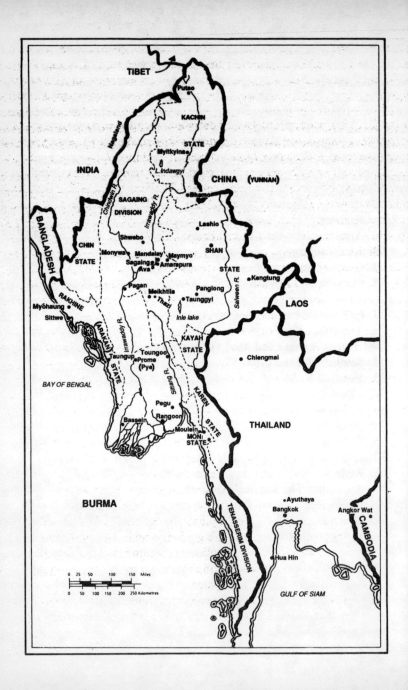

Dear Reader,

When I started writing in Mandalay my intention was simply to share my day-to-day experiences with you. As I became more interested in Burmese culture, I read up and included more about that; and as political matters started coming to a head, I recorded these too. In consequence it is only fair to warn that this book is neither fish nor flesh, though there may be some good red herring. If you are interested only in the modern narrative you have my permission to skip a historical chunk here, a cultural chunk there.

I wrote the Postscript well before the book was ready for publication, but I have let it stand. Since that time we have seen people-power working with almost unbelievable success in eastern Europe and within the USSR, and Mongolia is also on the move; yet many have forgotten, if they ever knew, that it was the people of Burma who tried it first and bled most. Rather than suffer an intolerable loss of face Ne Win slaughtered thousands, many of them students. Those who fled into the jungles have been hunted, tortured, executed. For the benefit of credulous (or just plain cynical) foreigners whom he depends on for vital foreign exchange, he has permitted the holding of a general election of sorts; but only after subjecting his main opposition leaders to house arrest or worse. Chief among these is Aung San Suu Kyi, reviled by his media because she is married to a foreigner: an Englishman. Lately, as if trying to hide Burma's wounds, he has attempted to prettify Rangoon and Mandalay, and maybe other towns. He has provided parks and potted plants; he has widened streets at the expense of trees and people's gardens; and he has used this campaign as an excuse for demolishing dwellings and displacing thousands of townsfolk by herding them into trucks and dumping them somewhere in the countryside.

The petulant vengeance, the xenophobia, the cosmetic tarting-up – all were predictable, all were in character, as I think the following pages will show.

G.A., June 1990

1. Arrivals

'You still want to go on this flight, is it?'

There had been a slight frowning of slender eyebrows as the Singapore Airlines girl looked at the two Burma Airways Corporation bookings; a hint of disapproval.

'Yes, please.'

After months of waiting for the Burmese Government to give the go-ahead; after decorating and preparing our house for tenants; after packing the crates and doing the paperwork necessary for their insurance and despatch to Rangoon; after driving my little white Suzuki jeep to Liverpool for shipment; after many an evening spent listening to Burmese exercises on cassette and trying to imitate the nasal vowels and the tones; and after the last goodbyes – after all this, we had stepped out of the Manchester winter, sunk into our Club class seats and, as the jumbo jet levelled out, enjoyed a free gin-and-tonic with hors d'oeuvres of smoked oysters and salmon. Liz sipped, nibbled, sighed, sat back and shed tears of pure relief and contentment. A superb meal with a good Bordeaux rouge, a liqueur, a doze. When I awoke briefly, we were landing at Athens and a Singapore girl in *sarong kebaya* was sitting opposite me, looking devastatingly demure. Then I slept most of the way.

During the necessary three-day stopover in Singapore, we had spent most of our time shopping for essentials: jerrycans and an extra spare tyre for the jeep; two big electric fans and a large electric kettle; plenty of insecticide sprays and a mosquito-killing vapour dispenser; and (found by Liz in a back-street shophouse after a search that took most of a morning) a couple of sturdy old-fashioned rat-traps of the sort that break your fingers if you set them clumsily. We were ready to go to Burma. We had read and heard enough about the country to know that it was 'different',

an exception to many rules; and here in the well-ordered, hushed
spaciousness of Changi airport, I had begun to feel the difference
already. There had been no large-scale maps of Burma anywhere
in town or in the airport's bookshops. There had been a hint of
a warning in the Singapore girl's momentary frown. Now here we
were, sitting in the Gate B24 departure lounge with only one other
passenger despite the fact that the flight had been called long before
and it was almost time for take-off.

It is very still. A security officer moves across the deep carpet to
open the exit door and finds it locked. He takes out a walkie-talkie.

'Hello. Bravo 2–4. Can you open number seven door or not?'

A junior-looking employee brings the wrong key and goes out
again. Departure time was 12.45 hours, five minutes ago. I become
aware of a faint hammering sound near the entrance to the lounge.
A corpulent Chinese-looking man is gesticulating and mouthing
through the thick plate glass. An armed security man opens the
door and there is an altercation in Chinese as the fat man hobbles
in, half a dozen heavy bags of hand-luggage bobbling about him so
that he can hardly walk. More passengers arrive, also grotesquely
overladen. One of them has a very large zipped holdall slung over
one shoulder, a camera bag over the other. With his right hand he
hauls behind him a groaning shopping-trolley, and in the other he
holds two bursting carrier bags; one of these is stuffed full of
cartons of '555' cigarettes and the other one clinks, so I know that
it contains a few bottles of Johnny Walker Red Label whisky. (It
has been well-known for decades that these particular yellow-and-
gold packaged cigarettes and this particular red-and-gold labelled
whisky are the standard 'presents' for Customs and security forces
personnel in Burma.) Now another altercation. A late-comer is
loudly protesting in English that he must go out into the main
concourse 'to get a drink of water', but the security officer is
adamant. After several more tries the 'thirsty' passenger demands
that, in that case, he must use the telephone. I wonder what sort
of shady business is being thwarted. The passenger gets his way
eventually and makes several calls in urgent, muted Chinese,
waving one arm as if attempting to dismiss everyone else from the
departure lounge. Urgent rearrangements are being made.

At last we move. On the bus, the Burma Airways pilot is
carrying, apart from the standard fat black case, a fat white carrier

bag closed with staples and clearly labelled in English: TO U HLA MYINT, SUPERINTENDENT OF CUSTOMS, RANGOON AIRPORT. The Fokker F28 looks a little puny compared with the Airbuses and Boeings. On board we find the first two rows of seats folded down to accommodate one Toshiba V75TR video-cassette recorder, one other VCR and a carton large enough to contain a couple of television sets. The rear of the cabin is also stacked with new electronic equipment. Presumably all this stuff belongs to the BAC crew and/or ground staff, since there is plenty of room in the hold for the baggage of the twelve passengers. We are the only Europeans on board. We pick a couple of seats and settle down. Liz leans forward and smashes a cockroach with a file that I have been reading. There is a perfunctory and incomplete demonstration of safety procedures by swaying Burmese air hostesses as we wobble across the tarmac.

Perfect flying weather and a perfect flight. Not a cloud, no turbulence, just blue sky hazing into blue sea. Now, through my starboard porthole, I can see below me as clear as on a map the Tenasserim coastline running northwards towards the Irrawaddy delta and Rangoon.

Arriving at Rangoon's Mingaladon Airport in a small BAC plane with only ten other passengers is a Very Good Thing. Whenever a Thai jumbo jet disgorges a couple of hundred tourists into its cramped and out-of-date premises, staffed by 'present'-hungry personnel, the process of entering Burma is bedlam. This we learned later. As it was, even without any cartons of '555' or bottles of Johnny Walker, we were through the formalities in no time. The only delay was caused by the one-year visas that the Burmese Embassy in London had given us. The standard procedure was to enter on a seven-day visa; tourists were allowed no extensions, and those on bona fide business had their stay extended grudgingly, a week or two at a time, until high-level permission for a year's stay was obtained. The Burmese Embassy's expansive gesture caused consternation at the Immigration desk. No one had seen one of these visas before, and while the officer dealing with us rummaged around in a drawer containing pads and rubber stamps other staff drifted over to look at the visa and look us over. Our passports were finally given a three-month endorsement, this being the longest extension that the airport was equipped – or perhaps permitted – to issue. This was my first taste of what I later called the 'institutionalised xenophobia' of Burma, a rejection of things foreign that owed very little to the prejudices of the Burmese but a great deal to the isolationist policy of General Ne Win, a policy he had enforced for a quarter of a century.

Rangoon was a depressed and shabby city full of cheerful and neatly-dressed people. In the first few days I became aware of two major facets of Burmese life: on the one hand the meagre material resources available to the vast majority of people and, on the other, the wealth of spiritual resource and physical resourcefulness that the Burmese can call upon in time of need. There is surely no other country so deeply Buddhist as Burma, where Buddhism is like an immense reservoir, calm, profound, and a source of unfailing power. To a good Buddhist, a lack of material wealth is not worrisome; all worldly goods are but a transitory illusion to be set aside if one is to continue along the path to nirvana. But in the face of real need, Burmese inventiveness comes to the fore, and something can always be improvised.

An early illustration of this was provided by our official visit to the Rangoon University Press. It was a rather grand name for a few small machines, efficiently supervised but with insufficient equipment and an uncertain supply of paper and ink. Passing from one wing to another after watching an old German press at work, we came across an unforgettable scene as we turned towards the connecting passage. There had been a continuous faint rustling and a hum of conversation ahead of us, but as we turned into the passageway with the supervisor of the press, the murmur of voices stopped and the rustling noise increased. Lining the long passage in front of us were two rows of men seated cross-legged on the floor and facing each other. Beside each man was a stack of freshly-printed sheets; it was his job to lift a sheet off the top, fold it over and crease it smartly with a thumbnail, make another fold and give that one a sharp crease too, lay the double-folded sheet on a slowly growing pile to the other side of him and at the same time lift off the next sheet to be folded. As we strolled along the gangway past thirty or forty men struggling to do what one machine would accomplish in a matter of seconds, the air was full of the sibilance of sliding sheets of paper and the rapid zip-zap of skidding thumbnails. As we turned the corner at the other end of the corridor, there came into my mind an incongruous picture of an English meadow in high summer, the air loud with drowsy insect sounds.

That afternoon we were scheduled to visit Kanbe Teacher Training College. Because of a parade that blocked all possible routes, we arrived no less than two hours late. The purpose of our visit was to see the college in normal operation, and we felt sorry that by arriving so late we would see only the tail-end lessons of the day. What made it worse was that three of the teacher-trainers were ladies who had, until a few months previously, been postgraduate students of mine for a full year in Manchester, and I didn't want to appear unprofessional. As it happened, however, the delay afforded us an introduction to another aspect of Burmese life. We had seen the 'improvise when necessary' principle in operation; now we were to see the 'improve on reality' philosophy at work. We climbed down from the LandRover to find the all-female staff lined up as if on parade immaculately dressed, as Burmese lady teachers always were, in their teaching uniforms – a spotless white blouse with decorous sleeves, and an emerald green *longyi*, similar to a sarong), ankle-length and unpatterned. After greeting and apologising to the Principal, we were offered tea and something to nibble, and I was able to greet my three friends less formally. Outside the staffroom everything was quiet and I thought perhaps the working day was over, but no: we were now invited to see the college in action. Two things almost immediately became clear. The first was that all activity had been frozen for two and a half hours so that the original programme could be seen in operation as planned; the second was that everything had been rehearsed as rigorously as for a passing-out parade. A patient trainee (probably the best in the college and especially selected for the occasion) was still waiting with her patient class, her elaborate visual aids at the ready. She went into action as we approached the classroom door, displaying her pretty pictures and asking her prepared questions, and her students produced perfect answers - including the lad who gave a perfect answer to a question that had not yet been asked. In a small, modern and well-equipped room, a teacher was drilling a handful of trainees in some aspect of English pronunciation. The normal thing to do – and the best – would have been to seat them in a semicircle and engage them in some informal face-to-face practice. But the occasion demanded the showing-off of the college's electronic equipment, so she was barking into a microphone and they, wincing between their headphones, were barking back to her (and to us) through the air. Apparently, a few yards of cable were no match for a few feet of air because every now and then a student would lift off the headphones in order to hear the teacher better. We moved on, to see the language laboratories in use. . . .

The whole show, for that is what it was, was far removed from the realities of everyday college life. I knew it, my three former students knew it, and they had known that I would know it. Yet none of us raised the matter later when, off duty, there was plenty of opportunity to do so. No one suggested that the episode was a sham, any more than my old sergeant-major would have suggested that 'spit and polish' or 'bullshit' was a sham. But it would be unfair to liken our visit to an army inspection without adding that, to the Burmese, it is important that people and things should be seen to their best advantage: one should be able to look at them and say *'Hla-deh, naw?'* ('Isn't that pretty?' or 'She looks attractive, doesn't she?') And if a certain amount of surface dressing hides a multitude of sins, like pancake make-up over pockmarks; and if it involves an element of self-deception; well, perhaps when times are bad the presentable appearance is a welcome change from the intolerable reality.

What was the reality? The truth was that in the quarter-century of Ne Win's military-style rule Burma had become impoverished; that his policy of enforced isolation had deprived the people of participation in the progress that was being made elsewhere; that in this stagnation opportunities for rewarding work were almost non-existent; that wages were appallingly low and were not keeping pace with inflation; that, just as the black market was an illegal but vital partner to the legitimate one, so private tuition (most of it unlicensed and therefore also illegal) was regarded by most parents who could afford it as a necessary supplement to schooling because the education system had degenerated into a masquerade; that virtually the entire population, outside a small officer cadre, was disaffected – some said 'cowed'; and that the expression of dissatisfaction was dangerous, even in private, because the feared

Military Intelligence network, or MI for short, had its sinister informers everywhere. That, and much more, was the reality. To many, it didn't bear thinking about, and all that one could do was keep up appearances.

Meanwhile, there were all sorts of matters to be dealt with at the British Embassy. There was the introduction to the Ambassador, for example. After the initial courtesies he asked, 'D'you play golf?'
    'No, I don't.'
    'Pity. Well, unless you have a pathological hatred of the game, I'd advise you to take it up.'
    I didn't exactly hate the game, but I did resent the way it used up acres of space that would otherwise be pleasant, unspoilt countryside open to the public.
    'Well why the bloody hell wasn't I told that, before I left England? But then you wouldn't expect me to buy clubs as part of my teaching equipment, would you? Or did you think The British Council would buy me a set at the taxpayer's expense? And anyway, isn't it only the privileged military slobs who play golf? Isn't that why golf clubs are just about the only goods free of import duty? I'm not here to teach those bastards . . .'
    That is what I *wanted* to say. Instead, I said feebly, 'Well, I do rather dislike the game.'
    'Ah. Well.' The Ambassador cleared his throat and changed the subject. It wasn't exactly an auspicious start.
    Then there were certain medical precautions to see to. Mandalay, four hundred miles to the north, had its share of rabid dogs and venomous snakes. It was advisable, we had learnt, to take with us some rabies vaccine and some snakebite serum.
    The Embassy man was brisk.
    'Rabies vaccine? I think we've got enough for two . . . yes, here we are. But snakebite serum, no . . . we've only got one in the fridge. No, no, no, you can't take that one. . . . Well, then *we* wouldn't have any, would we?'
    'But here in Rangoon you can easily . . .'
    'We'll send some up when the next lot arrives.'
    Again, I didn't say what I felt like saying.
    While various bits of red tape were keeping us in Rangoon, we were able to do some sightseeing. First on the list was, of

course, the incomparable Shwedagon Hpaya. Over the previous
four hundred years it had been described by many a traveller and
by some resident in Burma. In 1586 a merchant adventurer called
Ralph Fitch found it 'the fairest place, as I suppose, that is in the
world', where everything seemed to be covered in gold leaf and
where 'a man can hardly pass by water or by land for the great
press of people, for they come from all places of the kingdom.'
In 1898 Fielding Hall, a sympathetic observer of Burmese life,
described seeing the pagoda 'as you come up the river, steaming in
from the open sea, a great tongue of flame before you'. Seven years
later another British visitor, a painter called Talbot Kelly, rather
fulsomely described the scene within the precincts of the pagoda
as 'one of golden splendour amidst which a throng, clad in all the
most delicate tints of silk, move like scattered petals from a bouquet
of roses'. Move forward two decades and we find a dismissive
Aldous Huxley writing of the Shwedagon's 'merry-go-round style
of architecture and decoration' and seeing it as 'a sacred Fun Fair
. . . more fantastic, more wildly amusing than any Bank Holiday
invention'. Somerset Maugham in 1930 saw it as 'superb, glistening
with its gold, like a sudden hope in the dark night of the soul . . .'
and on arrival at the terrace as 'the most brilliant spectacle I had
ever seen.'

We walked from the Thammada Hotel where we were staying,
climbed the steep covered stairway and stepped out at the top
into the level evening sunlight. For a few moments, barefoot
and awestricken, I stood at the head of the stairway feeling –
what was it? – yes, unworthy. Then we strolled into the stunning
golden light.

One evening, under the dim golden light of a street-lamp beside
a wide road in the centre of the main administrative area of
Rangoon, we found a cluster of about two dozen people. They
stood silent, paying close attention to the sales talk – recognisable
as such, it seems, whatever the language – of some vendor or
other. We gently nudged our way into the semicircle of onlookers.
From somewhere unseen came a supply of power just sufficient
to produce a yellow glow in a single light-bulb. The sturdy,
shiny-faced vendor was sitting cross-legged on a mat, his assistant
squatting on the pavement nearby. Between them was a little low

side-table on which stood a huge glass container like a giant bottling-jar half full of dead coiled snakes which appeared to have been pickled like fish in a thick orange-brown liquid very like the oil that floats to the top of a cold curry. On the pavement in front of the vendor were three short rows of old bottles – the tiny brown glass bottles that pharmacists, in the days of my youth, would put pills and tablets in, and plug with cotton wool to stop these rolling around. Piled in loops over the vendor's legs and drooping into the hollow of his lap were two languid, tangled pythons, the larger of which might have been six or seven feet long. When he shifted, their bodies slurped and straightway settled back into torpor.

It was soon clear that the vendor was a great showman. He held his audience spellbound with a non-stop description of the wide range of ailments and malfunctions that his snake-oil would put right in no time at all. During one episode he leaned forward, wincing with simulated pain, one hand on the small of his back. Then a flourish of the other hand towards the great jar of snake-infested liniment, a straightening of the back, a strengthening of the voice, and all was well. Another episode was narrated in a lower, more confidential tone. As he spoke, his face became long and sorrowful, he bowed his head a little, his fingers fluttered limply about his loins, his voice solemn with mourning. The patient was obviously in a sorry plight, but – a half-hearted gesture towards the powerful golden pick-me-up, a tentative rubbing motion of the palm as if he were polishing an heirloom, a sudden spreading of the hands, a raising of the arms and eyes symbolic of resurrection, a change of expression from astonishment to triumphant vigour, and who could doubt the efficacy of this extraordinary embrocation?

Several faces were turned towards us. Throughout the performance I had noticed others glancing up to see what our reaction would be. As the whole business was plainly a very serious matter, they always found me looking either absorbed or impressed. A gaunt middle-aged lady waved a banknote. The assistant dealt with her change while the vendor reverently poured a tot of viper-juice into one of the tiny bottles. Whether she hoped the potion would cure her own stiffness or promote her husband's I could not say.

While Burmese red tape was still tying us to Rangoon, we

had time to go almost everywhere on foot, and became familiar
with much of the city centre. We ate various foods, Burmese,
Chinese and Indian, with no ill effects. We saw vendors who,
pitifully poor but chirpily cheerful, had spread on the pavement in
neat arrangements the detritus of some Thai Airways flight: little
plastic containers, paper napkins, toothpicks, in-flight magazines,
disposable cutlery. Necessity is the mother of recycling; and the
Burmese, I discovered, were very good at that. I learned how
little children had been trained by impoverished parents to greet
incoming passengers at Mingaladon or outside hotels and beg
from them the complimentary orchids that a Thai air hostess had
pinned on them. Touched by the children's eagerness to possess
the gorgeous blooms, tourists would unpin them, place them on
outstretched hands and then watch, first with indignation as the
grubby little fingers discarded the flower and then with pity as the
precious safety-pin, together with the wire that had secured the
bloom to it, was carefully pocketed. We leafed through battered
secondhand books sold by a man who instead of spreading them
on the pavement used some public railings as his display unit. I
tried bargaining a book down from fifteen *kyat*, and my Burmese
worked. The vendor looked quite pleased to get five, so neither
party had lost face in the transaction.

Walking through back-streets after dark, we had discovered
how rat-infested the city was. 'Rangoon is really dirty these days,'
said one of my three former students as we were strolling with
them one day near Sule Hpaya, the city's focal point. 'We used
to have Indians to clean it up,' she said wistfully. Like many of
the Burmese that I met later, this lady harboured a strong racial
prejudice against Indians and Indian-looking people – against *kalā*.
Once upon a time, this prejudice would have been understandable.
Even before the British seized Mandalay in 1885 and annexed
Upper Burma, they had been opening up the lowlands and delta
region of Lower Burma to rice cultivation on an ever-growing
scale. This attracted farm labour from Upper Burma and for
a time the earlier settlers helped newcomers to get themselves
established by lending them capital or giving them credit. But
this boom situation started to attract increasing numbers of
Chettiars, members of a Madras sub-caste with a long tradition of
commercial dealings behind them. More and more rice farmers fell

prey to Chettiar moneylenders and absentee landlords. Moreover
the British, who mistakenly and insultingly persisted in treating
Burma as 'Further India', relied heavily on Indian personnel to
fill administrative and technical positions. Consequently, by 1930
half the population of Rangoon was Indian and Indians held more
than half of all government posts. Resentment was widespread,
and no wonder. The problem did not disappear with Independence
in 1948 and it was not until 1962 - when Ne Win began a programme
of nationalisation, beginning with the British firms ICI and the
Burmah Oil Company – that the wind of change blew cold upon a
remnant Indo-Pakistani population that was still dominating much
of the country's trade and industry. The demonetisation moves
of 1964 froze them out. By the middle of 1965, nine out of
ten Indians, and four Pakistanis in ten, had left the country
– about 109,000 people. But that was long ago. What my former
student would no doubt have liked was a docile caste of *kalā*
sweepers to do the dirty work and kill the rats.

We were impatient to end our journey and settle down to
living and working in Mandalay. At last the all-clear was given
and in the grey early morning light we were back at Mingaladon
airport – I almost wrote 'aerodrome'. On the tarmac stood nearly
all of the Burma Airways Corporation's aircraft: two Fokker F28s
and three F27s. Not only was BAC poor; it also had a poor
reputation for reliability and safety. After half an hour's flying
among, into and over huge cumulus clouds that boiled up all
around, our plane surged upwards and then plummeted, like a
bus mounting an embankment, and plunging off a precipice. An
ancient white-bearded *kalā* and his son were clutching each other
and turning terrified eyes towards me, as if they thought I ought
to do something about it. I managed a wan smile that was meant
to be reassuring but probably looked like a rictus of horror, before
the force of gravity returned and crammed my innards back into
place. Liz affected not to be very much put out by all this, merely
remarking that the flight was a bit bumpy.

The plane lost height – gently this time – and the pagoda-studded
plain of Pagān came into view, at that height looking like the
science-fiction planetscapes depicted in *Eagle* and other comics I
had read as an adolescent, like a spired city blasted by intergalactic
forces. It was in reality the surviving splendour of a kingdom

sacked by Kubla Khan in AD1287 and then left to the slow ravages of time and the elements, and to the sudden whim of a seismic wave. We continued our journey northwards and as soon as the plane began to lose height again I craned over to see the approach to Mandalay. Although I could not at that time identify the locations, I could see the pagodas – some crumbling, some twinkling, some dazzling white – of a whole history of capital cities: Ava, Sagaing, Amarapura . . . then Mandalay itself.

2. Appearances

There was a moment of uncomfortable silence. The downtown
Chinese restaurant was shabby, but the food was good and the
conversation had been warming up, for our Burmese hosts spoke
excellent English. Apart from Liz, myself and the Cultural Attaché,
who had flown up with us that morning, there were a few of Liz's
future colleagues at the teacher training college – and my Head of
Department. He was a strange, spidery man with a voice that was
quiet and indistinct because of some slight defect. No one would
have heard what he'd said if there hadn't been a sudden lull in the
conversation.

'I don't think they should have sent Gerry to the university.'

He couldn't have said anything more un-Burmese, though
he was as Burmese as they come, or more inappropriate at
a welcoming dinner anywhere in the world. The party chatter
immediately started up again, a little too brightly, but my HoD had
got his message across: I was a joker in the pack, I would probably
rock the boat and upset the apple-cart, I was a nuisance. His tired
cynicism had communicated itself from the moment we had met at
the airport building, strolled towards the training college's waiting
pick-up with its star-crazed windscreen, tossed our cases in the
back and clambered in after them. He had tried to opt out of this
dinner party, first saying that his wife wasn't very well and then
protesting, 'But I am mending my motorbike.'

Next morning we were picked up and taken to see our places
of work and meet our other colleagues; and I was relieved to find
that mine were as pleasant as Liz's – quite unlike the HoD. In each
institution, instead of being given a desk in the staffroom we had
been allocated a separate room. For me a store-room, long, narrow
and high-ceilinged, had been cleared out and painted a bright blue

– Reckitt's blue, I called it. At the eastern end was a wooden louvred window through which I could see some sizeable trees-just outside, with one or two pigs rooting about underneath them; and just beyond, a small roundabout whose central island was fenced off and contained a shrubbery overgrown with bougainvillea. Somehow a cow had got in there. My long echoing room contained a large wooden desk, a chair and a bookshelf. I sat down at my chair by the window. This lone splendour was ambivalent. On the one hand my Burmese hosts were doing their best for me, as their culture bade them; but on the other, they were attempting to comply with the orders contained in a recently-issued circular which forbade them to have any dealings with foreigners unless it was unavoidable, in which case they were to write a detailed report on what had happened and what had been said. From time to time over the previous thirty years I had worked in a dozen countries, most of them in Africa and Asia; if Burma's people were among the most hospitable I had met, its government was certainly the most xenophobic.

By the time I left to go back to the hotel, the HoD had impressed it upon me that there was no point in turning up for work before ten, that I was not to push the Burmese pace, and that none of his staff was any good.

On that first day of work, I came out of the Mandalay Hotel and greeted a group of fellows squatting in a circle on the paving stones.

'*Mingalaba*,' they echoed with broad grins. Two stayed squatting, staring at the state of a game of draughts played with stones on roughly-drawn squares, but the rest ushered me round the corner, each pressing me to go in *his* horse-cart.

'*Ma-houq-bú*,' I objected. '*Saiq-ka shí-dha-la?*'

'*Shí-deh, shí-deh!*' shouted one of them, pointing to the only trishaw in sight, parked in the shade of a flame-of-the-forest. The bidding started at twenty *kyat* and came down to ten. Chatting as we went along, I couldn't decide which of us was poorer at the other's language: but we managed to establish that we were both married and both had three children. I couldn't, however, persuade him that *saiq-ka* was the English word 'side-car' borrowed by the Burmese. He appeared to be convinced that this type of pedicab was a Burmese invention and that therefore the word must be

Burmese, the Europeans having borrowed both the technology and
the term from Burma. I didn't contradict him; he had graduated
from Mandalay University the year before, and was fairly sure of his
facts. He wasn't right about the word – that I knew – but perhaps
he was right about the invention. A certain Major Raven-Hart, who
had canoed up 'the road to Mandalay' shortly before the Second
World War broke out, noted how cheap the trams were ('two miles
for a penny') and went on to mention:

> a curious vehicle invented I believe here. It is a cycle, not a motor cycle,
> with a diminutive side-car into which two people can fold themselves:
> there is about as much room for each as in a doll's perambulator. The
> side-car part is gaily painted. . . . (Raven-Hart, 1939:194)

The seats, facing fore and aft, could also be used for cargo.
A dozen mattresses could be stacked on the side-car, tied together
and lashed to the cycle-frame; and I once saw scores of cushions of
various brilliant hues, piled about three metres high on a *saiq-ka*
and wobbling their way through Mandalay like a vendor's clustered
balloons across a fairground.

The leisurely twenty-minute ride to work was very pleasant at
that time of year, January being cool and sunny. Groups of young
children all dressed in green and white were toddling off to school.
Their teachers, also in green and white, sedately pedalled along or
elegantly sat side-saddle behind a husband. Ancient small-nosed
buses, stuffed full of people and with a dozen men clinging at the
back and maintaining a foothold on a step or a piece of coachwork,
trundled past knots of cyclists and stopped to pick up yet more
people, only to be overtaken by the cyclists, then overtake and be
overtaken again. The tenor of town traffic was gentle. Occasionally
on a main route a private pick-up bus would come scorching into
town, slow down with a squeal and then dart impatiently among
cyclists, pedestrians and cows, overtaking anything except an army
truck, careening under its load of people and goods, half of whom
and most of which clung precariously on the outside of the vehicle,
and emitting a brassy blare every other second. But then it was
gone, and you were back with the creak and clicking of bicycles, the
chatter and laughter, the rumble of an old dilapidated 'line bus'.

Turning south on to 73rd Street we joined a continuous
flow of bicycles and trishaws all heading towards the university,

where the first lectures would be starting in a few minutes. The southward stream occupied the whole road, and the few motor vehicles heading north nosed their way slowly, like tugs going up a river. Through the main gate we glided into the campus and up to the little roundabout, around which the cyclists went to right or left as the fancy took them; here, by the steps leading up to the portico of the main building, sat long rows of students. This was where, morning after morning, I ran a long gauntlet of long stares – frank, unabashed curiosity written all over scores of bright faces – punctuated with mutterings, nudges and giggles.

Within a few days I was on friendly terms with my departmental colleagues and even with my HoD, who never ceased to exasperate me for the whole of my stay. One of those first mornings, just out of interest, I asked him where the men's toilet was. I wasn't dying to make use of it, and this was just as well. He paused before replying.

'Because, you see' (he had a habit of answering questions as if they all began with 'why'), 'we are not treated as we should be . . .' and he set off on a monologue of grumbles. I tried to steer him back to the question, but he spent half an hour not answering it. Then there was a pause into which I leaped.

'What do *you* do, then?'

'I try to make sure before I leave home that I won't need to use the toilet.'

'But when you *do* want to go, what do you do then?'

'I get on my motorbike and go home.'

He lived several kilometres away in the centre of town. I gave up and a colleague, who took me upstairs, pointed it out with no hesitation. I swear the HoD didn't know where it was. Some days later I bearded him again. I had asked in the staffroom about the BA and MA syllabuses and had been told that there were none there, so I asked him where I could consult them.

'Because, you see,' he began, 'we have to make do with what we have . . .'

This time I interrupted the familiar-sounding catalogue of woes several times. Surely there was something on paper informing both students and staff about the content of courses? My persistence made him testy.

'You can just concentrate on getting the Embassy to give us

(and here came a list of goodies including a photocopier and some cassette recorders). These will justify your presence here.'

With such egregious psychology, I discovered, he had alienated himself from every single member of his staff. Including me.

Thanks to some friendly and helpful Australians working on the Mandalay Water Project, we were able to move into the project's guest bungalow for a time, and there it was that Auntie Than Than came on her bicycle to see us one day. She was in her sixties and, having an ailing husband, had decided to become a 'broker', as she called herself – a sort of house agent. Older women like younger people to call them, in Burmese, 'aunt' or 'elder sister'. The word 'auntie', traditionally used by British youngsters when talking or referring to adult women, therefore fits Burmese custom very well. With Auntie, we walked or pedalled around the quiet streets of the old 'Civil Lines' area, where officers of the British administration used to live in the good old bad old days. They weren't bad as far as Auntie was concerned. She remembered the days that I had learned about when I was in primary school during the war, when most of the map on the wall – including Burma – was red, when Burma was the world's leading exporter of good rice and fine teak, when a farmer or teacher could earn a decent wage and buy decent things in the shops, when . . . Sometimes words would fail her and, after sighing 'Ah, Burma, Burma!' she would fall silent.

One day we were walking into a house for rent when Auntie rushed up from behind me, pushed past, wrenched some clothing from a washing-line strung across the door and threw it on to a nearby chair. It was women's underclothing, and I assumed that she had found it very embarrassing and therefore removed it fast; but I later found out that she was preventing me from walking underneath it, and was therefore saving me from sub-servience to woman – not (I think) that particular woman, but womankind.

Within a few days we had found a grand old house that we liked the feel of. Front steps under a portico led up to a floor that was well above any conceivable flood level, the doors were of adzed teak, the handles of solid brass, the atmosphere cool and dry. And, very important, the owner was a very likeable man. The house consisted mainly of five large rooms. On either side of the

centrally-placed hall were a living-room and a dining-room, and
above these were two bedrooms. The fifth room, above the high
portico, we earmarked as our study. A teak staircase wound up
from the hall. Each bedroom had a mosquito-netted balcony, one
of them with a little Buddha-shrine added, and from these balconies
you could look down on a bordered lawn framed by a semicircular
drive. To the rear was a long garden full of mango trees, coconut
palms, pomelo trees and saplings of lemon and lychee, and more.
A lofty water-tower was half-hidden by a banana tree.

Both house and grounds were rather large for only two people
(our children were now in their twenties and would not be staying
with us), but we had chosen with a view to the future. When
the time came to leave Burma, it was unlikely that another
husband-and-wife team would be found to fill our teaching posts.
Two families might have to share this accommodation for some
time if the Burmese bureaucracy was as cumbersome and dilatory
as we had been led to believe, and in this place they wouldn't be
forever falling over each other. Also, if our venture prospered and
it was decided to re-establish a British library in Mandalay (the
original one had been closed in the Sixties), there was plenty of
room for an extension or an extra building if you sacrificed a few
fruit trees. The house itself was – I hope it still is – a handsome
residence, a framework of massive teak beams bolted together,
the walls filled in with panels of brick nogging, the upper storey
floored with teak planks, the lower tiled. If it hadn't been for its
corrugated-iron roof, it would have looked from a distance very
like a Home Counties pseudo-Tudor dwelling. It needed some
refurbishing but was good value, and we had our hearts set on it.
We didn't know it at the time, thank goodness, but it was to be six
months before we were able to move in.

It was Union Day (12th February), a national holiday. Johnny,
a Burmese employee of the Embassy, was due to arrive on
the Rangoon train at 08.00 hours in order to go over the
house estimating the costs of work to be done and materials
needed. On my way to the station I was stepping carefully over
an area of broken paving when I almost fell over a man whose
head had suddenly appeared through the crowd at knee height.
He had advanced leprosy. Very little was left of his feet, and
his hands had gone. The wrist stumps were red and raw but,

as he spidered slowly across my path, he appeared to feel
nothing of the abrasion caused by grinding them along over
gravel and broken paving stones.

The train arrived at 08.30 without Johnny. When I went to
meet the eleven o'clock train, the stationmaster said it would
be a little late – perhaps 5 o'clock. Liz and I went to a bar
just inside the Myamandala Hotel which was full of Burmese
men enjoying a beer and sounded convivial. A waiter told us
twice to go the tourist bar inside. I gently pointed out that we
were not tourists and preferred this bar, and we were eventually
served a good cold Mandalay beer. The eleven o'clock train had,
as it often did, derailed itself. It arrived at five-thirty and later
we took Johnny to the same bar, where the same waiter did the
same things. I reminded him that we were not tourists and added
that my Burmese guest would not be allowed into the other bar.
After a long discussion in the bar and at the reception desk,
it became clear that there was no beer for the Burmese (a quick look
round told me that this was true, and that several Burmese customers
were awaiting with interest the outcome of the discussions) but
there *was* beer for the tourists. The poor waiter didn't make
these rules, and the staff didn't like having to operate this
partial apartheid system. It was clearly a way of ensuring that
there was always enough beer for the precious tourists, who
brought in the foreign exchange that Ne Win desperately needed
for buying arms to kill his countrymen with; and there was the
added advantage that it helped to prevent the Burmese from mixing
with the foreigners. Johnny was tired and hungry by now, so I
gave up. As we left, I told the staff that I was sorry they were
in such a difficult situation and that I did understand their
problem. There was an outbreak of smiles.

When the March weather got rather too uncomfortable for
side-car rides, I took to horse-cart travel. In the mornings, the
horses cropped what little grass there was as they waited between
the shafts in the thin shade of a roadside tree. As I approached, a
driver would give his gaunt horse a bag of greyish chopped hay.
A group of drivers had worked out an informal rota so that my
fares would be evenly spread. They greeted me with a chorused
'*Mingalaba, hsaya*' and a galaxy of smiles; they knew who I was (a

teacher merits the name *hsaya*), where to take me and how much I would – and would not – pay.

The Mandalay horse-cart is a two-wheeled trap on leaf-springs with a low-sided body and an arched roof of four or five iron ribs covered with a fitted canopy of plastic material. The body and wheels are brightly painted with red, yellow, blue and green, and the canopy is trimmed with similar colours and decorated with appliqué floral and geometric shapes. The registration number is painted brightly too – especially vehicles 999 and 1234, whose drivers are particularly proud of their numbers. The cartwheels are shod with rubber and each has an eyebrow-shaped mudguard of wood or, occasionally, of polished brass; some carts bear old coach-lamps which even on the darkest nights are seldom lit. The horse between the shafts usually contrasts sadly with all this finery. On these early morning rides, as I stepped into the sloping cart by the little rear door and settled down on one of the wooden side-benches, I would brace myself against the rhythmic farting (I refer, of course, to the horse) that usually accompanied the hoofbeat as the cart lurched into motion. That finished, I could then enjoy the coolness of a trotting-speed breeze in the shade of the canopy, whose scalloped hem was below shoulder level. Above the hem were one or two heart-shaped mirrors for the lady who wanted to check whether her golden 'Dancing Lady' orchids were still in place in her chignon, or the girl who wanted to see if the *thanahka* leaf-shapes on her cheeks remained unsmudged. I sat near the driver, looking forwards.

Most observers of the town have been uncomplimentary about Mandalay. At first sight the flat grid of dusty unkempt streets is a disappointment to those for whom the name Mandalay has Kiplingesque resonances; but there is always something interesting to see if you watch what people are doing. One of the simple everyday sights that I became fond of was the sugarcane crushers at work. Leaning against a shady tree there would be a few dozen tall sugar canes, and nearby a small stack of half-metre lengths. A squatting figure would be stripping the green skin off these and placing the juice-laden sticks ready for crushing, in a bowl by the machine. This was similar to one of those old-fangled mangles that used to squeeze water out of our laundry. Rotate the handle vigorously and the shiny metal rollers turned and we were kept in motion for some time by the large and heavy vertical flywheel, painted kingfisher blue and with spokes of various pastel colours. Around Mingala market and down 73rd Street the large technicolour wheels spun prettily, squeezing out a cheap refreshing drink which did not - as many bottled confections did – leave the drinker thirstier than before, and which cost a lot less.

Not far from the university gates, sitting back from the road on a patch of wasteland, was the emblematic and slightly disturbing figure of the paper-buyer. He sat at a low table that seemed always to be laden with used exercise-books, and before him hung the two large pans of his weighing-scales, which flashed in the morning light and gave his distant face an intermittent luminance. The weighing-scales were suspended from what can only be described as a little gibbet, and a sinister bunch of dead or dying flowers was tied to the top as if in memory of something. He bought all kinds of reusable paper, but exercise-books seemed to be his main stock-in-trade. Weeks, months, years of learning were weighed and found to be worth a few *pya* – enough to buy one glass of sugarcane juice. In my imagination, he was The Final Marker, sitting in judgement and pronouncing Education and Paper Qualifications worthless. The paper itself was useful, though: market and roadside vendors all over town used bags made out of folded and pasted newspaper, out-of-date official forms and leaflets, exam scripts, exam papers and, most of all, old exercise-books. We bought some local grapes in a bag that read:

1. I do not play. He does not play.
(or)I do not play, nor does he.

2. He did not go. I did not go.
(or) Neither he nor I went . . .

In the Department of English, those of us not teaching would sit and chat, sipping *ye-nwe-gyan* (green tea) from small cups. The staff were fairly representative of Burmese society: the Head, who seldom came into the staffroom and never stayed, was a Christian married to a Muslim lady; Charity was a Karen and a Baptist and was seldom without a spray of jasmine or some substitute in her silver-streaked hair; Abel was of *kalā* stock and consequently had grievances about the way his family had been discriminated against by the authorities; Kanti was a handsome and boyish Burman, a conscientious teacher; and Thant was the most hardworking of all, a slender, gentle woman, quietly efficient and with that toughness of spirit that few Burmese women lack. These were the teachers I chatted to the most. One day Ma Thant asked me, 'How do you come to the university?'

'By horse-cart,' I said, pouring more *ye-nwe-gyan*.

'Not trishaw?'

'No. I don't like the idea of a man having to push my weight along in this weather.'

'You feel sorry for him?'

'Well, yes.'

'I feel sorry for the horse; the horse has no choice.'

'Hm. I'll have to think about that one.'

On the way home a few days later, my *myin-hleh* overtook No. 131, which was being pulled by a tiny emaciated horse that would have been white if clean, and whose uncertain, knock-kneed legs kept up a brave trot only because the driver was clubbing its bony haunches with a heavy stick. The poor creature's tongue was lolling pink and obscene out of the side of its mouth, and its eyes looked anguished. A few days later I saw two men cursing and sweating as they pushed and pulled a cart on which lay a bag of skin and bones that minutes ago had been a horse. It wasn't the same one, but I thought of what Ma Thant had said and felt sorry for the poor underfed animal that was now pulling me along, for the afternoons were getting uncomfortably hot. The streets melted and black boils appeared under a skin of pale dust. The clip-clop of hoofs was muffled as the horseshoes branded the tar with deep glistening scars, and the road hissed like Sellotape as it unstuck itself from the wheels.

After a kilometre or so the horse's neck would go down and the pace would slacken to a walk. Morning flatulence was no longer a problem, but now there was another hazard. As the long hot day wore on, the drivers became drowsier, the horses wearier; but the flies buzzed more loudly and tormented the poor beasts more and more, so even the most exhausted animal preferred walking in the sun to standing still as a target in the shade. Slung just below the horse's tail there is a hessian dung-bag which is occasionally emptied into the street; but of course quite a lot adheres to the bag and dries off. Now even when a horse is trotting, a persistent fly can tickle or sting in a sensitive spot, causing the tail to swish; and this flourish sweeps dried remnants of dung into the slipstream, which carries it on to your face, into your hair and over your clothing. For some time I thought I was regularly being blinded by dust and chaff raised by a passing breeze or vehicle. When I discovered the true cause I decided to sit with my back to the horse at the risk of missing something interesting. Confucius he say, what might catch eye maybe not worth what eye might catch.

In our first two months we moved our things four times between the Water Project's guest bungalow and two hotels, project staff having priority when they came back from Australia or from drilling wells upcountry; but by the middle of March 'home' was a temporarily-rented house at the end of a lane on the eastern edge of the town. Beyond its gate was an overgrown pond, a canal and then miles of fields stretching to the fringe of the Shan plateau. A few of our things had finally cleared Customs and arrived in Mandalay. I had piled them into a horse-cart, loading it almost to the canopy. Then the driver and I had a good laugh when I had to travel spread-eagled, lying on my stomach in the little remaining space.

Having a house of our own was wonderful after operating from a small hotel room or guest room, but the house had one serious snag which became obvious as we walked home after dark. The lane was dimly illuminated at lengthy intervals by a series of light-bulbs tapping the overhead supply cable, which came to an end just outside our gate. As you approached our house, you moved from white lights to yellow and from yellow to orange, and the last few dwindled to dim red points, like distant stars receding from the earth. By the time the supply reached us, there was hardly any power in the cable. In daylight hours the current wasn't too bad, but at dusk the airconditioner would judder noisily and switch itself off, the fridge would fall silent, the lights would dim until it was impossible to read and the television would blink once or twice and go to sleep. Fortunately the people of Mandalay, a vast village of half a million souls, went to bed early. The lights would brighten and the television worked. (Not that there was much to see: broadcasts didn't start until 7 p.m. and closed down at 9.45, and the content was abysmal for the most part.) The fridge would start humming again; and by eleven it was possible to run one airconditioner and cool the bedroom.

The most exciting of the television programmes was an old American series in which a man called Charlie employed a small team of intelligent and highly capable young lovelies to do what the FBI could not do. *Charlie's Angels* was just about worth watching, in the circumstances. The first class that I had been given to teach was the second-year MA group. It comprised three young women, all attractive and each as different as chalk from cheese or chinaware. I had, to their amusement, dubbed them 'Gerry's Angels'. They proceeded to spoil me, bringing me little meals, providing me with Mandalay sandals, presenting me with small gilt and lacquered boxes for my pens and pencils, and so on. It was the traditional, delightful way of showing respect to one's teacher, one's *hsaya*; but the Burmese in general have a genius for making people feel good by giving them little presents. These young ladies were conscientious students. One was a Shan, pale-skinned and very fashion-conscious: whenever she thought she could get away with it, she wore her *longyi* well above ankle-length. I always knew when she was really absorbed in a task I had set, because she would slip off her left sandal, put her foot up on the seat of her chair and rest her left cheek on her *longyi*-covered knee as she wrote. The most intelligent was a tiny Burman, twinkle-eyed and with such a small high-pitched voice that I couldn't imagine how she dealt with a class of over a hundred students – a job which, as a junior tutor, she had to tackle every day. The dreamiest of the three was willowy and tall for a Burmese girl. She always looked as if she was thinking about some boyfriend, which perhaps she was, and she had a habit of saying in all innocence things which in the West could easily be misinterpreted. Once, at the end of the day's work, she came into my room and said softly: 'Sir, I want to take you to a hotel.'

Her father's soldier-driven jeep called for her every afternoon, and she was offering me a lift to the Mandalay Hotel. (Her father, an officer, put an end to that after this one occasion: being seen with a foreigner off-campus was not desirable.) On another occasion she sought me out and leaned across my desk.

'Sir,' she breathed. 'Do you like self-control?'

She waited for my answer, her head tilted, her dark eyes dreamy, her rosebud lips parted. It turned out that 'Self Control' was the title of a pop-song current in Burma at the time.

During the austere Forties, the British used to talk a lot about 'putting a good face on things'. The phrase summarised much of Burmese daily life four decades later, both in its endearing aspects and in its exasperating ones. Probably all societies have evolved ways of avoiding loss of 'face', but in East and South-east Asia these are complex and well-developed systems. The main purpose of the Malay Code of behaviour, called *adat*, is to preserve and to encourage due respect for the established social hierarchies: but since the Burmese are far less class-conscious than the Malays, their system, called *ānadeh*, is a very different way of maintaining social harmony, or at least the appearance of it. Its purpose is to avoid causing any awk-wardness, any embarrassment, affront or feeling of indebtedness. In conversation it involves asking oneself, for example, 'Should I say this, or might it put Mr/Mrs X in the uncomfortable position of wanting to disagree, of having to refuse, of feeling unduly obliged to me?' It is sometimes said that *ānadeh* means never saying 'No' and never putting anyone else in the position of having to say it, but it is not so simple as that. The English utterance 'No' has at least five possible meanings:

I am refusing to do something for you.
I am rejecting something you have offered.
I am denying something you have mentioned.
I am disagreeing with your opinion.
I am answering your 'Yes-or-No' question.

Burmans don't mind answering 'No' to straightforward ques-tions such as 'Is this Room 8?' However, they do avoid using the other types of 'No'. Incidentally, the opportunity of *voting* No never arose: the people had no vote, and the members of the Hlutdaw, an appointed Council of Ministers, were never free to vote against any proposal. But this was nothing new; Padre Sangermano, an Italian priest resident in Burma from 1783 to 1806, says of the Hlutdaw of the day:

> All orders or favours emanating from the Emperor . . . must pass
> through this tribunal, not because it has power to modify them, but in
> order to be registered and speedily put in execution. (p. 81)

As a lubricant against friction in everyday social matters, and
with Burmese cheerfulness as an additive, *ānadeh* contrived to
make life seem pleasant in circumstances that were beginning to
try the forbearance of the long-suffering public; but as a system
for avoiding or concealing the unwelcome truth, it was a massive
hindrance to reform. It evolved in days of old when the kingdom
was a court and a people, with no complicated administrative
hierarchy between king and peasant. Now, there was a Party
network spreading from the Chairman, Ne Win himself, down
through all walks and stations of life and pauperising the people
just as roots impoverish the soil. (Politicians seem unaware of
this implication when they talk smugly of the support they enjoy
'at grass roots level'.) This network was military in its senior
personnel and in its methods: even simply to get an electricity
supply and a telephone connection we had to await the decision
of a local committee chaired by a Lieutenant-Colonel. Within the
hierarchy, people at every level were afraid of the ranks above.
Occasionally there was an official announcement that constructive
criticism of government policies was welcome; but with things as
bad as they were any worthwhile suggestion would have been an
implied negative criticism, and when I drew such announcements
to the attention of my Burmese friends they would extend their
arms towards me with the wrists pressed together as if handcuffed
and smile sadly. From a cultural point of view it could be said
that *ānadeh* forbade any person to discomfit another by drawing
attention to an unpalatable fact; from a political point of view it
would be true to say that fear prevented anyone from admitting
the truth to a superior. The informers of the MI, the Military
Intelligence network, were said to be everywhere.

People went to great pains, in fact, to assure the authorities that
all was well. On one occasion, for example, when the Minister of
Education said he would like to speak to us over a cup of tea at
Liz's college, her colleagues gave her a thorough briefing: she was
not to mention the fact that for the second year running the trainees
had had no teaching-practice, nor was she to confess that the college
was unable to show its trainees how best to use the school textbooks

as the Minister himself had directed, because the college had not
been supplied with copies of the textbooks, nor was she to admit et
cetera, et cetera. Of course she avoided these topics; and when the
Minister turned to me and wanted to know how well the university
students spoke English, I said not 'Hardly any can speak English
at all' but 'Some of them are quite good at reading comprehension'
– which was true, but only just. But in most matters the disparity
between appearance and reality was so great that it was impossible
to believe that the authorities were really fooled; not even Ne
Win's officers could have been that stupid. They were taking
part in an elaborate tradition of pretence, a charade reminiscent of
The Emperor's New Clothes. In that story, no one dared to inform
the Emperor that he was stark naked, that his so-called finery was
non-existent; in Burma no one dared to tell Ne Win that it was
because his policies were threadbare that his country was in tatters.
On the streets, patchwork buses sidled along and broke down
with depressing frequency; on the railways, ancient rolling-stock
swayed and bounced and jumped off the rails; and from time to
time one of BAC's tiny fleet of Fokker Friendships would fall out
of the sky. For a couple of decades people had watched things fall
apart. Where they had been able to, they had mended; and where
they hadn't, they had pretended. It was a way of life by now, and
without a little boy to shout 'The emperor is naked!' things could
go on like this till kingdom come.

One day in the middle of May everything in our temporary home
stopped working. The electric pump raised no more water from the
well, and the fridge, cooker and aircon were dead. Having found
charcoal, candles and matches we made enquiries. A storm had
brought down a pylon at Thazi, we were told. This seemed unlikely
and, since insurgent groups such as the Karen National Union
were forever planting bombs on 'soft' communications targets, I
assumed that the storm was a euphemism. But it wasn't a KNU
bomb that had done the damage, as we heard later. Because of the
acute shortage of metals, people had been removing steel struts
from the pylons and replacing them with wooden ones.

The temperature for most of the day had been well into the
hundreds (Burma still used the Fahrenheit scale) and now a pall of
humidity drifted in, half-veiling the sun without tempering its heat.
The house, designed for airconditioning, became a sauna bath, but

it didn't feel any cooler outside. Liz slept on the living-room floor and I in the bedroom – except that proper sleep was impossible. I got through my classes the next morning, but as the day wore on the heat became stultifying. Liz tried sitting on the verandah, sitting on a swing under the palm trees, sitting on a cane settee from which the cushions had been removed – all to no avail. When the sun went down it failed to take its heat with it, and we sat in the twilight exuding trickles of sweat, our hair wet and greasy, the mosquitoes beginning to home in. Liz decided that enough was enough, packed a small case and went off to the Mandalay Hotel, which had its own generator. Another day and night passed before the power supply was back to normal, but then there was another little incident to remind me of Burma's fragility.

A few days later I had just started a lesson and was writing on the blackboard when a groaning and grating noise filled the air and the classroom seemed faintly to vibrate. I turned round to find the room empty of all but one last student, who was just flashing by me on her way to the door. Perhaps I am slow on my feet, but I think it truer to say that the Burmese react very swiftly to imminent danger. The students had decided that an earthquake was upon them and had made for the open, but it was not a tremor. As I turned to face the class I found the far wall, a massive timber partition fifteen feet high, falling towards me, its edges grinding against the side walls and producing a strident vibration. It hit the rear desks, screeched to a halt and hung just above the desktops in the dusty air. If it had fallen in silence, unhindered, it would have flattened my class and left me untouched as I wrote on the blackboard. (I was reminded of Buster Keaton in the famous 'falling façade' scene). I found a room without a timber partition and continued the lesson.

Almost everything takes a long time in Burma – I will explain the qualifying 'almost' later – and, having been appointed in Britain in October, having been given the go-ahead by the Burmese authorities in December and having arrived in January, it was now July before we were able to move into the grand old house we had chosen, now rewired, repainted and refurbished with mosquito netting. By this time my little white Suzuki jeep had arrived and Liz had acquired a secondhand car from a diplomat in Rangoon, not because we really needed two vehicles but in order to establish, for each teaching post, a set of precedents in the various rigmaroles for obtaining vehicle registration and insurance, a petrol ration and so on.

We had also acquired the services of Margaret, a Karen entering middle age, whose hooded eyes and thin lips could look sometimes puckish, sometimes prim and sometimes both at once. She knew little English and less about cooking but had been recommended (by other Karens of course) as honest and reliable. Concerning servants, our Australian friends had strongly advised us to employ Karens because they were more hardworking than Burmans, not to employ a racially-mixed group because there would always be bad feeling amongst them, and especially not to put a *kalā* with others unless you were prepared to put up with constant squabbles in the household. Consequently, as well as having Margaret as cook, we ended up with her husband U Kyit as gardener and her uncle U Po Bwin, elderly and cadaverously thin, as nightwatchman.

The only thing that did not take a long time in Burma was any activity whose purpose was to prettify, to please the eye, to flatter. Highways could be tidied and the boles of wayside trees painted white at a day's notice if General Ne Win's car was due to pass by. In no time at all, gaily-painted timber archways could be erected across roadways for such futile rituals as the annual ceremonial passage of the Union flag from town to town, the timber and labour being requisitioned ('donated' was the Party's word for it) on the spot. Again, things had been no different two centuries earlier according to Padre Sangermano:

> Whenever the Emperor wanted to construct a gate or bridge or building, it was the inhabitants who had to pay for it; and more was exacted than was needed. (p.91)

The Emperor in this case (Bodawhpaya) considered that his subjects' belongings were really royal property; in similar fashion, Ne Win always had first pick of the rubies, sapphires and jade at the annual Gems Emporium, a state-organised sale which earned a little precious foreign currency for his virtually bankrupt court.

Settling down in a house involved getting used to the prime example of Burma's ability to put on a splendid show in a matter of hours: the *pweh*. I would drive out one morning and see a few beams and sections of planking lying by the road nearby. When

I came home for lunch, these would have been transformed into a platform framed by an arch, and by teatime this would have become a stage, its brightly-painted proscenium resplendent in the yellowing light of late afternoon. Parked in the mud behind the stage, there would be an ancient dilapidated bus, battered and almost paintless, and a man sorting out cables for half a dozen huge loudspeakers waiting for disposition around the patch of wayside ground; watching him, a few silent boys; by the stage, a gaggle of excited schoolgirls; in adjacent windows and gardens, neighbours chatting. By dusk, they were all taking their places on woven mats, and vendors of titbits were lighting the lanterns in the stalls behind and beside the audience. That night, all night, there would be sequences of appallingly amplified clangorous and percussive music that accompanied high-pitched female wailings and male moanings; interludes of raucous repartee and laughter; and, rarely, short intervals of silence that reminded me, as I turned over in bed, how blessedly quiet a night could be in Mandalay.

A *pweh* is an open-air all-night performance, a sort of masque resembling in its lighter moments pantomime and music-hall or vaudeville, and in its more serious episodes rather more like ballet and opera – except that it is perfectly in order to chat to friends, get up and buy something to eat or drink and even to sleep during any part of the performance. Without understanding a word of what was said, foreigners such as ourselves could enjoy the slapstick humour of the clowning comics; sometimes a friend would explain something, but no one ever had the courage – or perhaps the vocabulary – to translate the obviously outrageous ribaldry which brought roars of laughter from the older folk but made some of the younger women tut-tut and then, as often as not, smile behind their hands.

Go and see one or two of these passing shows with their wandering players decked out in glittering finery and their faces glowing with cosmetics; watch them, victorious and defeated, tragic and farcical, romantic and coarse by turns in their little zone of brightness, a cocoon in a huge black silence; walk carefully into the darkness and look behind the scenes at those flimsy props, that tawdry discarded costume thrown on to the front seat of the half-darkened bus that acts as dressing-room, the weary leading lady smoking a huge cheroot, her dazzle gone, her make-up runnelled with sweat so that she looks at least fifty, which she probably is. Do this, and you will know, as the Buddhist audience knows, that all the world's a *pweh*, a passing show, a grand illusion.

3. Face Values

Appearances were deceptive, even – or rather, especially – in the case of money. Officially the pound was worth about ten *kyat* but if you hawked a ten-pound note around you could apparently get five hundred *kyat* or more. The US dollar was preferred though, and the higher the denomination of the banknote the greater the difference between the official and the black market rates. Ne Win didn't want aliens in his demesne but on the other hand he was constantly in need of foreign exchange, a commodity so high on the list of national preoccupations that *eff-ee* was to all intents and purposes a Burmese word – even people who couldn't speak a word of English knew what FE was. So Ne Win, alias Number One, had reluctantly introduced a one-week visa so as to allow a small but fairly continuous stream of tourists to fly in, rush around a limited tourist route spending their hard currency and fly out again before infecting too many people with exotic disorders that led to a craving for freedom of expression and association, to a demand for democracy – whatever that was. In the Electronic Age it was no longer possible to keep a population in ignorance of the outside world, but Number One did a fairly good job of keeping the outside world ignorant of what was going on in Burma. Very few foreign films were shown, the media were state-controlled and tourists were forbidden to bring video or movie cameras into the country. On entry they were supposed to declare all hard currency on an official form, change money only at Tourist Burma's official rate and on departure give proof of their financial transactions. But by underdeclaring in the first place, they could sell their dollars to a tout or taxi-driver for several times more *kyat* than the rate shown on Tourist Burma's blackboards would give them.

Most of the Burmese people I knew didn't set great store

by money. Wealth is of no account to a devout Buddhist, and the scriptures had certainly had some effect on attitudes and behaviour in this respect. The ubiquitous practice of spending part of one's meagre earnings on gold leaf so as to add one's own tiny contribution to the gilding of the Enlightened One's image, for instance, is an expression of devotion to the Way, the Noble Eightfold Path towards the elimination of suffering; but it can also be seen as symbolising the renunciation of wealth. However, it was also true that the people had plenty of worldly reasons for refusing to place much faith in money. There had been some unsettling changes of coinage from the silver rupee and the anna (in the days when the British had misguidedly administered Burma from Calcutta as a chunk of 'Further India'), to a brief Japanese substitute, back to the rupee in 1945, and then to *kyat* after independence. Then there had been the losses. Soon after Ne Win came to power his Demonetisation Law of 1964 had made all 100-*kyat* and 50-*kyat* notes worthless overnight. There was a refund mechanism, but the maximum refunded was five hundred *kyat* in notes of smaller denomination; then almost immediately a swingeing tax was imposed on all bank accounts containing more than a certain (quite modest) amount. These measures were deliberately aimed at the rich *kalā* moneylenders and businessmen, who now began leaving in large numbers for Pakistan or India; but of course many middle-class Burmese felt the blow. As Burma became what has been called 'a hermit country', the economy went from bad to worse. In 1975 there was a 30 per cent devaluation; the *kyat* was devalued a further 10 per cent only two years later. Stagnation and inflation continued a further ten years and then, a short time before we arrived in Burma, the replacement 100-*kyat* note had also been declared illegal tender. To augment the still valid notes of K25, K10, K5 and K1 the government had issued, to universal smiles of disbelief, notes of K75, K35 and K15. You didn't have to be a Buddhist to have little faith in the currency, but it helped. The people behind counters soon got used to stacking their banknotes differently: thirteen K75s wrapped in a K25 for a thousand, six K15s wrapped in a K10 for a hundred.

Whatever malady it was that had reduced Burma to chronic insolvency, it looked as if the British Embassy had caught it. Back in February, when we had been just one month in Mandalay, our prospective landlord, U Ko Gyi, had invited us to his house for a working dinner at which we would finalise the renting of his house. As we signed and shook hands there was a patter of applause from Auntie Than Than and an associate of hers, two contractors and Liz. Everyone was in a very good mood. U Ko Gyi was delighted that in a few days' time, on the first of March, he would be getting twelve months' rent in advance from the British Embassy; Auntie and her colleagues were looking forward to getting their cut; the contractors were smacking their lips (though I didn't know it at the time) at the thought of the pickings to be had when the Embassy sent paint, cement, corrugated-iron sheets and other rare and valuable commodities to Mandalay, and when they were given the opportunity to order (i.e. over-order) the locally-available lime, gravel and so on; and we were very pleased with our choice of house.

The very next day, word came that the Embassy couldn't pay any rent until April because it had run out of money. The landlord was keeping his part of the bargain and had already moved a lot of things out in anticipation. Liz and I were so disgusted by the thought of Her Majesty's mission in Burma going broke and breaking its contract that we sat down and put together every *kyat* we had. Our pay was sent up from Rangoon in a parcel, no bank would let us open an account in Mandalay and we had just been paid – so we had quite a sum between us. We counted out the bundles of notes, set enough aside for a month's basic expenses and found that we could just manage to give U Ko Gyi two months' rent in advance. Having composed an apologetic letter incorporating a receipt, we bundled the ten thousand *kyat* into a carrier bag and slipped the letter in. As an afterthought I took a glossy British Council brochure, cut from its cover the quarter of a Union Jack that it was emblazoned with, and slid this in as well. We then walked round to the house.

U Ko Gyi was there with one of the contractors. He was grim when he heard what I had to say, but took the news graciously and was pleased by our gesture of good faith. He protested a little, but then counted the notes, signed the receipt and looked a little happier. To complete the goodwill process I dipped my hand into the carrier bag, announcing solemnly that on behalf of the British

Government it was my pleasure to present him with a small gift. Mrs Thatcher was sorry, I said, giving U Ko Gyi the piece of card, that it wasn't a complete flag: that would have been too expensive. This cleared the air. Even the contractor, whose dreams of paint, cable, cement and corrugated iron had receded a little, managed a smile.

We discovered much later that this person was not a contractor but what is these days called a facilitator. He was also a shark. Just before our arrival he had tried to browbeat U Ko Gyi into giving him a percentage of the advanced rent; he'd also said that a truckload of goods would be arriving soon and that only a dozen of the bags of cement on board were to be unloaded – the rest would be taken away. I knew nothing of this at the time, but Auntie Than Than had advised me not to trust 'those people'. As the landlord had decided to stay on in the house to keep an eye on things, I had asked him to telephone me at work as soon as the truck arrived.

The call came when I had no further teaching to do, so I ran out of the university gate, jumped into a horse-cart and hurried slowly home. I had got the whole load checked off and all the cement (forty bags!) stacked away by the time the shark arrived. I had won the first round, but I lost the next two when a couple of pick-up trucks arrived unannounced and were unloaded before you can say corrugated iron, several sheets of which had plainly been removed. At some stage great heaps of bricks, sand, lime, stones and gravel appeared on the drive; I asked the contractor what on earth all the stones were for and he replied vaguely that they weren't for anything and would be taken away. Meanwhile, he had made it plain to U Ko Gyi that all left-over materials were to be his, the contractor's, property. I had other ideas about that but I couldn't stop the green paint being appropriated and the residue made up with lime and water. Two rolls of mosquito netting also 'walked'.

I had just pulled up outside the Department of English in my newly-arrived white jeep. I lifted out my briefcase, carefully locked the car door, and turning smartly towards the department, walked slapbang into the side of a large black cow that was passing. I managed to keep on my feet, but I had lost face. A student stood grinning widely as he undid and retied his *longyi* – an action which Burmese men must surely perform a hundred times a day. That little story would get around. The student strolled away and the cow sauntered into the grounds around the department, her velvety dewlap swaying like a theatre curtain that has just closed. I had never noticed how silently cows walk.

Early one Sunday morning the landlord telephoned again: would I please go round to the house as soon as possible? I arrived at the gate to find two pale lovely-eyed oxen, yoked to a cart, grazing peacefully on the grass verge. Reclining in the landlord's armchair under the portico and receiving the ministrations of some workmen was an elderly *hsayadaw*, looking like an enthroned emperor in his deep yellow toga-like robe. This venerable abbot had brought a note, written by the contractor, authorising the removal of the heap of lime. The contractor had clearly decided that if he couldn't get his hands on the lime itself, he would at least get the spiritual merit that accrued from contributing the stuff to a monastery, for the construction or decoration of a pagoda. I gently expressed my regret that the lime was not mine to give away. As the landlord was reverently translating this the contractor pedalled up to us and protested that he didn't want to sell the lime, only to donate it to the monastery. The *hsayadaw* smiled, nodded and turned his eyes back to me. I would with great pleasure donate the lime, I said, if it were mine. (This was true: the great white heap was blocking the drive.) In fact, if the contractor would care to write down his request, I would forward it to the Embassy – whose property it was – with a positive recommendation. This made the contractor look rather sickly; if he misappropriated the lime and donated it, the *kuthō*, the spiritual credit, was his; if the British donated it, what was the point? The workmen, hating to see a *hsayadaw* disappointed in this way, looked daggers at me as the old gentleman gathered his robe about him with quiet dignity and, inscrutable under his red and gold umbrella, departed in the bullock-cart.

I felt mean, and wondered whether I ought to salvage a little merit on my own account by using the stuff to build a small pagoda in the back garden.

At long last we moved into our house and Margaret, U Kyit and U Po Bwin now had their own quarters, a three-room billet of stout timber in the back garden. I went to the old British-built main post office to pay in advance for the installation of a telephone.

Above the massive panelled counter was a grille of lathe-turned teak, and far above there were ancient ceiling-fans that weren't turning any more. The woman behind the latticework took my form absent-mindedly, noticed the foreign name and looked up. I could almost hear her saying to herself, 'Oh yes, the English teacher at the university'. She made out a receipt in a little book leaved with brownish fibrous paper; coaxed some ink out of a faded and desiccated pad by working her circular wooden stamp around on it; smacked the stamp down hard; did the same with a rectangular stamp; set the two carbons further on in the book, ready for the next receipt; and then took from the counter a hacksaw blade, worn so smooth that the shine showed only a suspicion of waviness where the cutting-edge had been. She used this as a straight edge when she tore out my receipt and as a marker when she closed the book.

I took the receipt to a dilapidated wood-shingled building that still bore traces of old carving and was told airily that I would have a telephone within a week. I would believe that when I saw it. When I saw it six days later, I couldn't believe it. It worked.

The big trouble, the rebelliousness that was to lead to so much bloodshed, started on Saturday, 5th of September, when it was announced over the radio that the recently-issued K75 and K35 notes, together with the old K25 ones, were no longer legal tender. This time there were no arrangements for reimbursement, except that government employees were going to be paid again for the month that had just ended. The banks and post offices had just closed down for the weekend, Zegyo market closed down forthwith and there was general consternation at this daylight robbery. Some people had ten thousand *kyat* or more tucked away at home for a rainy day, mostly in high-denomination notes of course. There was a teacher who had just drawn out of the bank enough to buy a bicycle – which cost a year's salary; another who had saved enough to build a little house and had just withdrawn the cash; and someone else who had been about to buy a motorcycle that cost eighty thousand *kyat*, the price of two small cars in England. We now had the equivalent of ten pounds between us, plus banknotes that had been worth close on a thousand pounds; over the weekend there was nothing we could do about it though, so we relaxed.

Sunday morning. A whisper of breeze in the mango trees, a rustle as the coconut palm fronds shifted. Out in the lane, a neighbour started singing as he wove bamboo strips into a rectangular framework, making a replacement panel for a wall or ceiling. Two large black butterflies flirted around a lemon tree. Then a distant rumble, growing into a clangour, and a clopping of hoofs that were going at a smart pace. Trouble? I put my hands over my ears to keep out the din and peered through the bars of the garden gate. A horse trotted into view, then its prettily-painted cart appeared; then, at the end of a tow-rope, a very old and very large concrete-mixer came bounding and clanging and rattling, scattering scabs of dried cement along the road. The racket dwindled and died away, but soon Ma Thuzar and a friend of hers came cycling up the drive. These two youngsters worked at the Tourist Burma office in Mandalay Hotel and Thuzar had become very attached to Liz, treating her almost as a mother. This arrival was unexpected. What was up?

They had been besieged, they said, by enraged tourists who had suddenly found their money worthless. The hotel manager had received no instructions on what to do in this situation. The almost penniless backpackers had little or no hard currency to change and the better-off tourists refused to change any more of theirs. They had angrily pointed out that if the hotel could give them low-denomination notes for their dollars it could do so in exchange for their now worthless *kyat*, simply by backdating the receipts by one day. But tyranny smothers initiative, and the manager did nothing. Outside, the drivers of taxis, horse-carts and side-cars naturally refused to accept the worthless notes and, after arguments, settled for T-shirts or cigarettes or other bargainable goods in lieu.

Our two friends had come to warn us not to go out. There had been ugly scenes next door to the hotel outside the Mandalay Division People's Council headquarters, and there were large crowds of angry university students at Zegyo market. Ma Thuzar's sister had telephoned from Rangoon to say that as the university students there had tried to burn down the main assembly-hall, examinations had been postponed and the university closed. Our nightwatchman U Po Bwin cycled up with the same advice, and added that the police had shot and wounded a student and there were no buses running. I assumed it was the MI who had stopped them – they wouldn't want highly mobile groups of infuriated demonstrators all over town. We stayed at home.

I drove carefully to the university as usual on the Monday morning, my Confucian motto being 'There is nothing around a Mandalay cyclist'. (People would steer suddenly into the middle of the road to avoid a puddle or pothole, and stop or turn in any direction without warning.) There were large numbers of students standing around and sitting on the main steps, but they were just waiting to be sent home. For those who lived in the far north near the borders with Nagaland, Tibet and Yunnan, it would be a three-day journey at least. They had been issued with valid banknotes for this purpose, and the same was happening at Liz's college and every other college in the country. The state radio had announced that all educational establishments, from kindergarten upwards, were being closed early. Ne Win would never admit publicly that he had been frightened by the students into the hasty measure of closing down the universities; that would be a tremendous loss of face. Consequently future historians studying the records would note that the usual three-day break for *Thadingyut* was in 1987 generously extended to a six-week holiday.

The department was now very quiet. The Head, when he was present, inhabited a caged area within the departmental office, whose front was symbolically buckled and cracked because of the expansion and contraction of the absorbent 'cotton-soil' that underlay the city. Here, like a bored gibbon, he would sit for long periods without even pretending to do anything, even when a term was in full swing. If the department's head was in the clouds, its feet – there being no syllabuses, no set books, no duplicator, no supply of paper and stencils and in any case no clerical staff able to type in English – stood in a small private agency in town where a copy-typist hammered away at an old typewriter whose type had lost its face. At the beginning of the year (not earlier, because classes always started a week or two late) a lecturer took a set of last year's handouts to the agency (the old stencils had fallen to pieces) and got them retyped (no point in changing anything and making life even more complicated). These already brittle, yellowing sheets were gummed together in the top left-hand corner, staples and paper-clips being impossible luxuries. Once the stencils had been typed and corrected, and recorrected several times, thousands of copies were run off because every student of every year had to do English. The copies were a bit faint because the typewriter was old and because duplicating ink, available only on the black market, was expensive. The agent was then paid with the money advanced by each student for this purpose. Any surplus would go into the departmental fund; or perhaps it wouldn't.

Hordes of students then came to collect their sets of handouts. First-year BA students turning up for their first classes found themselves wedged into a room with about two hundred others. Like the ink on the handout, the lecturer's voice was a bit faint; she was insecure and nervous because she herself was only an MA student, and anyway a lady shouldn't raise her voice too much. The following weeks were characterised by boredom, stuffiness and torpor; by the middle of the year the class was only fifty strong but then exams loomed and the immemorial hum of memorising was heard throughout the land. Desks appeared in the corridors where there was a little movement of air and, among a small proportion of the students, a sort of religious fervour set in. Like monks in a cloister, students sat or slowly perambulated, keeping up an intoned liturgy.

Outside my door one morning a student was pacing up and down the corridor repeating something over and over. As he passed by, I heard:

'It is an . . . It is an . . . IT IS AN . . . It is an . . . It is an . . .'

This left much unsaid. I wanted to get down to work, but my ears would not abandon the message. They tracked the student to the end of the corridor, where there was a pause. The suspense was terrible. Then he approached me once more:

'It is an . . . exceedingly complex operation . . . EXCEEDINGLY COMPLEX OPERATION . . . exceedingly complex operation . . .'

What sort of operation? This was ridiculous. I went to the door and was just leaning forward to listen when a colleague came in to discuss something and we nearly cracked our heads together. I never did find out what sort of operation it was that was so exceedingly complex.

The exams would be done, the scripts marked; the scores would be atrocious; and when the results were published, everyone would have passed. Not because the students were unintelligent, but because they hadn't really been given a chance, a BA (English) could not be taken at face value. Besides, failure would be a loss of face, which would lead to trouble.

As I drove towards Zegyo market I saw ahead the clock-tower built to commemorate Queen Victoria's Diamond Jubilee. When the British took Mandalay (and thereby Upper Burma) in 1885, they would surely never have imagined that within fifty-seven years they would be ousted – and by Asian power, at that. What face they lost when the Japanese forces swarmed over Burma in 1942! It was lost irrevocably; and although Japan suffered a military defeat, Britain then suffered a commercial one, for there were no radios, televisions, motorbikes or cars on sale in Mandalay that were not Japanese. It was significant that the British Embassy had not had a 'man in Mandalay' for twenty-six years and that, now they had one, his little white jeep with its quarter of a Union Jack in the windscreen was a Suzuki. To crown it all, I saw as I passed the tower that the clock-face bore the name SEIKO. I don't think the old lady even bothers to turn in her grave any more.

What? said the voice. I repeated the question.
   No, the Embassy wouldn't be able to replace our money.
   What if I sent a blank cheque?
   Sorry old chap, no valid notes left. Better borrow some.

I passed some construction work and noted once again that most of the heavy work was being done by women, who manage to look composed and assured in their working clothes and have a bearing that makes their menfolk seem to be of a different species. A willowy figure helps, of course, but they are not all slender; and it doesn't depend on money. Two of the most striking women I saw in Mandalay were very poor: one was a vendor of tit-bits in Mingala market and the other was a bricklayer's mate. This young woman was little more than five feet tall and was dusted with cement and lime, which she had been mixing with sand. Now she was carrying bricks. She sank gently to a squatting position in front of a stack of them, her back upright. Placing a coil of cloth on top of swept-back hair grey with dust, she stretched her arms forward to take a brick in each hand and began to stack them – two front-to-back, two crosswise, two front-to-back – until after ten bricks her delicate-looking arms would stretch upwards no further. She then rose effortlessly under the little column of bricks and, gliding over to where the bricklayer (always a man, it seemed) was working, folded herself down again and off-loaded the bricks two by two. All this she did so gracefully that you noticed her actions rather than her features. It was when the women (especially the well-to-do) dressed to kill or to show off that they looked their worst . . . at weddings, for instance. Their clothes tended to be too gaudy, they had too many accessories (rings, bracelets, necklace, earrings and pretty reticule), the make-up was too heavy and the hair-do too ornate. The bricklayer's mate had none of these, and she was every inch a queen.

She wouldn't have been able to afford make-up, but she could afford to do without it anyway. She could even smear her face with *thanahka* and get away with it. This is a fragrant and astringent yellowish lotion that she makes herself. In the market she buys a short section of the branch or root of the tree *Limonia acidissima*, enough to hold comfortably in the hand. At home, she hold it horizontally and scrubs it around on the abrasive surface of her wetted *kyaukpyin*, a stone disc rather like an old-fashioned bread-board in shape and size. A very fine bark paste begins to form, and as she sprinkles water on it from time to time the paste drains into a groove running round the *kyaukpyin*. She tips this *thanahka* into a container and continues until she has made enough. A daub on the cheeks may be enough to refresh her, but in the worst of the heat she might rub it on all over after taking a bath. Apart from cooling, it also protects the skin against the fierce sunlight. Young girls often have a circular blob on each cheek, and perhaps a stripe down the ridge of the nose, which makes them look doll-like or clownish. Older girls may trim the blobs into the shape of a bodhi-tree leaf, sometimes roughly, sometimes with a fine tracery of leaf-veins.

Many Western observers have found the use of *thanahka* ugly. I found it attractive, perhaps because of the hint of primitiveness in its resemblance to war-paint. Anyway it was reasonably cheap and it kept its face value.

★   ★   ★

I had renamed my MA classes 'staff development sessions', since most of my students were also junior lecturers, and under this guise, I continued to teach. My colleagues had drawn their replacement salary in K15 notes, but they earned so little that I couldn't ask them to lend me any. Then, of all people, my HoD made me feel ashamed of my ungracious attitude towards him by pressing a wad of K1000 into my hand in spite of my protestations.

A week later there was a radio announcement: all coins and all banknotes of values K1, K5, K10 and K15 would (people held their breath) continue to be legal tender (sighs of relief). Two new currency notes were to be put in circulation the following week, of denominations K90 and K45 (snorts of derision). Immediately there were jokey rumours that the old K10 and K5 were to be replaced with K7½ and K3¾ notes.

The contractor continued to turn up, at home or even in the staffroom, demanding cement or more money, sometimes both. The Embassy eventually did the honourable thing and replaced our demonetised *kyat*. But the Burmese did not forgive Ne Win for robbing them, and from this time onwards there were the makings of a popular unity against this common enemy, a unity they had perhaps never felt since those heady days that followed Independence which had in their turn been followed by the assassination of the man in whom they had placed their hopes of a united Burma: Aung San. Now, a feeling of solidarity in adversity was growing. It was to be almost a year before matters came to a head. The stage was not yet set, but the planking was lying in the grass in readiness for the staging of a bloodthirsty *pweh*.

4. Golden Land

As soon as we had a car we couldn't wait to see a bit of the country. Most of Burma was out of bounds since the authorities could not guarantee our safety from insurgent attacks if we were to go beyond the normal tourist destinations. As foreigners we were told to make official applications for any travel outside Mandalay district, stating dates, routes and hotels in advance; but Liz's application to go on one brief trip across the river to Sagaing, only half an hour away, had been so lengthy and complicated and the system was so restrictive that for short trips I decided to ignore the rules and see what happened. Nothing ever did.

Once the temperature had entered the hundreds, Maymyó beckoned. Life had been a little restrictive in Mandalay and out on the open road I enjoyed an assortment of new impressions: bamboo leaves glittering in the bright morning; haystacks which, being on the raised floors of small open-sided barns, not only foiled the approaching monsoon but also provided shade underneath for the cattle; the water-trickles left by decrepit trucks as they toiled up the winding road, each with a cistern above the cabin which ingeniously replenished the leaking radiator; the coolness as we hairpinned through the pines and levelled out on the plateau; and then the trees in blossom.

Beside the road stood a jacaranda in full bloom disturbingly beautiful and quite undrivepastable. It was almost leafless but was shrouded in a dense mist of bluish-mauve that reminded me of my very first paint-box. I had seen jacarandas before, but the sight still gave me a little momentary shock, as when I had looked at colour negatives for the first time and seen my world all dyschromatic. There was a passing uneasiness, as if something in nature had gone awry and a patch of hot summer sky had got caught in winter

branches. The cherry-blossom on the approaches to Maymyó and
in the Botanical Gardens was past its best, but many other species
unknown to me were in bloom. There were trees with pendent
yellow flowers as large as hollyhock blossoms, trees with crimson
petals rising from the dark twigs like flames seeping through
fissures, and trees clothed with sleeves of pink all along the boughs
– no room for leaves – which reminded me of the bobbly cardigans
that mothers used to knit for baby daughters. But none of these
could match the jacaranda.

We went to stay in one of the several buildings which,
before Independence, housed the government of Burma when
it retired from the heat of the plains for a few months. They
now constituted the Nann Myaing Government Rest House, but
the gardens flaunted their British origins. We admired the sweet
peas clinging to their tepee of canes, the neat rectangular bed
of petunias, the carefully and colourfully mingled stocks and
snapdragons and larkspurs, the nasturtiums trailing over rockery,
the flimsy California poppies bending in the warm wind – and the
careful labelling of all these in English. We might have been in a
Surrey park. To complete the illusion, a cuckoo called three times
from a nearby group of trees.

The town showed, perhaps more than most, that it had seen
much better days. It was only a century old and had begun as little
more than a British army base. The town (*myó*) was named after
Colonel May of the Bengal Infantry, who was posted there to pacify
the area soon after the annexation of Upper Burma. For a decade or
more, the British were harried by ill-armed but courageous bands of
guerrillas led by ruthless but valiant patriots such as Maung Yaing,
who dislodged a garrison of Gurkhas down by the Irrawaddy at
Shemmaga, and Ta Te who, rather than surrender, died hurling
masonry and defiance from a pagoda wall when his ammunition
had run out. Then a prosperous town grew around the garrison
and became Burma's counterpart to Simla or Murree, a somewhat
glamorous hill-station. Now, as you walked around the town centre
by the Purcell clock-tower and the large blue-and-white painted
mosque, you saw only shabby and ill-stocked stores where *kalā*
proprietors once displayed stacks of British goods, from saucepans
to sola topees, from gabardine to golf-clubs. An old Muslim of
upright bearing who seemed to know I was British from a distance

of fifty yards greeted me and shook my hand, told me he was ninety-three and then asked what had gone wrong.

'Before 1942 you could buy anything here,' he said, using both arms to indicate the shophouses and stores on either side. 'Anything. All British. After the war, nothing. Then, all Japanese.' He was simply reminiscing and regretting. He didn't really expect an explanation, thank goodness.

The Maymyó equivalent of the Mandalay horse-cart is a four-wheel closed carriage which is probably a descendant of the Victorian cab. It looks like a one-horse stagecoach, but is as brightly painted as its cousin down in Mandalay. A little north of the town centre, past the Golf Club Repairing Shop, some of these carriages were parked on the dusty verges of the Lashio Road outside some ramshackle eating-houses. Two or three of the drivers wore local wide-brimmed hats. It would have made a perfect scene for – forgive me – an Eastern Western.

We visited Maymyó several times, choosing to stay only once in Candacraig, the former 'chummery' of the Bombay Burma Trading Company. Now the Maymyó Rest House, it had gone downhill since Albert Bernard, its last living link with the days of the Raj, had retired in his eighties a few years earlier. He had been in charge of the catering in the Twenties and had run the place himself for the last sixteen years. The Chinese temple with its circular gateway was picturesque only in a pretty-pretty way – I felt as if I was on a stage-set – but the large market was always interesting for its mixture of ethnic types and variety of produce, which included fresh strawberries. A row of stalls offered antiques and bric-à-brac. Some of the articles had acquired the natural patina of age, others had been given a little assistance in the difficult business of ageing gracefully.

We were able to drive a few miles north along the Lashio Road to a pleasant picnic area beside a waterfall, but didn't risk going any further. Heading south for home, you might if you were lucky see one or two beautiful flying carpets – thick-piled mats of freshly picked yellow or coppery chrysanthemums completely covering the roofs of pick-ups and jeep taxis further down the zigzag escarpment road. Almost all of these blooms would end up in a pagoda, or *hpaya*, at the feet of the Lord Buddha.

In 1960 I happened to be in the small, quiet town of Chiengmai in the north of Thailand when the Water Festival came round. I was driving along the main street in an open car when a gallon of cold water, shot from a bucket at a first-floor window, smacked down fair and square on my head and shoulders. The cold jolt and blurred vision didn't cause a traffic accident that time, but quite often did. This New Year festival, called *Thin-gyan* in Burma, comes in April before the monsoon and at the hottest time of year. Here too the traditional boisterous dousing, from which no one except the monkhood is exempt, is often taken to extremes. In 1882 Shway Yoe (J.G. Scott), noting that the wetting was considered a compliment and that dirty water was never used, added: 'The barbaric innovation of squirts is a sign of decadence.' (p.351)

Now people were using whatever they could find, including large hoses. Not everyone was happy that what had probably begun as a rain-making ceremony in pre-Buddhist times was now all too often degenerating into a bullying free-for-all. When we set out for Taung-gyi we were escaping not only from the heat but also from *Thin-gyan*.

We sped south across the baked, desert-like 'Dry Zone', stopping on the outskirts of Meikhtila to pay our respects to a Spitfire, set up as a monument on a pedestal near the roadside. Wheeling in formation like migrating geese, silver Japanese planes had pattern-bombed the town at their leisure, for there had been only a subsidiary airstrip here in 1942. In March 1944, while the ferocious battle for Mandalay was being fought, here in Meikhtila – in the words of Field Marshal Sir William Slim – 'the struggle for the airfield was savage and continuous'. Spitfire UB409 probably had quite a story behind her; she now proudly bore the Burmese colours gold, white and blue, but sparrows nested in her nacelle and from her weathered propeller thick coats of paint cracked and bubbled and flaked away. I lowered my camera when a soldier appeared and forbade me to photograph this secret machine. I didn't tell him we'd already taken several shots.

The car seats were drenched with sweat, the dark wet patches rimmed white with salt. We tanked up with a pint of iced sugarcane juice each and headed eastwards, hoping that our Tourist Burma friend Ma Thuzar had managed to book a hotel room for us in Kalaw. This town, another former hill-station on the rim of the Shan plateau, lay among clouds of jacaranda in a vale surrounded

by pine-dotted hills, where substantial old buildings, like Home
Counties mansions, stood among the trees. The Kalaw Hotel was
of the same vintage. Like Candacraig, it had gardens and a tennis
court, a solid teak staircase, solid teak doors, solid furniture and
solid food. A heavy fragrance dropped from the pink-clad branches
of a tree just outside the door, a sweetness that reminded me of
raspberry-and-vanilla ice cream. Behind the tree was a hedge, and
beyond the hedge a railway line. Hearing a whistle, we waited for
the train to appear. It approached a bend in the line slowly, half its
passengers sitting on the roof, it seemed. When we waved, many
of them – they were all men – grinned, waved back, shouted
greetings, stood up and did a little dance of high spirits. They sat
down laughing and gave a final wave as the train curved out of sight
among the pine trees.

We were expected. In this cool climate we slept like logs,
polished off a brave imitation of an English breakfast, booked for
a stop-over on our return journey and headed north for Pindaya
across a rolling plateau of pale terracotta soil sprinkled with trees.
Tribespeople, probably Pa-O, could be seen from time to time
apparently walking from nowhere to nowhere clad in black except
for the cloths, patterned with bright red, that the women wore
turban-style.

We cruised down into the pretty valley where Pindaya nestled
beside a small and placid lake, past a lakeside meadow shaded
here and there by a massive tree; past a bullock-cart being backed
into the shallows so that the clear surface water could be baled
into its mounted water-tank, once an oil-drum; past a cluster of
brilliant white *zedi*, like perfectly symmetrical stalagmites, each
spire crowned with its umbrella-like *hti*, some of these rusting
away, others newly coated with glowing gold leaf; past a row of
tall coconut palms where the curving road hugged the lake; and on
round the lake to the modest one-storey hotel where again (thank
you, Thuzar) we were expected.

Apart from its cool air and pretty setting, Pindaya's attraction
is its cave complex, halfway up the steep hillside behind the hotel.
The large main cave is full of Buddha images set thickly on the
ground and up the sloping walls almost to the roof, where dark bats
hang in clusters like rotten fruit; the figures range from massive
to life-size to minute, some carved in white marble, some cast in

bronze, many entirely coated with gold leaf and therefore probably made of brick or plaster; and they exemplify a range of styles from old to new. Everywhere you look you see from various angles that same impassive smile – thousands and thousands of times. Like caves everywhere, these had acquired superstitions. People came from far and wide to effect some cure or seek the fulfilment of some wish, yet there was no historical or even legendary account of how or why or even when those tens of thousands of images came to be there.

The next day, we drove on to Taunggyi marvelling at how good the road surfaces had been all the way from Mandalay. Passing by Inle Lake we were already at about three thousand feet, but there was a further bit of zigzagging up a sharp incline before we reached the town, which lies at the foot of the great hill (*taung gyi*) after which it is named. Founded by Shway Yoe (Sir George Scott) in imperial days, this is the capital of Shan State, where people proudly regard themselves as so distinct from the Burmans of the plain that they talk about 'going down to Burma'.

At lunch-time, having booked in at the Taunggyi Hotel and done a little shopping in the market, we put our heads inside an eating-house called Lynn You. Immediately, one of two nearby customers looked up and muttered something about Mandalay to his companion. This nettled me, because I thought we had escaped from the parochialism of Mandalay, where everyone knew everyone else's business; so I showed off a bit by ordering a meal in Burmese as far as I could, hoping that this might embarrass the fellow who had so openly talked about us. But of course this merely broke the ice, and they turned out to be very friendly – the one a Shan mechanic and the other an Intha from down by the lake who made very good furniture, he said, but couldn't speak Burmese very well. We chatted in English for a while and, as they stood up to leave, the quiet Shan made some casual observation about our car and added that the registration number was T 951. We had left the car some distance away about two hours earlier, but he was right. I don't think he was an MI man or informer but here was a reminder, if one were needed, of how conspicuous a European was – especially one with a car. I checked my unreasonable annoyance.

'That is so,' I said sweetly in Burmese.

After breakfast the next morning we sat sunning ourselves on the hotel steps by the petunia beds. Liz went to a vendor for a glass of sugarcane juice and came back chatting to some lively boys. More came, and soon we each had a small class of town toughs squatting and standing around us. One of my group showed by gestures that he wanted a light for the discarded cigarette-end in his mouth. I shrugged.

'I don't smoke,' I said truthfully.

'Disease!' volunteered a bright-eyed boy of about twelve.

'Smoke no good,' added another with a wag of his forefinger.

Having established in broken – well, shattered – English that smoking was bad for the health, I pointed up at the *taung gyi* and asked how long it would take to get up there. We used the phrase 'on foot' and I tried to get them to say '*by* car' instead of '*on* car', though since people do travel on the tops of vehicles in Burma perhaps it wasn't really a mistake to say 'on'.

'One hour?' I asked. Incomprehension. 'One *nayi*?'

There were snorts and head-shakings and one boy said, 'Two *nayi*.'

'Two hours?' It must be farther than it looked.

'Two hour, yes.'

Distractingly pretty in their best holiday clothes, two young Shan ladies came by. Deadpan, the bright-eyed lad pointed to one of them and said to me, but loud enough for the girl to hear, 'She is my sweet.'

Everyone, including the young ladies, laughed at this precocity; and I had just got them practising 'my sweetheart' (though I preferred 'my sweet') when the ten or so pairs of smiling eyes became grave as they focused above and beyond my head. A khaki-clad figure was telling them that they should not be talking to foreigners and that they must leave. Our precocious little joker was indignant and said I was only a *hsaya* teaching them some English, but the security man was adamant. As I began to say goodbye I saw an unforgettable expression of contempt on the lad's face: his lively eyes had narrowed, there was a furrow between his eyebrows, his nose was wrinkled with disgust and the corners of his mouth were turned down. I thought he was going to spit, but he threw me a sidelong glance conspiratorially and hissed a rapid string of syllables not one of which I understood. Yet I understood the whole utterance perfectly. It meant, 'Aah, these bloody idiots – they make me sick!'

Or something like that.

This little incident put me in a rather negative mood for the rest of the day. We strolled down to the museum, which had some intriguing exhibits. I liked the buffalo-horn air-compression cheroot-lighter, for example – I hadn't realised that the compression of air could create enough heat to light tobacco. But there wasn't enough information, in Burmese or in English; there was a Shan bamboo rocket, for instance, and a photograph of one being launched, but I wanted to know a lot more about their history and how they were made. The small Natural History room downstairs was crammed with specimens, but most were in poor condition; the Bengal tiger, now pretty rare in Burma I should think, was lumpy all over and looked as if had been stuffed with crumpled newspaper. The poor creature had suffered an even worse indignity: the area where its genitals had been was crudely patched with leopardskin. Then the hotel staff informed us that we couldn't climb the *taung* because it was a forbidden area. It was true that the road a few miles beyond the hotel was held by Shan rebels, but the whole hillside was visible from our window and it was difficult to believe that it harboured insurgents. After a good evening meal at the Tha-Pye restaurant and a look at the night market where goods smuggled in over the mountain passes from Thailand are sold openly, we began to walk back to the hotel. We looked at a bookseller's shabby old paperbacks spread on the pavement, whereupon, taking us for tourists, the vendor asked us if we had any books, T-shirts, dollars, *anything* for sale. (We were used to this by now. We could have made a small fortune by playing the market, but always rejected such approaches because we felt that we were there to help Burma, not to milk her; some of our friends thought us naïve in the extreme.) The vendor's reaction on hearing that we were teaching in Mandalay was to wonder aloud why on earth we had come from England to work for 'this bloody silly government', as he put it. A few yards up the road a diminutive soldier told me off for walking on the pavement in front of a bank; and to cap it all I discovered back at the hotel that, as in the Myamandala in Mandalay, there was a separate bar for the Burmese in which we were not particularly welcome.

It wasn't just my negative mood. The men who had to tell us about the hotel's apartheid were unhappy to do so, and as time went on we learned not to put people in the position of having to do this. Burma the Golden presented you with tens of thousands of gently smiling faces, but there were times when a face slipped and revealed the resentment behind the smile as if it were a fissure beneath paint or mouldy plaster behind gold leaf.

That night, we saw a convoy of trucks packed with armed soldiers pass by, heading eastwards into rebel-held territory. Ironically, not far along the road was Panglong; there, forty years earlier, the leaders of Burma's ethnic minority groups had signed an accord with the Burmese government to work peacefully to achieve their eventual autonomy. Farther along and much nearer to the borders of China, Laos and Thailand than to Taunggyi lay Kengtung, capital of the infamous Golden Triangle; and behind Kengtung's gold lay opium-growing and interminable suffering, gun-running and sudden death.

In the small hours I found myself suddenly alert, having moved from sleep to wakefulness without the bleary transition I usually experience, and I knew immediately what was happening: a cockroach was exploring the area around my left eye. Its mandibles seemed to be nibbling among the roots of the eyebrow hairs. My hand swung up to flick it away but already it was scuttling down my face. My nostrils wouldn't close like a camel's but my lips were pressed together as I swung again and knocked it off my chin. In the pitch dark room I had no idea where it had gone so I picked up my pillow and bashed it, threw back the bedclothes, got out of bed and swished my forearm back and forth over the bottom sheet. In the other bed Liz heaved a sigh of disapproval in her sleep. Satisfied the intruder wasn't lying in ambush, waiting to pounce on another part of my anatomy, I lay down again and watched the window turn grey. The familiar two-note call of a cuckoo drifted down the hillside; then from nearby came the piping decrescendo of the Plaintive Cuckoo, whose song has the rhythm of a dropped ping-pong ball coming to rest; then sleep returned.

I met one of my students near the market, and she and her

sister and little nephew joined us on a trip down to Lake Inle. On arrival we found that we had missed the Tourist Burma boat, and a young lady employee told us it was forbidden to hire one of the many private boats. My student explained who we were but the girl shrugged. She was sympathetic, but all *kalā-byu* (white foreigners) were tourists, and tourists had to use Tourist Burma boats. She was just a decent girl trying to keep a decent job. We went to Yaunghwe market, where Liz moved off to take some photographs, leaving me literally carrying the baby, now half-asleep; the two Shan girls showed me round the market. It was amusing to watch the reactions of the Pa-O women selling their dried fish, vegetables, spices and cheroots. Their steady stares would move from me to one of the girls to the now sleeping toddler, and then from me to the other girl and back to the little boy on my shoulder. Then without taking their eyes off us they would lean slightly together and exchange a few muttered theories. Just when one group appeared to have decided which girl was only my sister-in-law, Liz appeared and completely upset their calculations.

From the coolness of Taunggyi and Kalaw it was down once again to the hot dusty glare of Thazi, on through Meikhtila and then north along the straight and almost empty trunk road to Mandalay. There was an occasional truck thundering southwards, men sitting in the shade of a wayside tree – sitting not by the road but on it, with their legs stretching out over the tarmac as if playing some Burmese version of 'Chicken'. A third group on the outskirts of a village had parked all their bicycles on the road at right-angles to the verge rather than off the road altogether or at least parallel to it. These scenes would not be worth mentioning if they had not been instances of a rule that I had formulated. Without being aware of it most of the time, the English make way for others walking towards them along a corridor or pavement; the behavioural rule is automatic. In Burma, there is a rule which says, 'If you can narrow a gap, do so.' Let me illustrate.

Outside our kitchen door the gardener used two large potted plants to halve the width of the path. It was not on the spacious driveway but in the narrow alley at the side of our house that visitors always chose to leave their bicycles and thus cut off access to the back garden. Outside the front gate an old cowherd always tethered his cow on the drive, never on the much broader grassy verge. The narrow road outside went over an even narrower bridge a few yards away, and it was there – not on the bank of the stream – that the young men parked their bikes and sat on the parapet with their feet in the road, making it a point of honour not to move as I squeezed past in my jeep. On the way to and from the university, students cycled up to five abreast and on arrival (in our department, at least) parked their bikes across the corridors rather than along the walls. And so on. It was almost as if everyone had attended an intensive course on How to Block the Way. Was I exaggerating? Was I getting paranoid? My doubts were dispelled when I read the following in a pamphlet written by an oldtimer in 1945:

> At Tharrawaddy three young Burmans tired after a night's fishing went to sleep on the Rangoon highway just in the lee of a blind humped bridge. Before going to sleep, as was disclosed at the inquest, they had discussed the dangers of sleeping on the highway and the possibility of being run over by a lorry, which actually proved to be the fate of the one nearest to the middle of the road. Not infrequently they slept on the railway line and thus passed to their next existence via painless decapitation. (Richards, p.19)

The corollary of that rule was, 'Where there is a narrow gap, squeeze through it.' Again it was the male cyclist (and motorcyclist) who most faithfully obeyed the rule. My first experience of it in operation was when I was walking across a quiet back-street, watching where I was putting my feet because of the bullock-dung. I was about to step up on to the verge when a cyclist swished past my face, almost bowling me into the mire. The road was otherwise empty. But of course it was only when I saw it happen to other people that I was able to formulate the rule. A monk halfway across a wide road looked at an approaching motorcyclist and rightly judged that if they both proceeded he would arrive at the other side well before the arrival of the vehicle. He continued, walking if anything a little faster. But the motorcyclist accelerated and veered towards the verge, forcing the monk to stop as the machine flashed between him and the kerb. I also saw a cyclist hit a Burmese gentleman in exactly the same sort of situation. The gentleman merely looked daggers and retied his *longyi*, and the cyclist merely gave a sickly grin and retied his *longyi*, before going on their

divergent ways. It is a strange rule, because in Mandalay's heavy
heat a cyclist will at all other times do anything, break any
rule, rather than accelerate or stop – either of which means
extra sweat.

Standing on Mandalay Hill with his favourite Ananda, Buddha
prophesied that twenty-four thousand years after the establishment
of his following there would be founded at the foot of the hill a
great city, a centre of the faith. Mindon Min duly obliged, more
or less on time. Standing on Tangyi Ridge and looking eastwards
across the Irrawaddy (so ran another old tale), the Gaudama told
Ananda that a great city would rise on the far shore; and of
course there arose on that very spot the glorious kingdom of
Pagán, towards which we were now heading in a little white jeep
laden with full jerrycans because I couldn't draw my petrol ration
in any but my appointed garage. There had been rain about, but
a grey veil ahead had slid aside leaving the countryside looking
as if it had been freshly painted. A distant range of hills was as
blue as the bloom on a grape, the floodwater in the patchwork
fields a deeper blue around the tufts of newly-planted *padi*. The
older plants formed carpets of a glowing greenness that grass
never quite equals, while beside the road the bullock-cart tracks
meandered like red river-beds, not yet fading. As they dried, they
would crumble into fine dust. Even the metalled road ahead had
a blue sheen. The white lines on the road had indeed been
freshly painted, and so had the white bands around the trunks
of the few roadside trees. Ne Win must have passed this way
very recently.

   After a hot two-hundred mile drive under the October sun I had
visions of a tall, cold, golden beer. The output of Mandalay beer
was drying up for lack of certain ingredients; but we had decided
to stay in the Thiripyitsaya, a pleasantly appointed hotel with an
unreliable cuisine, and they would be bound to have some for the
tourists. We checked in and went straight to the bar. Yes, there
was beer but only for those who booked for dinner. To hell with
blackmail. Back in our chalet we broached our emergency supply
of Scotch, hot from the car, diluted it with warm water and went
outside to watch the day fade across the river and behind the ridge
called Tangyi-taung.

We decided to try an open-fronted wooden restaurant-cum-souvenir shop in the village. No, there were no river-prawns because Ne Win had been staying nearby and for security reasons no fishing-boats had been allowed on the river for two days.

Oh? Had he come by river?

No, by helicopter.

Oh.

But there would be prawns tomorrow.

We ordered what was available and sat at a round wooden table with traditional tapestries hanging overhead. Child-sized marionettes, white-faced and gaudily dressed, lay slumped against a wall. Another dangled from the ceiling, his head on his chest, like a clown that had just been hanged. When the food came the friendly owner and his wife joined us and we chatted in English augmented by bits of Burmese. Relatives strolled in, kids gathered round and soon we were joking about the government and commiserating with each other on demonetisation losses. They had lost far more than we had. The tasty and ample meal for two cost only about a pound, so we ordered curried prawns for the next evening.

Long before the time of Gaudama Buddha the peoples of Burma were, along with their eastern neighbours, animists. There were spirits in their surroundings – in trees, rivers, caves, mountains, everywhere. Houses had guardian spirits that needed propitiating. A Burmese tale tells how once upon a time a man felled a tree to build a house for himself and thus made the tree-spirit homeless. The spirit promptly sued the fellow, who was ordered by the court to build in his compound a tree-home substitute where he must regularly leave little gifts of fruit and flowers for the offended spirit, or *Nat*. In Burma, a sort of national pantheon of *Nats* evolved:

> At first the *Nats* who were worshipped were impersonal and local, as for example the *Nats* of the banyan tree, the hill and the lake which were just outside the village. Later on, thirty-six personal and national *Nats* came into being who were distinct personages with their own life histories and who were worshipped all over the country. They did not replace the local *Nats*, but diminished their importance. (Maung Htin Aung, 1962:2)

The system of beliefs that developed in the kingdom of Pagān involved planetary gods, Hindu deities, *Nats* and magic; and feast days involved drunkenness, abandoned dancing and animal sacrifices on full-moon days. This was the state of affairs when Anāwrahtā, Burma's greatest king, came to the throne of Pagān. Becoming converted to Buddhism, he determined to do all in his power to foster and glorify the faith, and by the time of his death Pagān was the world centre of Buddhism. He had tried hard but unsuccessfully to stamp out the *Nat* cult and eventually came to a clever compromise, as Htin Aung tells us:

> The figures of the Thirty-six Lords were taken from their shrines and placed in the king's great pagoda in an attitude of worship; he declared that the number was now thirty-seven, because Sakra, the king of the gods and guardian of Buddhism, was at the head of the pantheon. (p.4)

If you can't beat them, join them to you! In much the same way, the early Church in England had made the pagan symbols of vitality – holly, ivy, mistletoe – serve the celebration of Christmas; the Venerable Bede had borrowed the name of a goddess of Spring (Ēastre) for another important Christian festival; and 'blessing' by anointing with holy water had once been 'bletsung', the sprinkling of sacrificial blood.

To the present day the Burmese have continued to respect and cherish the thirty-seven lords, and the local *Nats* have not greatly diminished in importance. In long-term matters such as the pursuit of merit, or *kuthō*, the Way of Buddhism is supreme; but in workaday affairs the household and local *Nats* are listened to and appeased. One terrible day in 1885, people living on the lower slopes of a mountain in Wuntho heard ominous and terrifying noises: a funereal boom as of heavy guns and a mournful wailing that echoed across the valley. They knew this was the anguish of the mountain *Nat*, but did not know the cause of such sorrow. Weeks passed in that remote valley before the news arrived that Mandalay had been taken and the king and queen exiled. Upper Burma was now British. Even today the drivers of buses and taxis on the road to Maymyó, knowing that a complement of nine passengers would anger 'The Nine Lords', will not proceed before picking up a small rock from the roadside, naming it, and then putting it on board as passenger number ten. (Nine, the most intriguing digit in mathematics, was probably a mystic number in pre-Buddhist cults.) The ancient belief in the powers of astrology and palmistry is still very strong even among the well-educated, and even alchemy – the ultimate aim of which is to secure eternal youth and power – is not dead.

I had thought it necessary to find out a little about *Nat* history because the two most important ones (apart from Sakra, or Thagyā Min) were and are the guardian spirits of Pagān: The Lord of the Great Mountain and his sister Lady Golden Face. Each has a niche in the portal of the city, where the only surviving part of the ninth-century wall stands, and each is given fresh flowers every day. I drove out to the village of Minnanthu, which lies on the sixteen-square-mile area of pagoda-studded plain, and on the way was intercepted by a young man on a bicycle who indicated that he would go and get the keys for the nearby pagodas. I had seen Angkor Wat and Ayuthaya in the Sixties and was not overawed by the scale of Pagān, massive though it was. But here in a temple called Thambula were frescoes over seven hundred years old that had survived sacking and despoiling, centuries of humidity and the 1975 earthquake; and here was our helpful young guide leaning on them, his sweaty palm pressed over the face of some female dancer painted in 1255 or thereabouts. In another pagoda, Hpaya-thonzu, I found him drumming his sturdy fingernails over a beautiful and well-preserved fresco. Later, in Manuha Hpaya, I found that slap-happy decorators had splashed limewash across some of its paintings. It was all a little depressing.

Our guide, Aung Lin, insisted on taking us to his home. Minnanthu village is surrounded, in the age-old manner, by a fence of brushwood and thorn. We drove through a gap in the fence, our arrival causing some commotion among the villagers nearby. Aung Lin said they hadn't had any tourists driving into their village before. Still tying her *longyi* across her chest, an old lady bustled out to see what was going on and was so surprised that she let it fall.

We had a look at the village. In a thatched outhouse stood a sesame-seed press, a giant mechanical pestle and mortar: the great pestle was connected by a horizontal bar to a wooden seat. You poured seed and hot water into the mortar, sat on the seat, pushed off backwards and swung round in a wide orbit. This made the pestle roll ponderously round, crushing the seed and releasing the oil, which the hot water helped to flush out of the drain hole near the bottom of the mortar. In another compound the village ox-cart maker was at work. It took four men a month to make one from scratch, he said, and judging by the one he was just completing I could well believe it. It was beautiful. Every one of the sixteen spokes on each wheel was shaped to fit into the hub almost invisibly and each was decorated with a pattern of brass-headed nails. There was some delicate carving along the sides. The part of the yoke that would rest on the two bullocks' necks was padded with leather, and all the woodwork had been rubbed over with filtered engine-oil to protect it. To my eyes it was a triumphant marriage of form and function – good to look at and oozing reliability – and I couldn't bring myself to ask how much it cost. I felt it would be disparaging even to mention money.

Back at Aung Lin's home, we went into the earth-floored room under the building proper – a good timber building because his father had been Chairman of the local People's Council. His mother gave us slices of pale watermelon which we ate gratefully, as a chicken and her chicks scrambled over our feet. The old lady sat at the table, one foot on her chair (the way most Burmese will tend to sit on such Western contraptions), and continued making large cheroots, finishing off each one in the straw-coloured sheath of a maize-cob and securing it with a couple of turns of cotton and a knot. Looking past us she noted the arrival of her husband but appeared to take no further interest in him, putting one of the fat eight-inch cheroots into her mouth and lighting it. We greeted the head of the family and sat down again. This was the first time I had seen, close to, a Burmese woman 'a-smokin' of a whackin' white cheroot' as Kipling put it. She was now holding it between the thumb and forefinger of her right hand; underneath the cheroot, held by the other three fingers against the palm of her hand as an ever-ready ashtray, was an enamel bowl like a very small chamber-pot. She took a great pull as I watched, her cheeks caving in and her eyelids drooping. The massive end of the cheroot became a bright golden disc, like a sun breaking through grey cloud, and a few small sparks fizzed out. Breathing out the blue smoke and tapping off half an inch of ash, she leaned across the table and passed cheroot and bowl together to her husband. It was only then that I realised: although neither had said a word to the other, this was her way of welcoming him.

The incredibly well planned and skilfully constructed pagodas of Pagān – they were once said to number (of course) 9999 – could not fail to impress. It is a surprising place to find such a high level of technological and artistic know-how expressed in architectural, sculptural and pictorial forms: the massiveness of Dhammayangyi, the loftiness of Thatbyinnyu, the grace of Gawdawpalin, the elegance of Ananda, whose proportions are perhaps the most immediately pleasing to the Western eye. But I can never read a phrase such as 'built by Kyanzittha in AD1091' without thinking how unfair history is. It wasn't built by him and it wasn't, I'm sure, built in one year. Ananda was built by hundreds of subjects little better than slaves, many of them probably only reluctant Buddhists, who cut, hauled, raised and fitted the stone blocks no doubt with great loss of life and limb; by masons and sculptors, skilled artisans like the bullock-cart maker; but not by a king. Yet when it was finished it was he who got not only the credit in the history books but also the merit that would stand him in good stead in his next incarnation.

It was after our delicious prawn curry that the restaurant owner invited us to see his gold mine.

On our way through the narrow back-lanes of the village the following morning we could see that almost every backyard had a deep hole in it, surrounded by heaped earth. In the small compound we visited was a pit two metres square and more than a metre deep. Near it were two small circular pits full of muddy water and connected by a shallow channel. Standing nearby were a bamboo tripod from which hung a bamboo sieve-tray and, raised on bamboo framework, a chute (a bamboo chute!) about waist-high at the end nearest the larger circular pit, and sloping down so as to empty into the smaller one. Fixed on to the head of the chute was a lidless wooden box with a perforated metal base. The ramp itself was covered with a sheet of plastic, then hessian, then fibrous palm roots; and on top of these three layers was a lattice of bamboo strips weighted down by three lumps of fossilised wood.

Most of the extended family were there. The father cut soil out of the big pit with a mattock. A young son staggered across the pit floor with a loaded basket and lifted it up to a lad squatting by the tripod who sieved the contents, discarding stones but retaining any nails or others pieces of metal. Another son took the sieved soil, basket by basket, to a tall cousin who was standing in the larger of the two pits. The soil went into the box, whereupon the cousin picked up a large can in his left hand and a piece of roof-tile in his right. He withdrew a canful of muddy water from around his ankles and, pouring it into the box, stirred the resultant mud with the tile so that a thin slurry flowed through the holes in the metal base on to the waiting chute. As the brown rivulet rippled its way down over the bamboo lattice it deposited its heavier particles in the roots and fibres before running into the small pit, causing an overflow covered with putty-coloured froth to slide along the channel and round the cousin's ankles, ready for recycling.

When fifteen baskets of soil had been processed the lattice was removed and the hessian and roots were placed into a large enamel basin, where another lad carefully washed them clean of adhering particles. He let the sludge settle, carefully poured off the water and then tilted the basin for yet another boy to scoop out the silt with a small enamel bowl. It was this lad who did the panning. Slapping some silt into the family wok and pouring water on it until the pan was half full, he shook the thing backwards and forwards vigorously, then changed to a slower, circular motion. The swirling water spilled over the far lip of the wok until there was little left, and we examined the residue: the steel tab of a zip that had somehow not been screened out, some tiny pieces of lead, a fragment of meteorite. None of these was discarded. More water, more panning, then . . . yes, several small flakes of gold. Each was gently dabbed out on a fingertip. A small glass phial of clear water was unstoppered and the fingertip placed over the narrow mouth. One shake, and the flake of gold fell shining through the water to join others at the bottom of the phial.

Perhaps a thousand monsoons had passed since a hand had applied that gold leaf to an image of the Great Teacher in a gesture of devotion. The Mongols had come ravaging in 1287 and then over seven centuries the earth had from time to time twitched its skin like a dreaming beast, snapping Pagān's spires, scattering bricks, dislodging blocks of stone, toppling images. Torrid heat, wind, rain and roots had completed the levelling. Now the people of Pagān, Ne Win's serfs, were poor enough to rummage in the dust of its glorious past. As a tourist resource this tract of fertile plain spiked with the spires of surviving pagodas is pure gold, a hard currency earner. It is pure gold too in less literal but more enduring ways: historically as a magnificent heritage and a focus of national pride; artistically as an archive of architecture, the plastic arts and painting; and above all spiritually as a source of inspiration, especially when the hidden sun kindles the clouds, or when the pagodas are silhouetted against a golden river, and Tangyi Ridge is dark against a saffron sky.

Five days after leaving Pagān we heard on our radio that yet another of Burma Airways Corporation's handful of planes had plunged out of the skies. It had been carrying thirty-six tourists to Pagān. There were no survivors.

5. Burmese and English

In 1959 I went to teach in Thailand and in four years picked up quite a lot of spoken Thai. I got the hang of its five tones, but not before going through a stage when I was likely at any minute to say a rising tone instead of a falling one, or a high instead of a low, or whatever. The worst occasion was when I leant forward over a taxi-driver's shoulder, meaning to ask the time. I was told afterwards that I had, very politely, said 'Dog shit'. The driver had somehow prevented his careering Austin A40 van from crashing as he rocked with laughter, brushing away tears of mirth with one hand. By 1986 I think I was getting a little old for language-learning. Burmese 'felt' very difficult.

True, it had only four tones; but it was a different sort of tone system from that of Thai. And true, there was only one consonant that could end a word – the glottal stop that Cockneys use instead of the t-sound – but this simply succeeded in making too many words sound similar to each other, so that it was difficult to remember which was which. In its attempts to remember, my poor mind got up to all sorts of tricks. Knowing how important toilet-paper was likely to be in a country not noted for its public hygiene, I set about memorising the Burmese word, which sounded like '*seq-ku-leiq*' (q = the glottal stop). Yes, I thought, that word sounds like 'circulate'; 'circulate' is like 'revolve'; when you pull toilet-paper the roll will revolve. Hey presto! Even now, I remember '*seq-ku-leiq*' as an endlessly revolving spool of tissue-paper, a photograph (*daq-pōu*) as a duckpond and a table (*sa-bweh*) as a subway.

I learned no more than the most basic elements of Burmese grammar, but people were so pleased I'd tried that they made me feel I knew more than I did. I didn't, for example, get to grips with the classifying words that all Southeast Asian languages seem to have. I think the nearest we get to these in English is when, in inventories, we write things like:

Stair-carpet	1 length
Curtains	8 pairs
Cutlery	4 sets . . . and so on.

In Burmese, 'three children' has to be said as 'child-three-person' (*kalé thōu yauq*) for example; and I remember that Thai has a classifying word sounding like '*towa*' which means 'having-four-legs, unless it's an elephant', so that you speak of four dogs or four tables as 'dog-four-(*towa*)', 'table-four-(*towa*)' . . . but not elephants, which are royal and therefore belong to a different class of being and therefore belong to a different class of word. Once upon a time, Burmans were so ethnocentric that their language classified non-Burmans as non-humans. Shway Yoe tells us:

> Foreigners – regarded as aliens and indeed not entitled to rank as human beings at all, since they have never worn the yellow robe – receive but scant reverence from the tongues of the older people.
> . . . the same auxiliary being applied to them as would be used in speaking of a buffalo or a pig. Thus you would say kala hni'gaung, foreigners two animals, or 'two beastly foreigners'. This has, however, now almost died out, certainly in regard to Europeans, and is only occasionally heard with reference to some of the least civilised of the hill tribes. (p.563)

It wasn't easy to pick up more Burmese because people who spoke some English, however little they knew, wanted to practise it. What I did learn was that it was necessary to modify the way I used my own language, especially in the matter of questions. I learned to avoid asking questions beginning with 'why'. Why do people . . .? Why isn't there any . . .? Why has the government . . .? – questions like these were nearly always politely evaded. As I came to know Burma and her people better, I realised firstly that one doesn't ask awkward questions, and secondly that in any case proper answers would have been so complex that only the foolhardy would have embarked upon them. In other words, I learned a little about *ānadeh*.

Even here the gulf between the official and the actual made itself felt. If you wanted a realistic answer, your question had to be phrased in an appropriate way. For instance, you could be shown into an empty, shuttered and clearly long-undisturbed library, ask 'Can students borrow books from this library?' and receive the answer 'Yes'. Your courteous and thoughtful guide would not expect you to pursue the matter any further – a Burman certainly would not do so; but if you were then to break the rules by asking (say), 'If I bring some students here, will you lend them some books?' then that would be a different matter entirely. In English, the answer would be 'No' in both cases. In Burmese English, the answer to the second question would be, 'Well, you see, the Principal is not here, and he has the keys to the cupboards.' Or 'Well, unfortunately the librarian has been transferred.' Although either or both of these answers might be true, the library, even with its librarian and keys, would not be open for borrowing; but your guide would have successfully avoided saying 'No'. No Burmese person likes to refuse a favour or service. Similarly if, at nine-forty-five, you asked a passer-by, 'Does the post office open at nine-thirty?' you would be told 'Yes'. If you said, 'I'm going to the post office now. Will it be open?' the chances are that the answer would be different. The official opening-time was 09.30, but it seldom opened before ten. In fact it was possible (I did it deliberately once or twice) to ask the same person both types of question consecutively and to get contradictory (or rather, apparently contradictory) answers in the space of a few seconds.

With a few exceptions, it was only people within a certain age-band who knew enough English to be able to converse fairly easily; of these, few felt able to speak freely, in a political sense. The very young had not been able to learn enough, and the very old had forgotten too much; so it was upon those in their forties and fifties that I relied most for information and advice. A few anecdotes, and a little history, may make it clear why this was so.

Once, when I was on campus waiting in my car for a colleague, a delightful little gnome of a man toddled up to me. He was getting on in years, and his puckered face looked as if it had been squashed until the eyes bulged brightly. This, together with his small stature, made him look a little frog-like.

'How do you do?' he said slowly.

'How do you do?' I responded, with a smile. Somehow I could see by the look in his eyes that he was trying to peer backwards in time and was stumbling through decades of linguistic rubble in an attempt to find his lost command of English. Then he stuttered away for some time while I politely pretended to understand his drift. A long pause, then:

'This country . . .' And he stopped again, looking helpless.

'Is getting better now,' I prompted. (This was when things seemed to be improving.)

'Better,' he agreed, 'but . . .' and then came an incomprehensible stream of sounds.

'Hm,' I nodded pensively.

'And this country . . . this country . . .' He was looking earnestly into my eyes as if he might find the words he wanted there. Another long pause.

'Accuse me,' he apologised. 'I have forgotten my mind.'

And with a wave, he toddled off.

He must have been in his upper seventies and had gone so long without using English that he now found the language irretrievable. Auntie Than Than had been about eighteen when the Japanese had arrived in Mandalay, and was now sixty-four. Her English was so rusty that at first communication proceeded in fits and starts, with many a pause while Liz and I suggested words until the right one came up. As time went by she became more fluent but, like me, found speaking a foreign language very tiring. Nevertheless, she would occasionally come out with a beautifully-turned phrase, as when she once said of Ne Win's regime, 'It is everything for appearance and nothing for reality.' In conversation one day she went misty-eyed as she thought back to the English lessons of her own school days. She hesitated for a moment and then said:

> O wait for me by moonlight,
> O watch for me by moonlight,
> I'll come to you by moonlight . . .

Her memory petered out at this point, but I had recognised Alfred Noyes' poem *The Highwayman*, which I too as a moony teenager had been stirred by.

'That was 1941,' she added.

She liked that sort of poetry, she said, but hadn't seen that poem for forty-odd years. I searched through old textbooks and anthologies, found it eventually and gave her a photocopy. The poem still brought a tear to my eye.

Coming further down the age-scale, the majority of educated people in their forties and fifties spoke English well – many of them extremely well. The only grammatical mistake I noticed fairly frequently was the use of 'too' instead of 'either': 'I can't too,' they would say. Many had difficulty with the sound 'oi', pronouncing 'oily' in the same way as 'wily'; they spoke of 'bwiled water' and 'fertile swile', and when our landlord referred to one of the flushing lavatories in our house, he gave it the glamorous name: 'twilit'. Burmese has no 'oi' sound, and I assumed that this was the cause of the difficulty. Apart from that, their pronunciation was excellent.

Most university students and people in their twenties and thirties spoke little or no English, except for some of the side-car and horse-cart operators who had frequent contact with tourists. Half of these cheerful but poorly-dressed lads seemed to be graduates. They had got their degrees without learning any English to speak of, and for this my disaffected and cynical Head of Department was largely to blame. They had then picked up a great deal of English in a few months of driving or pedalling, and for this they had themselves to thank; for in my view they made very good language-learners – chatty and inquisitive, with a good sense of humour and a good memory.

If the secondary school students knew only two words of English ('Hey, you!'), the young children seemed to know only one. Everywhere we walked, they ran to greet us. Invariably, their opening gambit was to advance as close as they dared, stick a hand in the air with the first and second fingers making a V-sign exactly like Winston Churchill's (*not* like an angry sportsman's), and then to shout 'Piss!' and grin from ear to ear as they waited bright-eyed for our response. We soon realised, of course, that the kids were saying 'Peace!' but we wondered how this mode of greeting had come about. Surely it wasn't, like the ubiquitous old jeeps, a relic of the Second World War? No, just a long-outmoded greeting used by American hippies in the Sixties, I later discovered. In true British fashion, we would answer, 'Good morning/afternoon/evening' as appropriate or just 'Hello', and smile back as brilliantly as we could. This worked, and soon I would hear parents exhorting their toddlers to say 'Hello' and older children practising to themselves 'Gu maw nin . . . Gu maw nin'. 　　★　　★　　★

The crumpled old man, Auntie Than Than, the civil servants
we came across who were in their forties or thereabouts, the
university students, the schoolchildren – using these age-levels
much as an archaeologist uses layers of débris, you could chart
the recent history of English in Burma. But perhaps we should
begin at the beginning. The use of English in the country dated
only from the British annexation of Lower Burma in 1853, and at
that time there had been no state system of schools, no syllabus into
which the British could insert 'English' as a means of propagating
the language. Just as education in medieval England was in the
hands of the Church, so in Burma it was in the monasteries that
people had traditionally learned how to read and write and study
the scriptures. British administrators, almost always unwilling to
interfere with religions in the territories of the Empire, decided to
leave the monastic schools alone and to set up an alternative system
of lay schooling; but the Governor did nothing to curb the mission
schools that were already appearing, and which used English for
teaching all subjects. The Catholic and Baptist missions seem to
have been especially active in education. The lay system comprised
three types of school. There was the English-medium or 'European
Code' school where everything was taught in English: originally in
these schools Burmese was an optional alternative to 'Additional
English' or French, but as from 1933 Burmese became a compulsory
subject. Then there was the 'Vernacular' school in which everything
was taught in Burmese or a local language such as Shan. The third
type was the 'Anglo-Vernacular' school, which used Burmese in the
early years (English being only a subject) but increased the number
of lessons taught in the medium of English at the upper end of
the school.

The teaching of English then entered a period of ups and downs
that lasted for several decades. With the arrival of the Japanese
Army in 1942, schools closed for a while. When they reopened,
each found itself part of a unified education system under Japanese
military administration, with Burmese as the medium of instruction
and no English lessons on the timetable at all; the mission schools,
however, seem to have been left alone. After the war, with Burma
once again part of the Empire but moving towards independence,
an official report on education stressed the importance of Burmese
to the nation's well-being and supported its continuation as the main

language of instruction; and in 1948 it became the official language of the Union of Burma. Naturally, there were still plenty of people in education and in the Civil Service during the Fifties and Sixties who were fluent speakers of English; in fact, unlike their peers in India and Pakistan, educated Burmese speakers of English had an accent so unobtrusive as to be virtually unimitatable. And the English-medium mission schools remained, tending (as they did everywhere in the imperial and post-imperial times) to cater for an élite and to turn out articulate anti-imperialists who became patriotic leaders and administrators.

But in an expanding education system run on a dwindling budget in troubled times the quality of learning suffered generally, and the forces of nationalism tended to be demotivating as far as the study of English was concerned. In 1964, soon after Ne Win seized power, the last bastions of quality in English language learning fell when the mission schools were 'nationalised' along with the rest. Burmese also replaced English as the medium of instruction in the universities and colleges. During the first seventeen years of Ne Win's appalling misrule, the once-excellent standard of English declined drastically as older staff retired, to be replaced by youngsters who had learnt hardly any English. All this time, Ne Win had been insulating Burma from an outside world which was becoming more and more dependent upon English as an international auxiliary language. (For example, English had become the sole language of international communication in civil aviation and was soon to become the maritime lingua franca too; and most of the world's top-ranking scientific papers were now appearing in English, whatever their national origin.) Realising that a certain amount of English language expertise was necessary for access to the technology Burma needed for economic development, Ne Win announced at an education seminar in 1979 that a mastery of English was required of the country's students. This was an unexpected turnaround. It was said that one of his daughters had just failed the TOEFL test (an English language examination in which a pass was needed for entry to American universities) and that this had made Number One realise the depths to which English had sunk in Burma. Be that as it may, the announcement set in train a flurry of activity in the Ministry of Education.

Unfortunately, neither Ne Win nor his military goons had any idea of how to go about raising the standard of English, and those lower down in the hierarchy merely made it their business (as usual) to comply with Number One's wishes with due, or rather undue, haste. The mixture of ignorance, eagerness to please and true enthusiasm produced quite the wrong decisions; English studies were henceforth to begin in the kindergarten year and, at the same time, were to be introduced into the first five years of primary schooling as well. The schools suddenly found themselves faced with the task of introducing English to three million little beginners, despite the fact that there were now hardly any teachers at that level trained to do the job or even able to speak English themselves. Of course, these teachers were able to accomplish very little in their English lessons, and those giving private English tuition flourished as never before. At the same time, at the upper end of schooling, the official medium of instruction for Maths, Science and Economics was switched from Burmese to English. No one had bothered to find out how many teachers of these subjects were actually able to teach in English. Few could. Even if they *had* all been able to, their students would not have been able to understand the lessons; and that (of course!) would have been the teachers' fault, not the government's.

All of this was just one more facet of life in what could be called a 'schizocracy': a society in which the rulers construct and maintain a system of appearances totally severed from the corresponding realities. Even the education system was in danger of being turned into a non-education system. The outrageously underpaid teachers had to find some way of earning more in order to feed their families properly; they therefore gave private tuition (the word had been borrowed by Burmese and sounded like '*tew-shen*'), sometimes even during school/college/university hours; they earned far more from a few illegal lessons than from days of legal teaching, so there was no point in imparting information too efficiently during official teaching time; and it was not surprising that a few teachers were actually withholding information in school so as to create a demand for it in '*tew-shen*'. Just as Ne Win's cock-eyed economic policies had led to the creation of a vast black market which the Party had ruled unlawful, while at the same time depending upon it, so his education policies had given rise to an outlawed tuition system supported by every family that could afford to make use of it. The symptoms of Ne Win's own schizophrenia – this was my own diagnosis – included a flight from reality into illusion, and he was creating a social system in his own image. I assumed that the process was unintentional.

Naturally, the Burma Socialist Programme Party (BSPP) had its own brand of English, the main function of which was to conceal, or more frequently to contradict, the truth. As soon as I read my first copy of the *Guardian* (Rangoon) I thought of Orwell's 1946 essay 'Politics and the English language', and I later reread it. In it, Orwell maintains that bad prose, especially bad political prose:

> . . . consists less and less of words chosen for the sake of their meaning and more and more of *phrases* tacked together like the sections of a prefabricated hen-house.

Later, using another image, he says that it:

> . . . consists in gumming together long strips of words which have already been set in order by someone else, and making the results presentable by sheer humbug.

Where political writing is *not* bad, Orwell says, it is generally because the writer is 'expressing his private opinions and not a "party line" '; and he adds that political writing is largely 'the defence of the indefensible'. How he would have revelled in dismantling the hen-house of BSPP prose! I enjoyed it myself, and began to compile a Dictionary of Party English; a few of its entries are offered below.

A Dictionary of Party English: Some Examples

affluence, socialist society of   society in which wealth flows from the people to their leaders, thus qualifying the State as country of 'Least Developed Status'.

correct   that which we (see **we**) consider convenient for our purposes, whatever they may be.

destructive elements   insurgents, university students, their teachers and others who disagree with us (see **we**); not, as in British English, natural phenomena such as frost, etc.

eliminate   see **eradicate**

eradicate   slaughter; e.g. 'eradicate all destructive elements'.

further   meaningless euphemism intended to suggest that things are already quite satisfactory; e.g. 'further raise', 'further enhance' = raise, enhance.

indigenous people of Burma Burmans in particular, but more loosely everyone born in Burma except those of Chinese and Indian (especially Indian) stock.

just war a maiming and killing of people in circumstances of which we (see **we**) approve.

literature writings that are **correct**.

loss and wastage theft, esp. by underpaid and hungry elements.

necessary guidance advice considered essential by the Party and useless by the recipient; advice normally (and fortunately) ignored.

rally large gathering of workers forced to attend a Party function and chant slogans at the end.

remote border area places such as the Embassy of Czechoslovakia in Rangoon or in the Rangoon-Mandalay railway line, where insurgent elements operate.

spirit of self help realisation that the BSPP can do nothing for you.

voluntary service compulsory labour.

we a few of us top dogs in Rangoon who are going to keep things as they are, whatever you (see **you**) want.

you anyone other than **we**.

Party English was instantly recognisable as a variant of Marxist/Leninist/Stalinist propagada, but Burma had her own brand of what Orwell might have called 'unnews'. For example, every so often throughout most of our stay the *Guardian* carried a headline that ran: DIRECTIVE NO. 75 EXPLAINED IN (name of town). This directive seemed to be so important that, whenever I saw that it had been explained yet again, I read on in the hope of finding out what it was about. I never did find out; nor did any of my Burmese colleagues. The explanations were always done at large meetings specially convened for the purpose, and without exception the newspaper reports simply listed the dignitaries attending the gatherings and ended by saying that someone 'explained the directive and then gave replies to the points raised.' You were never told what points were raised or what replies were given, but the names and titles of those officiating were very convenient for filling several column inches, especially when you could mention people like: Rangoon Division Party Regional Committee Area Central-level, Paddy High-Yield Cultivation Supervision Committee Chairman and Party Central Executive Committee Member U Hla Tun (12th September 1987). There were frequent accounts of 'ceremonies'

at which insurgents 'asked for forgiveness of the working people
for their past misdeeds' in front of officers, officials and
a thousand or more villagers herded together for the ritual
humiliation. The close of such meetings was pure *Animal
Farm*: 'The ceremony then came to an end with the chanting
of slogans.'

The *Guardian*'s editor wisely refrained from expressing his own
opinions and had adopted the motto 'Whatever you say, don't say
anything.' He simply gummed together the Party's own strips of
words. In the educational field, for example, two of the Party's
tired slogans were 'all-round development' and 'education within
the reach of all'; the leader-writer was able to expand these into
several paragraphs without adding anything new, so that all one
noticed was the numbing repetition:

> The State has been making efforts to bring basic education within
> the reach of all . . . ensures all-round development . . . with a view
> to bringing basic education within the reach of all . . . measures for
> all-round development. . . . The State has been making every effort for
> all-round education development. (12th September 1987)

Since most people could not read English, I wondered why the
Party went to the trouble and expense of printing such claptrap in
my language; and even the Burmese versions of these columns were
in a jargon alien to the Burmese people.

The most celebrated piece of real Burmese English was a phrase
displayed outside pagodas and other sacred places telling the visitor
that within the precincts it was forbidden to wear anything on
the feet. The Burmese always go barefoot in such places, and
foreigners are expected to do the same as a mark of respect. It
was easy for me to kick off my Mandalay sandals, and my feet
soon became hardened to gravel and to hot paving stones; but it
was difficult to credit that the British of imperial times stubbornly
rejected this opportunity to show respect for people's feelings. At
first, the Burmese had not voiced their objections; but by 1920
notices prohibiting the wearing of shoes had started appearing
in the most-frequented pagodas. Maurice Collis, an administrator
posted in Rangoon but visiting Mandalay for a few weeks, saw the
well-known Burmese English notice:

> In the Mandalay of March 1920 the shoe question, as it came to be
> called, had not yet reached this state of definition. I had barely heard
> of it, and though the notice 'foot wearing prohibited' was already up
> outside the Arakan pagoda, I did not think it would be enforced against
> me. (*Into Hidden Burma*, p.56)

That delightful phrase was still the one in use outside the Arakan
Pagoda – or Mahamyamuni Hpaya, or (as everyone in Mandalay
called it) Hpaya-Gyi – in 1988. Collis was more sympathetic to the
Burmese than most, and knew that he was doing the wrong thing,
having already annoyed a bystander.

> It suddenly struck me that I was committing a rudeness, and I wished
> I had not come.

In dealing with 'the shoe question', the British seem to have
been infuriatingly arrogant, accusing the Burmese of simply trying
to belittle them by making them go barefoot. Yet a British captain,
Hiram Cox, had noted as long ago as 1796:

> By the orders of the Government [i.e. the court of Bodawhpaya] no
> person is allowed to go up to the pagoda with their shoes on, but I
> saw many Europeans and native Christians break through the order
> with impunity.

That impunity was enjoyed on sufferance, but the irreverence
shown by failure to remove footwear always rankled. Collis knew
Burma well, but he didn't take his shoes off: to him the only answer
to the problem was not to visit pagodas!

Much more recently another Burmese English instruction had
been added to some notices: LADIES MUST NOT WEAR BRA-LESS.
If this sentence no longer appears, it may be my fault. A Tourist
Burma employee one day asked me to go through the notice and
make corrections. I would have left that sentence alone, but he
knew it was wrong.

Those in search of 'quaint' English might find a little humour
in a hoarding erected by a vegetarian religious group. It probably
still stands on the roadside opposite the south side of the fort in
Mandalay. It said: BE KIND TO ANIMALS BY NOT EATING THEM.

Those bent on nostalgia could find occasional echoes of Raj
days. The inventory in our Mandalay Hotel room listed the
wardrobe as an *almirah*; this was a word that had passed from

Portuguese into Urdu and then into Indian English, but only a few elderly Brits would recognise it these days. For some special occasion Liz once went to college in a dress instead of her usual white-blouse-and-green-skirt teaching uniform, and an elderly lady colleague said, 'I like your gown.' Liz was wearing what I called a 'dress'; when I was a boy people would have called it a 'frock'; I supposed that 'gown' was the word that preceded 'frock' in the days when the strains of the latest foxtrots and quicksteps floated on the moonlit air in old Rangoon and Maymyó, but I was probably just letting nostalgia run away with me. Another colleague one day used the word 'bioscope' for filmshow – a word I'd hitherto heard only in South Africa. On another occasion I was stepping into a horse-cart when an old man stopped and asked why I was travelling by 'gharry', an Indian English word derived, like 'tonga', from Hindi. I said that I had no car and that I was in a hurry.

'Very well,' said the old fellow, as if giving permission. But I think he considered it *infra dig* for a sahib to use that form of transport in this day and age.

Sic transit gloria imperii.

6. Twilit Scenes

In the previous quarter of a century, there had been very little money available for the upkeep of public buildings (except for the mansions occupied by the Party, Police and Army headquarters staff) or private dwellings (except for the residences of Party chiefs, officers and – of course – those in charge of Public Works Department supplies). There were plenty of fine but shabby old houses, of which ours was one, in the area that used to be called the Civil Lines in the bad old days of Empire. Because they were made of teak, or of teak and brick, the structures were generally sound; but any surviving bathroom and lavatory fittings were of some antiquity. No one could tell us how old our house was. I should think it dated only from the Thirties; though the lavatory cisterns were crazed like Ting bowls of the Sung dynasty, the porcelain bore such unclassical names as 'Armytage Ware' and 'Twyford's Civic'. It is the only house I had ever lived in that had three bathrooms, each with a Western-style sit-up-and-beg toilet. Since there were two upstairs, Liz and I enjoyed the luxury of having one each.

At some point in the distant past someone must have dropped the lid of Liz's cistern, because it bore not only the fine network of Sung-like crazing but also a coarse mesh of jagged cracks from which the cement had oozed as some patient repairer had endeavoured to hold the mosaic together long enough for the cement to set. On one corner, he hadn't quite managed to prevent it sagging, but it had held together and done its job and I regarded it as a minor monument to Burmese persistence. I had got to know this lid quite well because the flushing mechanism beneath it had once or twice failed and in removing and replacing the lid I had always handled it as if it were indeed Sung porcelain. With

an adjustment here, or with a bit of wire there, I had managed
to keep it going until now; today it wouldn't flush, didn't even
gurgle, merely sighed. In the toffee-coloured sludge at the bottom
of the cistern I found parts of a heavily-rusted broken washer and
a few pieces of some unidentifiable material. I had to go to work;
a guest was due to stay with us the following day, so we asked the
landlord to get the repair done as soon as possible.

When I got home at lunch-time the landlord was sitting on
a seat under the 'plum' tree in the front garden. Indoors, over
a cold lemon barley water of local make, I ascertained that he
was well, that his family were all well and that there was no
news of much import. He then ascertained that we were well
and that we had no news or rumours to pass on either. All
this time, there had been intermittent hammerings and tapping
noises issuing from the bathroom upstairs, accompanied by cries
of exasperation and followed by silences punctuated with grunts of
disappointment. The landlord informed me, rather superfluously,
that the plumbers were upstairs 'mending the twilit'. They were
upstairs, sure enough; but 'mending the twilit' sounded a little
optimistic. U Ko Ko Gyi, the landlord, went up to join them
while I grabbed something to eat.

I then went up to the bathroom to offer moral support and
peered in. The place was a shambles. It looked like an abattoir
in which someone had just slaughtered and dismembered some
denizen of the deeps, something large, aqueous and rubbery –
a giant cuttlefish, perhaps. The tiled floor glistened and was
streaked with reddish-brown veins which converged upon a hole
in the corner and slowly drained themselves. Splashes of the same
gory colour dribbled thinly down the white-tiled walls. Flabby
strips of some flaccid matter lay strewn across the floor, their
undulating outlines contrasting with the angular and business-like
shapes of a large knife, a monkey-wrench and a hammer.

Squatting in the midst of this carnage were three slender
male figures in threadbare, spattered shirts and *longyis*. Two were
intently watching as the third made some adjustment to the arm
that held the ballcock; they were so engrossed that they had not
noticed my arrival, so I had time to study the chilling remains
that littered the floor. A dark amoeboid shape turned out to be a
sheet of black rubber – part of a truck-wheel-sized inner tube –

from which a large disc had been cut and whose scalloped edges
showed that it had provided many a smaller disc; the alarmingly
flesh-coloured sac lying collapsed in a corner was the wet and
tattered bladder of a football, also with a large circular hole in
it; and the semi-transparent thing leaning against the foot of
the lavatory pedestal was the upper half of a large celluloid
X-ray plate, minus a disc that had been cut out of someone's
right lung.

The ballcock and its arm were now being fitted together and
replaced in the cistern, and the landlord joined me. I pointed to
the membranous tissues on the floor and said I assumed we now
had a plunger made of inner tube, football bladder and X-ray
photographs – was that right? He drew closer. Yes, exactly, he
said. Of course, there were some things that were rather more
suitable for a twilit but, because these were not available. . . .
I nodded sympathetically, like a fellow surgeon conferring over
the internal chaos of some hapless moribund patient. There was
a sudden seriousness in the air. The mosaic lid was brought
like an offering and placed on the cistern, the handle turned.
A rushing of water but, oh dear, a leak. Honour was at stake,
I felt, as the man who appeared to be the foreman took the
wrench and tightened a large nut. Flush. No leak. Looks
of triumph.

'*Kaun-gaun-deh,*' I said. '*Theiq kye-zu tin-ba-deh.*'

Three very wide and very white grins answered these few
words of appreciation, and the plumbers filed down the stairs
with heads held high, followed by the landlord. The next day Liz
used the toilet and when she depressed the handle it swivelled
uselessly around. With an adjustment here and a bit of wire there,
I fixed it. There was absolutely nothing wrong with the plunger,
and it continued to work without fail for the rest of our stay.
(Incidentally, by the time the lid of the downstairs toilet had got
smashed, the patient porcelain repairer had obviously had enough
of mosaic work: he had simply shaped a slab of teak so that it
sat snug on the cistern, and then painted it white to match. Why
have a shatterable lid?

Thursday, 5th November was the full-moon day of *Tazaungmon*,
the eighth lunar month of the Burmese calendar. In many homes

a special seasonal dish was being prepared and, as in so many
traditional Burmese matters, the colour yellow was involved: in
this case it was the pretty flower-clusters of the *'may-za-lee'* tree
(Cassia siamea), which somewhat resemble those of the laburnum
tree. The buds and tender leaves were used in the making of
a clear soup and also in a savoury mixture of a stuffing-like
consistency. Our landlord brought us a dish of it, and we found
it a pleasant enough confection but unremarkable; it seems,
however, that its flavour is not its most important quality.
According to a Burman traditional belief, at this time of the year
the guardian *Nat* of the *hpyauq seiq* (the constellation Pleiades)
comes down to earth and stays with his good friend, none other
than the *Nat* of the golden-blossomed *'may-za-lee'* tree. The *Nats*
of all the other trees also converge on the *may-za-lee* to welcome
him. It naturally follows that if you eat the buds and leaves
gathered on this night, you can imbibe the medicinal properties
of all the trees in a single potion, and thus be assured of health,
strength and longevity.

In England, the kids would now be pestering passers-by for
'a penny for the Guy', and, at dusk, burning their scarecrow-like
effigies of Mr Fawkes. Among Burman youngsters, there is a
tradition that has some affinity with the April Fool's Day
hoax and with Hallowe'en pranks. The youngster has to steal
something from a neighbour's premises without getting caught
out, and then put the stolen property in some public place
where the shamefaced owner will have to reclaim it in full
view of the wisecracking neighbours. A youngster who is caught
in the act is punished by being made to perform some useful
social service, such as clearing a small piece of ground. That
was the tradition. By now, the range of pranks was not, it
seemed, confined to the removal and deposition of other people's
possessions.

Another feature of this *Tazaungmon* festival is the weaving
competition. Within the precincts of certain pagodas, teams
of unmarried girls compete in the weaving of new robes for
presentation to a nearby *kyaung*. At the pagoda called Set Kya
Thiha the night before, five teams of girls had laboured on as the
full moon swung slowly overhead, hastening to weave the strips
of cloth that would be sewn together to make a *hpongyi*'s robe.

I had understood that the robes were to be made from scratch, the process beginning with the raw cotton and ending with the finished garment. Two of the teams did have an older woman who spun the cotton into thread for the weavers, but of course this natural cotton was being made into white cloth, not the saffron worn by a monk. The other three teams were turning out coloured cloth, but they were using ready-spun thread that had already been dyed. Maybe this was another example of a custom in the process of change, or perhaps decay.

As for the colour of the robes worn by the *hpongyi* of Burma, I had tried without success to find out why it was that so many wore maroon, scarlet, dark brown, orange, chestnut, even geranium-red robes, and so few the saffron colour that was traditional and which I had grown used to during my four years in Thailand as a young teacher. The traditional dye, gamboge, was prepared from a substance exuded by a tree (*Garcinia hanburyi*), of the same family as the mangosteen, which is found in much of South-east Asia. (The name *gamboge* derives from *Cambodge*, which is what the French called Cambodia before its *padi*-farms became the killing-fields of Kampuchea.) The juice of the tree was collected in much the same way as the latex of the rubber tree, but was then allowed to harden into orange-brown lumps. In water, the gamboge would form a deep yellow emulsion which gave a vivid golden hue to the cloth steeped in it. I had read somewhere that the bark of the jack-fruit tree also yields a suitable dye. It seemed that hardly any robes, at least in the Mandalay area, were now dyed in the traditional way, and no one seemed to know why. One person suggested that the monks chose different colours because they like to cut a fine figure, but I think this was a mischievous interpretation. Another was of the opinion that the aniline-dyed black-market cotton mixtures might wear better and be more comfortable than the customary cloth; I would have thought the reverse was true. Whatever the truth of the matter I often felt that a group of monks or novices, instead of presenting a marvellous splash of glowing gold, had a rather ragged look in their variegated robes.

The Deputy Rector and I strolled outside, ducking under some stout crosspieces of bamboo scaffolding, and turned to look at the neo-classical façade of the solid old university building with its foundation stone dated 1921. The whole frontage, including the imposing pillars at the top of the stone steps, had just been painted a creamy yellow except for the floral mouldings, shaped like Tudor roses, that bordered the high arched doorway. Each of these had been picked out in other colours: candy pink, baby blue, pastel green and then again pink, blue, green . . . The English Department ladies had said these colours were awful, I had agreed, a male colleague had added that the portico looked like the entrance to a Hindu temple (and what insult could have been worse?) and I had offered to try to get the technicolour flowers restored to their normal monochrome.

'In England they'd be the same colour as the wall,' I said.

No response. The Deputy Rector obviously liked the colours.

'At most they'd all be the same colour.' That was a mistake.

'What colour?'

'Oh, er, . . . white, maybe.'

The next day all the flowers were white and my colleagues were looking reproachfully at me. They didn't like white. It was the colour of mourning.

All this was part of the preparations for the visit of Anne, the Princess Royal. Very soon after arriving in Burma I had expressed the hope that, since all previous book exhibitions had been held in Rangoon and the books donated to Rangoon University, the next lot ought to go to Mandalay. I was getting more than I had bargained for: not only a book exhibition but also a princess to open it. A British aircraft of the Queen's Flight had brought a group of bigwigs to carry out a dummy-run of the royal visit. They had found a spruced-up campus: the mud and litter had been shovelled away from the gutters, the roads weeded, the overgrown bougainvillea on the roundabout neatly trimmed and the red carpet rolled down the wide flight of steps. I had peered at their arrival, squinting through the wooden slats of my window, and then turned back to my chores. There were the usual lizard droppings to brush off my desk and chair; and what was I to do with the fascinating network of white ant channels that I had been studying as it spread up the wall and then branched out into space towards the back of my chair like delicate antlers? I regretfully cracked off all the tiny tunnels in case HRH should call, sprinkled insecticide powder all round my bookcase and then settled down to work.

Gangs of workers settled down amid heaps of lime and gravel along 73rd Street, and kerbstones began to appear. Meanwhile cows, oxen and pigs continued to meander through the campus. Cattle sometimes strolled up the steps of the main building, stood under the colonnade wondering why the flagstones sprouted no grass and then relieved themselves before moving on to pastures new. I conjured up all manner of hilarious encounters for Princess Anne. Inside the lofty main concourse, the walls, pillars and ceiling had been coated with Reckitts blue emulsion; the echoing hall possessed all the dignity of a large municipal indoor swimming-pool.

But alas, it was not to be. The Burmese authorities were worried about security – that is, of course, lack of security – and switched the venue to the Town Hall. The Karen National Union had written to Her Majesty saying, in effect, that she shouldn't send her daughter to Burma; and the Kachin Independence Army had endorsed this view. Amnesty International was also making noises about Burma's atrocious human rights record but eventually, one week before the event, it was announced that Princess Anne would visit Burma 'in the near future' – no dates, no itineraries, no purposes were given. So there were to be no hilarious encounters with cows, no stories to dine out on. Still, the campus looked much better now. Except for the white flowers, of course.

Liz's secondhand car wasn't ticking over very smoothly so we took it to the garage of an elderly man whom we knew as Peter and whose son was called Ivan, though there was no Russian blood in their Chinese veins. Peter was square-faced and stocky, and his grizzled hair bristled like a chimney-brush. He would sit in his open-sided workshop reading English and American novels and occasionally issuing instructions or advice to Ivan and his mechanics, and he spoke faultless English as if taking part in an academic debate in pre-war Oxbridge. We left the car in his hands but had no sooner arrived home than he and Ivan turned up in a smart new car. Dramatically, Peter held up two sparking-plugs.

'These are plugs one and three,' he announced unsmilingly, putting them into my hand.

In each case the lower part of the L-shaped electrode had snapped off at the right-angle.

'Was this really how they were when you took them out?'

'It was indeed. I've never known a car continue to run with plugs in that condition. Remarkable.'

The two pieces of metal had obviously gone into the works, and I was worried that they would cause some damage.

'Well, they are quite soft,' said Peter. They might be lying harmlessly somewhere in a corner. Or they might have been blown through on the exhaust stroke.'

'Can't we take the top off and check?'

'Ah, but you're between the devil and the deep blue sea.'

'Why?'

'Well, my dear sir, have you got a spare gasket?'

'Oh, I see what you mean.' In taking the top off, we would almost certainly ruin the existing gasket.

'Might I offer some advice?' said Peter. I nodded. I knew nothing about engines. 'I think we should drain the engine oil off, as you intended in any case, and fit new plugs. Then you should drive it for a short time. Should there be any sign of malfunction, you would bring the car straight to me. You see, a piece may become attached to a valve, in which case regrinding would be necessary. Or possibly the . . .'

Peter was, I could see, entering upon a lecture; so I cut him short by agreeing. Outside stood the brand-new Toyota saloon they had arrived in.

'Nice car,' I said admiringly. At a sign from his father, Ivan opened the bonnet.

'Very nice,' said Peter. 'Transverse engine, but whereas the traditional . . .'

I didn't want to cut him short again, but Liz managed to do it nicely for me.

'Is it yours?' she asked. It was a very effective conversation-stopper.

'Ah,' muttered Peter, closing the bonnet, signalling to Ivan and moving towards the passenger door. 'Er, no.'

'Whose is it?'

In answer, we got the thud of a closing door and a brief wave in the gathering dusk.

In his Town Hall office the recumbent colonel was on some sort of drip-feed. (People of other countries take their tonics orally, but the Burmese who could afford it were taking theirs intravenously.) Apparently the authorities in Rangoon had agreed to a three-day book exhibition but the local People's Council Chairman had said that only one day was possible because there was to be a puppet-show in the big hall the day after the opening of the exhibition by Princess Anne. Burmese officials have always been good at offering excuses that are also slights, but a small Embassy team was now overcoming this little obstacle. The negotiations were coming to a close when it was noticed that the inverted bottle was empty and air was about to enter the vein of this Party Pooh-Bah. After a hurried disengagement of the apparatus, the team left with permission to set up the exhibition the following day (Saturday) and to leave it open until Monday afternoon. The royal opening was to be on Sunday morning, but in Burma it is normal for all preparations to be carried out at the last moment.

In the big hall the next morning there were two great piles of pale hairy rugs that looked like trimmed polar-bear pelts, several huge drum-shaped objects which turned out to be rolls of the obligatory red carpet, some display stands and grimy cabinets from the university and, all over the parquet flooring, a curious random criss-cross of purple lines. Knots of Burmese workmen stood around uncertainly, like warehousemen half an hour before knocking-off time. When I got an E-shaped layout organised and began to get it laid out, it became clear what the strange purple floor-markings were. Not having a suitable red carpet, the workmen had improvised by rolling out what they had and spraying each length with the nearest colour available. The pale rugs had then been needed to cover up the network of stains on the floor. The glass fronts of the cabinets were cleaned with lime and water and placed in position, then filled with books and cassettes on English Teaching; the stands were aligned and covered with forty Shakespeare posters; and the rugs and carpets were carefully disposed. Filthy and exhausted after three hours of heavy work, I slept like a baby for two hours after lunch, until the squirrels frolicking on the corrugated-iron roof woke me up with their imitation of a steel band.

'Princess Anne's gonna love you in that get-up,' said the Cultural Attaché.

It was Sunday, and I had gone to the door in shorts, dirty patched sawn-off jeans. The wearing of a suit is an indignity to be suffered only under considerable duress, and I had been hoping to get out of attending the opening ceremony. But our presence was required and half an hour later, clad in our best, we hopped into the jeep under the proprietorial and approving eye of Margaret. As our gardener, U Kyit, opened the gate, his mouth fell open too.

Somewhere in every Burmese town there must be a depot full of potted plants, for any building that is to house an official function sprouts flower-covered shrubs and potted palms overnight. The hall looked like something in Kew Gardens and was thronged with soberly-clad men and brilliantly-dressed ladies. I hid behind the crowd but the Attaché found me and positioned me just behind the row of dignitaries lined up to meet HRH. On reaching the end of this line the Princess, obviously well-briefed, said to the CA, 'But haven't you got a lecturer here at the university?'

'We have indeed, ma'am.'

It was a put-up job, and there was nothing for it but to step forward and be introduced. When she moved on into the exhibition she was dogged by my HoD, whom no one could detach from her presence. I could have sworn I saw her cast her eyes heavenwards at one point, but of course no princess has ever done that sort of thing in public; but then again, no princess had ever met my HoD before.

Liz and I got away as soon as the royal guest had left. Liz was off to Singapore that evening to attend a conference and was also going to take the opportunity of getting an expert diagnosis of a small lump that had appeared in her right breast. It was sunset when I took her to the station and settled her into an ancient sleeper waggon. I marked exam papers all evening, and turned in just before midnight. I had just put the light out when the house hiccuped; beams creaked, the things in the bathroom cabinet rattled, then all was still. Only a minor tremor, but the Burmese had made me quite superstitious about earthquakes, and I felt a twinge of uneasiness.

I had insisted, against stiff opposition from my colleagues, that I should do my share of the marking. It was only fair – the stacked-up bundles of scripts in the department office looked like a model of Manhattan. In the end I was given a light load as a compromise: only 1616 scripts. Each took about twenty minutes to mark with any reliability so, given a forty-hour week doing nothing but marking, my share represented three months' hard labour. I was marking some bundles done by the First-Year Honours students, or 'Horners' as many of them called themselves, one young hopeful even styling himself 'Hornest'. The text in their exam was about how pickpockets are trained, and how they 'graduate' by removing a wallet from a dummy figure that has bells in its pockets. Switched on to automatic, my mind was now guiding my red pen through the answers at speed. There was evidence of extensive copying, and soon I found a whole batch calling the thieves 'prickpockets'; this soon failed to distract me but when script after script insisted that the dummy had its balls in its pockets, I had to clock off for a while.

There had been no news from Liz, but we had always agreed that 'no news' meant 'good news', so I wasn't worried.

I got back down to my marking and immediately felt, as I always did, very sorry for the students. Knowing that their English was so weak, they memorised chunks – often proverbs and aphorisms – as all-purpose components to be fitted into any possible essay topic that might come up in the examination. For the essay on 'Studying for the examination', some were able to produce a flattering account of themselves, e.g. 'I very hard work and intelligent and I will pass this exam.' Some were more aware of, or honest about, their limitations and had in their hundreds reproduced their versions of a 'chunk' suggested by some bazaar crammer or private tutor: 'Some are born bright. Others are dullards. But I am mediocre.' One lad's version ended: 'But I am medorice' (he could say that again); another preferred: 'But I have

top: The stunning golden
light of Shwe Dagon
Hpaya
middle: Our grand old
house
bottom: Gerry's Angels

Kalaw in jacaranda-blossom time

top: Dhammayangyi Hpaya,
Pagān
above: Woman selling spices,
Yaunghwe market
right: Carved teak panel, Shwe–
kyaung–gyi

previous page: Karaweiq
barge on Mandalay Palace
moat
top: Novices greeting Liz:
'Piss!'
middle: Thanahka in the
shape of bodhi-tree leaves
bottom: Teachers wearing
padang flowers

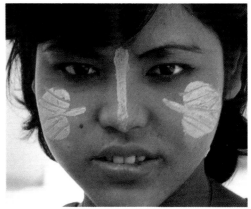

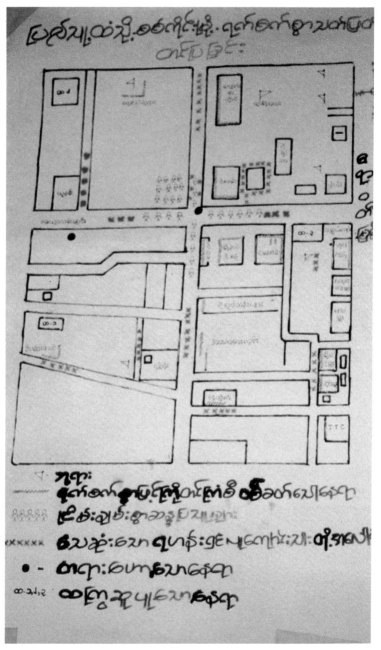

Sagaing exhibit in the students' news display, Mandalay University

top: The Ava Bridge at
sunset
middle: In the market,
Maymyó
bottom: Banner with
photos of Sagaing victims,
Hpaya Gyi

left: Protest posters on a *chinthe* below Mandalay Hill
below: Buddhist nuns demonstrating below Mandalay Hill
bottom: 'A euphoric multitude shepherded by the monks'

medicare' – lucky boy! A few grovelled: 'I am very try but not good brain.' One student, who had managed to memorise the most 'chunks', had produced a truly dazzling second (and incidentally final) paragraph which went as follows:

> I hope, the examinations well success. God helps those who help themselves. Avoid evil and it will avoid thee. Do not tell tales out of school. A wise man changes his mind sometimes, a fool never. Extremes are dangerous. Therefore I am not extremes studying for the exam.

I piled on extra marks for that final bit of logic.

We had brought to Burma some seeds of what we called the Moonflower, a type of convolvulus whose real name we did not know. We had come across it in Kampala, where it sprawled over fences and entwined itself with hedgerow plants, producing hundreds of incandescent white trumpet-shaped flowers that scented the dusk. We had collected seeds to grow in pots on the balcony of our flat on the campus of Makerere University. One evening I had noticed a flower-bud, a long slender pale green neck with a bulbous tip furled spirally like a closed parasol. I got up to make our sundowner of *waragi* and fresh lime juice and came back to find a fully-opened satiny white trumpet that glowed in the half-light. It had opened in a matter of seconds. After that, we got a great deal of pleasure from watching them opening at sunset. They were very punctual but opening-time did vary a little according to the amount of light and warmth still coming from the west. When we moved into a house on the campus that looked westwards across a little valley, I built a little bamboo fence along which we trained more moonflowers and we encouraged the local kids – all sizes, from toddlers to teenagers – to come and watch at the appointed time. Their eyeballs and teeth glowed white with delight as the trumpets opened. Once, a flower had snapped open so suddenly that the tiny tot nearest to it had jumped and fallen backwards, to the good-natured jeers of his playmates.

We had taken the seeds back to England, but they didn't do well; so we saved them until, two years later, we went

to Cameroon where Liz had obtained a post in Bamenda.
There they had grown well and we had again saved seeds;
these were the ones that we had brought to Mandalay and
which were now producing buds. A plant in a pot up on the
balcony carried one bud which, I knew from experience, would
open this very evening. Margaret seemed impressed when I told
her all this.

'You want to watch, Margaret?'

'Yes.'

'About six o'clock?'

'OK.'

But it opened early. Fortunately, on my way downstairs to get
a cup of tea soon after five, I noticed that it had already started to
ease open and ran to fetch Margaret. We squatted, our noses only
inches from the bud, and the flower obligingly opened within ten
seconds while Margaret was exclaiming 'Oh . . . OH . . . AWE!'
She went off to chirp at her husband in excited Karen, and I
returned to my marking. After a few hundred scripts, the topic
of 'Studying for the examination' was getting a little boring. But
lo! The first script of this batch began: 'I am studying my hard.' I
read on with renewed interest but discovered only that while some
are born bright and others are dollars, the writer himself was not
extremes – just medoicre.

That evening I went to a friend's farewell party which,
though attended almost solely by expatriates, was brightened by a
performance of Burmese music by Mu Mu Thein and her troupe.
Mu Mu herself sang expressively and accompanied herself on the
hsaung, the Burmese harp. A girl on each side of her sang the
parts that in the West would be called 'choruses' and also danced
a little. At one end of the row of performers was a violinist and
at the other end a drummer. This man spent some time 'dressing'
the small standing drums he was going to play. He pulled over
each one a sleeve of colourful cloth; then he tuned them by
rubbing a sort of paste on to the hide until it produced the right
tone when tapped.

Mu Mu's hsaung was a beautiful instrument shaped like a boat
whose tall narrow prow curved back a little and then forward,
like the neck of a swan; or perhaps it would be truer to say that
the instrument as a whole resembled a swimming waterfowl. The

bird's back (or the boat's deck, if you prefer) was of stretched
hide, the rest of the body (or hull) of tough *padauq* wood; and
the thirteen strings stretched diagonally from the back of the
neck or prow to the centre of the bird's back or ship's deck.
The upper, thicker strings were of silk cord, the lower ones of
nylon. In former times all would have been of silk, of course.
They were all held to the neck by loops of thick red cord
which could be loosened and retightened for rough tuning, and
finer tuning was achieved by twitching the loops up or down the
curved neck.

As she played, I watched Mu Mu's expert hands and noticed
that whereas European fingers would be angular and knuckly
when plucking the strings, hers curled inwards and curved back
in flowing movements as if they were made only of ligament.
The boat-like sounding-box was producing a pleasant tone with a
surprising resonance, and I was enjoying my unimpeded front-seat
view. After a few minutes of the performance, however, the people
sitting behind me started chatting. One man was clearly in danger
of getting some blood into his alcohol-stream and made a noisy exit
to the kitchen where cans of Foster's were carving their shapes
into chunks of ice in a huge bowl. Another guest lolled back and
rested his feet on a stool, not realising that by presenting the
soles of his feet to Mu Mu he was insulting her. I would only
have added to her embarrassment if I had caused a scene, so I
let it pass.

The old nightwatchman U Po Bwin was opening the front
gate as I turned off the road. I parked the jeep under the 'plum'
tree and walked across to have a word with him. The full moon
was brilliant in a clear sky and the air was chill with dewfall. I
told the old man to bring his chair under the portico; then bade
him goodnight. The light of the high full moon of Natdaw, the
respected *Nat*, even as a reflection off wall and roof and tree,
shone on my bedroom curtains so that the window was as silver as
a cinema screen.

Sunday. Beautiful morning, but . . . back to my marking.
The students in this batch insisted almost to a man that the
Rector was very kind, that they themselves (through medorice)
loved their teacher much and that therefore (another delicate piece
of logic) therefore they would pass with flying collar and perhaps

even with destination. Occasionally I was shocked to find a bit of real communication. One hopelessly poor candidate wrote:

> I am lazy to learn my lessons. I did not study. So I worry for this exam. I am not interested in my subject. Schoolboy injoyed in my study. Now I am unhappy my studen life. Forgive me my tutor.

I gave him lots of marks for actually telling me something about himself. Another lad was more confident. He told me: 'I was repaired for examination.' I think he meant 'prepared', but in Burma one can never be sure. Yet another went out of his way to be helpful, ending his woefully inaccurate three-sentence essay with: 'Stop hear.' I complied unhesitatingly and went to pour myself a whisky-water. I had been at it the whole day, except for brief breaks for lunch and tea.

Liz telephoned from Rangoon and said she'd been advised to go to England as soon as possible for further diagnosis. We both knew the implication, and she tried to cheer me up by telling me about all the things she'd bought in Singapore. As I greeted her next morning at the station, two muscular lads lifted all her heavy luggage on to their shoulders, assured me that they knew my vehicle and disappeared into the press of travellers and welcomers. When we finally emerged they were standing by my jeep, grinning amiably; and when I paid them off they said, 'Thank you, teacher' in Burmese. It says a lot for the people of Mandalay that I had not been worried about the cases; and it was little incidents like this one that were making us feel very much at home there.

Liz insisted that I should stay and carry on as usual, and in the few days at her disposal she was utterly thorough in clearing her desk, getting her classes taken care of and briefing me in matters domestic. Just over a week after arriving, she was leaving again and our friend Thuzar, the young woman who worked for Tourist Burma, was kissing her a not-quite-tearful farewell at the airport.

Back to the marking. One First-Year Horner informed me that Bell invented the telephone in 1976. I was aware that Burma was in the grip of a time-warp (an old joke said that when you arrived from Bangkok you had to turn your watch back thirty minutes and your mind back thirty years), but this was going too far. I think I was probably kinder to the candidate who wrote:

> Telephon or Bell was invited in 1786 by an American. He first enabled to speak his assistant who was 100 yards long. It was a great improvement. Listener received a massage in form of signals.

Days later and in a daze of ticks and crosses, I was startled by an explosion of singing in the lane beside our house. Eleven o'clock was very late by Mandalay standards, and it was pitch dark, but a couple of dozen souls were singing lustily to the twanging of a guitar. Laying aside my red pen, I went down to where our Karen nightwatchman sat reading his Bible under the portico. The song, which I hadn't recognised, had come to an end. In the silence a baby wailed and was comforted; then there was only the clicking of bicycle chains and the creaking of saddles. I asked U Po Bwin who they were.

'Arsey,' he said dismissively.

'Who?'

'Roman Catterlick.'

'Oh.' The penny still hadn't dropped.

A light appeared at the house opposite and the group burst into song again.

'Eyesore delight!' they chorused. 'Eyesore delight!' Then came a Burmese version of *They'll be Coming Round the Mountain*, which I assumed had less bawdy lyrics than the ones I had learnt in the Army. Finally, barked out in unison, came: 'Meh-yi Kissmass tu-yu-aw!'

I had completely forgotten that Christmas was almost upon us. The house opposite was then darkened, and the bicycles clicked and creaked off into the night.

Late the following evening Liz phoned from Manchester. A biopsy had confirmed that the little lump was cancerous. Over such a distance and in the knowledge that some Military Intelligence thug was probably monitoring the call, big things remained unsaid as we took refuge in small-talk. Although it was very late when I put the phone down, I took further refuge in the marking that had to be done. But the essay topic 'An important day in my life' elicited no gems of humour – rather, nuggets of philosophy. 'An important day in my life is I was born day.' Who

could deny the truth of that? 'I had an important day in my life.
I have already forget that day.' Life's like that. 'I am very happy
staying in my life.' Quite so. The student is teacher of the tutor.
I went to bed.

I nearly jumped out of my skin the following night when
the silence was shattered by a deafening 'Merry-Christmas-to you
all!' that exploded beneath my feet. The Karen carollers were
in the portico directly below my study, and had broken into a
calypso-rhythm carol backed by several guitars, a tambourine and
maracas. As they were finishing this opening number, I opened
the doors. I wasn't feeling very jovial but, spreading my arms
expansively to match my smile, I said 'Merry Christmas!' as
heartily as I could. Back, with the precision of a machine-gun,
came a thunderous 'SAME-TO-YOU!' They performed more
songs. During a beautifully-sung version of *Silent Night* I looked
across at U Po Bwin. He gave me a smiling shrug, which said,
'See? Much better than Arsey.'

I was stuck on number four. 'For each statement write TRUE or
FALSE' said the exam question, and the candidate had put:

1 Flase
2 Ture
3 Flalse
4 Flure
5 Ture

I made a mental note that the next year's paper should, as an
experiment, ask the candidate to write TURE or FLASE. As I
hesitated over item four, the door-bell rang.

'I am the son of U Kan Hlaing,' said the young man on the
step. Oh, Lord, would the contractor-saga never end? He wanted
to pick up the heaped stones and gravel left behind six months
before, which theoretically belonged to the Embassy. As it was a
public holiday, I said No he couldn't; but as it was Christmas, I
said Yes he could, some other time.

A colleague had invited several of her staffroom friends to
come and sample her husband's cooking. Ma Ma Charity, who
was Margaret's aunt, and Ma Thant were among the guests.
After a meal of good Muslim food, during which I surreptitiously

observed the antics of a couple of rats that were exploring goods
stacked against the wall, I took Ma Ma Charity home, and
Ma Thant then took me to see a twelfth-century pagoda in
Amarapura. Shwe-kyeq-kyá Hpaya stands on a riverside knoll a
little upstream from the Ava Bridge, still the only bridge across
the Irrawaddy. Built by the British in 1935, deliberately blown
up by retreating British forces in April 1942 and not repaired
until 1954, the bridge itself was nothing to look at. What pleased
the eye was the skyline of Sagaing on the far bank. The sacred,
pagoda-studded ridge is beautiful in any light, but when a low sun
bathes the scene, morning or evening it can be incredibly lovely.
As we watched, the sun sank behind a thin band of cloud near
the horizon, the sky became a great gilded dome and the vast
expanse of water slid by like flowing gold. A flight of large birds
flew eastwards across the river and into the gathering bluish dusk,
and below us three small boats sent ripples of black into the gold
as the last fishermen gathered up their lines and paddled for the
now shadowy shore.

   Such peace. Such a lovely place to have a bloodbath.

7. Creatures Great and Small

It was now Independence Day (4th January) and I had received no Christmas mail, no word from Liz. All must be well. I went to see the traditional canoe races on the northern stretch of the palace moat. Behind my moat-side seat I could hear the rumble of the bullock-cart races, which I was beginning to think might be more exciting than the canoe-racing; but then a great double-breasted ceremonial barge sailed into view. It was shaped like a pair of *karaweiq* (a mythical long-bodied waterbird) swimming side by side and supporting on their backs a large pagoda-like structure. The whole craft was mainly (of course) golden-yellow, with details picked out in red, blue and white. Along the back of each *karaweiq* sat a file of brightly-dressed maidens in thick make-up, paddling prettily in unison; but they were only paddling the air, and when the barge slewed round for a return run I saw that it was propelled by two ancient and raucous outboard motors. It was a stately, glowing spectacle. I would not have been surprised to find that the sole passenger was an oriental Cleopatra on a burnish'd throne; but under the 'pagoda' was a traditional orchestra, while on the bow two women in spangled red and glittering headdress danced sinuously. Four ceremonial canoes wove in and out, manned by oarsmen dressed as generals, courtiers and ministers of a bygone age. On the narrow prow of one, a male dancer cavorted to ear-splitting amplified drumming without any apparent fear of losing his balance and plunging into the moat.

I recalled that when the British flotilla had been on its way up the Road to Mandalay in November 1885, the man that King Thibaw had sent southwards to deal with the problem had been the Master of the Royal Barges. I wondered whether his job had hitherto been simply to arrange regattas such as this one on the moat. He certainly had no fleet or warships under his command. All he could do was pretend:

November 24th was another day of peace, yet that same evening Ava's Commander-in-Chief, the Master of the Royal Barges, sent a telegram to King Thibaw, announcing a great victory over the British. (Foucar, 1946:139)

Thibaw no longer ruled over Mandalay; nor did the conquering British; but Mandalay still had her barges.

A week later Liz got through on the phone: the tumour had been removed and she was out and about already. Another week, and a great heap of mail arrived, containing five letters from her, just two days before I flew down to meet her at Mingaladon. She came striding across the tarmac as chirpy as ever and then, for a whole week, took part in a teacher-training course in Rangoon. Margaret was especially glad to see Liz back, I think, because Master appeared to have been going funny in the head. He had taken to prancing about in the garden barefoot and almost naked in the blazing sun, scampering from bush to bush shouting 'Ow!' or worse. I had taken some fine photographs of leaves a split second after gorgeous butterflies had taken wing, but I wasn't going gaga.

While driving to and from the university, I had at various times narrowly avoided flattening humans of various ages, dogs of various shapes and colours, pigs of all sizes from frisky pink piglets to lengthy mud-covered sows, goats, bullocks and – biggest of all – great, placid buffaloes that lumbered across the roads, slow, single-minded, unstoppable. (I had long ago in Thailand learned that when hit at, say, twenty miles an hour by a decelerating car, a water-buffalo will often just walk away, leaving the vehicle badly damaged.) I thought I had encountered all the jaywalkers that Mandalay had to offer – human, canine, porcine, ungulate – but I had not. The road to the university, 73rd Street, was beginning to get busy again and, driving towards the main gate, I was behind the usual group of five lads cycling in line abreast, talking and laughing as they dawdled along, each with one arm on another's shoulder. I accelerated round them in second gear, then stood on the footbrake as hard as I could to avoid a head-on collision with an elephant. Fortunately, there was just room to pull over and let the towering beast pass. The man leading the creature out of the campus gave me a look that left me in no doubt that he was questioning my sanity, and I realised what I had done: as I overtook the cyclists, I had sounded a warning hoot which must have appeared to be for the elephant. As is so often the case, one sees the humour of the situation only after the event. Had I run into the poor elephant and been squashed into a subsequent existence, I like to think that some latter-day Orwell would have written my obituary and entitled it 'Hooting an Elephant'.

Some time later, I saw the elephant coming back past my room with a Burmese-style howdah on its back. The *oozi* or mahout sat in the centre of the howdah, and on either side of him sat a boy resplendently dressed in *shinbyu* robes - the finery worn before entry to the novicehood in a monastery. On either side of the elephant walked a young man holding a traditional red-and-gold umbrella to shade the boy riding above him; the handles must have been about ten feet long. The elephant passed out of sight, carrying the two young *maung shin* on a triumphant yet solemn journey that symbolises the relinquishment of the riches and vanities of this world which Prince Theidat (Siddhartha) had achieved when he left his aristocratic comfort, first to become a wandering mendicant and then, on attaining enlightenment beneath the bodhi tree, to become the Lord Buddha.

On reaching home (or, if they were not brothers, the place agreed by their parents), each lad would set aside his finery, have his head shaven and washed ceremonially and, on assuming the saffron robe, become for some time a member of a monastery. This period was, according to the old custom, the four months of Buddhist Lent; the novicehood thus corresponded roughly to the rainy seasons. But that was true only of devout families. As far back as 1882, Shway Yoe observed:

'A few boys remain only twenty-four hours in the yellow dress, long enough to enable them to go once at least round the village begging from door to door . . .'

But he added that it was 'considered hardly decent for the *shin* to leave under seven days . . .'

Summer had arrived. A week earlier, the temperature in Rangoon (where it was generally much cooler, though more humid) had reached 104°F. I had no means of knowing what the local

temperature was, but all the symptoms of high summer were
in evidence. The street corner by Mingala market was once
more melting and folding itself, like something out of a Geology
textbook, into hills and valleys of hot and wrinkled tarmacadam.
The city's cyclists were more dazed and dozy than ever, so I
constantly reminded myself: 'There is nothing around a Mandalay
cyclist.' My colleagues, whose diet was far poorer than mine, were
complaining of the heat, though it was not bothering me yet. In our
garden, various birds were courting and nesting, and the mangoes
were now an inch or more long; and some other trees had shed
many of their leaves. It felt as if spring, summer and autumn had
all arrived at the same time.

And the reptiles had reappeared. The turquoise blue lizards
dormant in all the gardens were now to be seen on almost
every tree-trunk, sunbathing or nodding vigorously to themselves
or chasing dowdy little brown females up and down and round
about; I had seen a couple of vipers on the road in the last few
days; and the first domestic snake of the season had been seen at
the water-tap in the back garden. I had received a copy of a circular
sent to the friendly group of Australians working on the Mandalay
Water Project, who seemed to have made us honorary Aussies. I
had known before coming to Mandalay that Burma had the world's
highest incidence of death by snake bite. This circular pointed out,
among other things, that 90 per cent of snake bites in the Mandalay
area were those of the Russell's Viper, one of the world's more
deadly snakes. This creature and the cobra were common enough
and venomous enough to warrant caution. I made a mental note
to be more careful now when scrambling about on hillsides, and
especially among old pagodas, whose sun-warmed bricks and cool
crevices provided near-perfect living conditions for snakes.

The python is non-venomous and kills by constriction. But
unlike its cousins, it grows to be quite a size and has made a
name for itself in Burma over the years. In the Thaton district
in 1927, for instance, a twenty-foot specimen swallowed a sleeping
hunter whole, feet first, presumably after first crushing the poor
fellow. The python was discovered in a state of post-prandial
lethargy and killed. In 1972 a python of similar dimensions ate
an eight-year-old boy. Fortunately, the city was not crawling with
pythons. However, the Russell's Viper was fairly common and,

although the hospital had a supply of the right serum, there were likely to be unpleasant side-effects, the nature of which remained unspecified. (About rabies, the circular was less optimistic: the hospital possessed only the old type of serum, which had to be administered in a lengthy series of painful injections into the stomach lining. I had already decided that, since one had twenty-four hours in which to get initial treatment, if I got bitten I would fly straight to Rangoon for the quicker, less painful modern treatment.)

Another creature that had recently emerged was the tucktoo, a largish lizard that inhabits trees, roofs and walls, usually outside rather than inside buildings. I preferred the more onomatopoeic Thai name – *took-eh* is the nearest I can approximate to it in English spelling. The name comes from the series of hiccups-cum-belches that these lizards produce from time to time, day or night, but more noticeably at night. They warm up with a short crescendo of single syllables (took-took-Took-Took-TOOK–TOOK) and then stop this stuttering to announce TOOK-EH! TOOK-EH! for up to a dozen times in a slow decrescendo. On this particular day, the one outside my office produced eight hiccup-belches; thirty years earlier, my Thai colleagues had told me that seven brought good luck to the hearer - seven, no more, no less. They had also told me that if a *took-eh* bit your finger you would never be able to free it from the creature's mouth without killing the lizard and cutting its jaws away. They never told me why or how anyone might contrive to get his finger stuffed down a *took-eh*'s throat in the first place.

The *took-eh*'s lesser cousin, a small house-gecko called in Thailand *chingchook* and in Malaysia *chichak*, is *ein-myaung* in Burmese. No room is complete without a dozen or so of these semi-translucent putty-coloured lizards. They scurry up walls and across ceilings – especially near lights, where insects gather – and snap up, often audibly, mosquitoes, flies, beetles, insects of many kinds. I had once watched a three-inch *chingchook* in my Bangkok house catch and deal with a resting dragonfly whose wingspan was almost twice as broad as the lizard was long. It was a long and noisy struggle, the *chingchook* chattering occasionally between its clenched teeth, the dragonfly's wings vibrating against the kitchen wall and all but lifting the lizard into the air. For fifteen minutes the stricken insect buzzed its four powerful iridescent wings in an attempt to take off; but whenever it rested for just a moment the reptilian jaws jerked the insect's thorax a fraction deeper into the gecko's throat. Two wings floated to the floor. The two opposite ones continued to vibrate for a minute or two before dropping off. The *chingchook* then bashed the dragonfly's body repeatedly against the wall by swinging its head in a paroxysm of triumph. The dragonfly's large head flew up in an arc and clattered across the stone floor of the kitchen. The *chingchook* had then wriggled the remaining thorax and abdomen slowly and voluptuously into its gut.

These little house-lizards will tackle almost any insect except ants and certain species of beetle. Being indoor creatures, they do not hibernate during the cool weather. They occasionally fall on you as you open a screen door or move a curtain, whereupon you feel a brief cold wriggle like a weak electric shock; then you hear a faint 'splat' on the teak floorboards and you see a dazed little thing that you feel sure must be badly injured; but as you look it scuttles to the skirting-board, leaps on to the wall and scurries behind a picture or a bookcase or whatever to nurse its headache. Occasionally, you wake up to find that you have rolled over in your sleep and squashed one; sometimes you crush one between door and jamb; and once as I opened the door of the freezer compartment of our fridge I startled a young *ein-myaung*, which leapt into the ice-box and quick-froze itself. But, on the whole, the creature cannot count homo sapiens among its natural enemies. The ones that inhabited my room at the university were a bit of a nuisance in that every morning I had to sweep their droppings off my books and papers; on the other hand there was one in my study at home that appreciated my guitar playing and would chirrup as soon as it heard the first strumming.

I don't much mind snakes and other reptiles, though naturally I was always wary of snakes because unless you are an expert you can seldom tell whether a particular specimen is harmless or deadly. (An old Indian handbook of mine says that 'a certain amount of precision in its identification can only be acquired by noting the characteristics of some of the important scales' – which means getting well within striking distance.) A lot of harmless snakes are therefore needlessly killed all the time. But harmless or harmful, snakes don't make my blood run cold. Large spiders do. I went one morning down the garden of our temporary house to look at a well that supplied us with all our water. Lifting off the corrugated-iron cover, I could see nothing at first but the reflection of a bright sky, motionless palm fronds and the silhouette of my head. Then there was a minute movement of a point of light a foot or so from my right eye, on the brick-lined wall of the well. A huge spider was watching me. It was the colour of dark soil and had the squat body and powerful legs of a small crab. And it was bristly. Two of its eyes were glittering at me, taking in the sudden foreign light and refracting it like tiny shattered windscreens. I was being eyed with circumspect efficiency by a born killer that was much too close for my liking. Gently I straightened up and gently I lowered the cover into place and allowed myself to breathe again.

We weren't often bothered by spiders, fortunately, but scorpions were a constant problem. I narrowly missed scooping up with my bare hands a large dark one that had taken up residence under some emptied-out packing material. Discovered, it scampered straight for my bare foot, whereupon I executed a standing leap towards a broom and then executed the scorpion by using the broom as a sledgehammer. Sweating, I swept the bits outside. I always sweat when I have to kill something. Liz is cooler about these things. One day she opened the door of our Mandalay Hotel room to find a scorpion on the carpet just inside, waiting to welcome us. She picked up a standard lamp and planted it heavily on the creature before it had time to think, then called one of the staff to take away the remains.

After we had settled into our stately home, we came back one night to find a land-crab running under our portico and on down the drive. (It reminded me of a morning long ago in Bangkok during the rainy season, when I had come out of my house to see a fish waddling across the drive. While I stood and gawped at this marvel, the gardener ran out into the rain and caught it for his lunch.) But this, Liz and U Po Bwin agreed, was a crab; so when, some days later, I was about to relieve myself in the downstairs twilit and saw two pairs of pincers protruding from a small hole near my left foot, I thought I'd find out more about these creatures. I got down on all fours to have a look. The hole between wall and floor was too narrow, the claws too slender, too black: it was a scorpion, ebony claws held akimbo, dead still.

I called Kyit, our Karen gardener, who sucked air through his teeth, said 'Aw!' like a crow, ran off and returned a few seconds later with the carving knife. (I had tried in vain to get Kyit and Margaret *not* to use my favourite Spanish carving knife for stabbing blocks of ice apart, prising mortar off bricks; I hadn't mentioned the killing of scorpions.) Kyit slowly positioned the blade against the wall then brought it down hard like a guillotine. The black pincers clicked into life and started working like some netherworld mechanical digger. As he dragged the knife away from the wall other sets of legs and a squat black body came into view, the tail finally whipping out of the crevice and striking the blade with its venomous sting. After a while it unbent itself and fell flat to the floor. It wasn't the biggest scorpion I'd seen – that had been one we'd come across in a Borneo forest – but it was the blackest. When Kyit had removed the thing, I prowled around the twilit recesses to make sure the scorpion's mate wasn't nursing revenge somewhere. Confucius he say, wise man relieve mind before bladder.

That wasn't the last of the household's scorpions. Just before going to bed one night I stopped at the foot of the stairs, unaware for the moment why I had stopped. Then I knew that I had registered some detail in the dining-room that was different from usual; then I knew that it was something to do with the corner opposite the door I had just closed. That was all. I turned round, opened the door, flicked the light on and walked over to the corner. Jutting out from under the teak skirting-board was a pair of black-pincered legs, held akimbo. Sweating, I half-heartedly tried to crush it with a piece of wood that was handy, but I was far too slow. I warned Liz, as she got up first in the morning, to watch out for it. The next morning Liz brought me a cup of tea and said casually, 'That scorpion, I got it.'

But, as usual in the tropics, it was the smallest creatures that did the most damage. Mandalay could probably boast of dozens of species of ants; the ones we suffered from were some normal-sized ones that ran like the wind and some minute reddish ones that bit like tigers. Close-packed hordes of these little red devils had long ago succeeded in achieving all the usual feats, invading the kitchen, colonising the cupboards, committing mass suicide in pots of jam sealed with screw-top lids and drowning in an alcoholic stupor in the dregs of wine and beer. Then for a fortnight or so they disappeared. Had they moved on? Was the ant season over or something? No. One morning I moved my radio cassette-recorder and found under it a heap of black dust. The ants had pulverised the cassette-to-cassette recording mechanism.

When the really hot weather came, the ant High Command decided that an airconditioned bedroom might be preferable to a sweltering kitchen. Patrols and search parties were sent out under cover of darkness into the bedclothes. Encountering vigorous resistance and chemical warfare, they retired to regroup elsewhere. This new rendezvous turned out to be the study, where they found huge reserves of edible glue in book-spines, lampshades and furniture joints. When they took to climbing up the chair I was sitting on and marching into my shorts armed to the mandibles with formic acid, it was my turn to retire for a drink. I found their dark, fleet-footed cousins living very comfortably in our ancient, dying refrigerator.

It was the middle of May and Liz was down in Rangoon working on a teacher-training course. Margaret started clearing away the breakfast things, and said casually, 'Master like flog?' (I never succeeded in getting her to call me anything but 'Master'.) I knew Margaret's English, and her strict Baptist background, well enough to know that she wasn't suggesting a session of steamy masochism while Liz was away.

'Yes,' I said, 'I like them very much.'

'Er? Uh?' She looked at me askance with disbelief. Challengingly, she added, 'You like tomollow dinner?'

'Oh yes, Margaret. Yes please.'

With her hand across her mouth she laughed incredulously, as if only the Karen could possibly like eating frogs, and managed to convey that it had been her uncle, the old nightwatchman, who had jokingly suggested to Margaret that she should ask me if I'd like to try a meal of frogs. (I could just imagine the conversation – in rough translation – of the previous evening: 'Mm . . . These frogs is good. 'Ere, tell you what. Ask His Lordship if 'e would like a nice Karen frog curry. Go on, dare yer. Watch 'is face. Be a laugh, won't it?')

The frogs, curried with a lot of chilli and ginger, were served the next evening. They were excellent, and I arranged that frogs would be on the menu the first evening after Liz came back from Rangoon. When Liz too pronounced them good, Margaret was struck almost dumb with joy and amazement.

That little culinary episode was a happy one, but our experience of eating another little creature was not quite so delectable. It was mid-October when little mounds of fresh dark earth started appearing along the edge of the drive and on the lawn. Moles? But the little heaps were much smaller than molehills. While I was eating my breakfast one morning, I saw Kyit the gardener delving into one of these tiny piles of earth. As he didn't speak English, I called Margaret outside.

'What makes these, Margaret?' I asked, pointing to one of the heaps.

'We call *hpayit*.'

'It digs, like this?' I put the backs of my hands together in front of my face and made cramped breast-stroke movements, as if I were parting thick undergrowth as I staggered through the jungle.

'Yes, Yes!'

'Ah. Moles. We call them moles.'

'Can eat.'

'Moles? No, I don't think . . .'

'Karen eat.' A smile of beatific triumph suffused her face. These *hpayit* were obviously not only a delicacy but a challenge. I thought we might as well try one or two, if they were that good.

'Has Kyit caught any?'

'Aw yes, plenty.'

'Can we have some for lunch?'

Margaret's eyes widened. 'You try?'

I nodded. Mole meat ought to be quite tender, though you'd probably need two or three to make a complete meal. Margaret chirruped at Kyit, who ran off towards the garage. 'U Kyit bring,' she said.

He came back holding something between thumb and forefinger and held it up for my inspection. It was about three inches long and was clad, not in glossy black fur but in what looked like a copper coat of armour. If you were to cross a cockroach with a very large grasshopper, the outcome would be something like this creature: a flat, plated body, a pair of long and powerful hind legs for jumping, a pair of short and powerful forelegs for digging and another pair for good measure. As these limbs groped the air a few inches from my nose, I tried to maintain an unruffled expression on my face. I forced myself to say what I had intended to say. 'Yes, we'll have some for today's lunch.'

Leaving Margaret and Kyit looking at each other uncertainly, I started to walk back indoors when a terrible thought crossed my mind. I remembered how, in Cameroon, a boy had pounced delightedly upon a great green grasshopper that had landed on the bonnet of our car. He had torn the legs off, stuffed the twitching body into his mouth and crunched it up with a grin before my very eyes. These *hpayit*, these – yes, they must be mole-crickets – I knew I couldn't eat one of these *raw*. I stopped.

'Er, Margaret.'

'Yes, master?'

'The *hpayit*. You fry?'

'Yes, fry very good.'

Thank God for that. I asked her not to tell Liz but just to serve them up as part of lunch. But when the time came, she served up the usual type of meal and stood just inside the kitchen holding a plateful of *hpayit* and saying 'I bring?' in a stage whisper. By now, of course, Liz knew that something was up; besides, you could hardly mistake the brown carcasses, belly-plates and leg-stumps uppermost, for prawns.

'What are these?' asked Liz in a voice edged with suspicion and a touch of indignation.

'Mole crickets, I think. Burmese delicacy,' I said. 'Fresh from the garden.'

'Right, I'll try them.'

We tried one each, watching one another to see the effect. They were a disappointment. The outside was very leathery and the inside very oily. To give them a fair chance we ate a couple more, but they were too rich. We weren't enjoying them, so I took the rest to Margaret, who accepted them with an 'I-told-you-so' look on her face, popped one into her mouth and put on her smile of beatitude; only the Karen palate, she was saying, could appreciate to the full the juices of the *hpayit*. My whole afternoon was punctuated by mole-cricket-flavoured belches and in the middle of the night I was awakened by a shrill stridulation that I assumed was a *hpayit* love-song.

In the morning there were fresh little mounds in the drive. Two boys, who were supposed to be helping a carpenter to fix something in the servants' quarters, were engaged in catching the creatures. They squatted by a mound, carefully brushed aside the freshly-dug earth to reveal the insect's tunnel and then poured water down a hole. It might take several pints before the *hpayit* decided that enough was enough and emerged, to be nipped by waiting fingers and popped into a plastic bag.

A little later U Ko Gyi, the landlord, arrived on his bicycle, as he often did on Sundays. He carefully untied a cloth bundle to reveal a pot . Oh no, not . . .

'*Hpayit*,' he beamed. 'Cooked by my daughter.'

Margaret said later that they were very good.

But that had been back in October. At the end of February, six weeks after returning from England and proudly showing me her scar, Liz went off to Manchester again for routine post-operative radiation treatment. She would be away for almost three months.

8. The Other Woman

Liz had phoned from Manchester a couple of times to confirm that she felt fine and that her treatment was going well. In Mandalay the days were getting hotter and hotter. One pleasant place to visit when the weather was hot was U Bein Bridge, down in Amarapura – only a half-hour drive away. In the dry, hot weather the bridge is an elevated walkway of stout teak timber crossing a sandy plain, and looks like a long rickety pier at low tide. Here and there the bridge widens to form a roofed resting-stage where the visitor can sit on a bench and cool off in the gentle breeze; but if you cross the bridge without stopping, it is a fifteen-minute stroll. The soil below is dry and sandy but, being a flood-plain, very fertile and capable of yielding two crops per dry season. However, the source of the Irrawaddy is hundreds of miles to the north in the lower reaches of the Himalaya – not very far from what (if the Chinese haven't yet claimed it) is the highest mountain in Southeast Asia: Hkakabo Razi, 19,297 feet (5881 metres) high; and when the faraway snows begin to melt, turning the hill streams into roaring brown torrents; and when the monsoon looms overhead, airlifting tons of water from the south-west; then very soon the great river begins to seethe and rise like boiling soup and to overflow its banks. At this spot, by the bridge, the overspill creates a lake with a depth of fifteen feet or more. It extends on either side for many square miles, and although it is only seasonal it bears the name Taung Thaman Lake. The walkway is then only a few feet above the surface.

I had some photographs, the product of a previous visit, to give to some novices of a monastery on the other side of U Bein Bridge, and my good friend Thant agreed to accompany me. She and her friend Ma May had gone with Liz and me on a visit to Ava and another to Monywa; when Liz was away, May had cooked various meals for Thant and me; Thant had shown me several pagodas and monasteries; all in all these two were, in true Burmese fashion, spoiling me.

I parked my little white jeep among the stately trees and crumbling pagodas of the old capital city, Amarapura, and Thant and I walked down to the old bridge. I had last seen it when the choppy floodwaters were high; now the shallow valley was carpeted with vegetable crops, with a few *padi*-fields and duck-farm areas where there was still a little standing water. It was now possible to drive to the opposite bank but, when I saw the great wall of dazzling dust rising behind a truck coming across, I decided to go further along and walk over the bridge to the other side. On the approach to the bridge, under the great trees, there is a cluster of stalls that offer the sightseer prawn fritters, grilled fish and other titbits. We ran the usual gauntlet of frank, dark-eyed stares from vendors and customers alike, and strolled on to the bridge and into the blistering sunlight.

The massive teak pillars and the structural timbers were firm and in very good condition, considering their age, though some of the walkway planks were in need of repair or replacement. The bridge always reminded me of two very Burmese traditional features: the shifting capital and shifty contractor. When, after centuries of glory, Pagán fell in 1287, successive kings established their capital cities in various places – among them Sagaing, Ava, Toungoo and Pegu. Without going too far back in time, we might start with King Hsinbyushin: he came to power in 1763 and within a year had shifted his capital from Sagaing to Ava, on the other bank of the Irrawaddy. Within twenty years, Bodawhpaya was transferring it a few miles northwards to Amarapura; but forty years after that, Bagyidaw moved it back to Ava. Eighteen years later, it was back in Amarapura, this move being perhaps at least partly prompted by the destructive earthquake of 1838. Whatever the case, King Tharawaddy had not long settled into his new capital city before he died, leaving his rather incompetent son Pagán Min himself, to succeed him. We shall hear a little more of this man shortly; fortunately for his subjects, he was deposed after seven years of maladministration by the far more regal and devout Mindon Min and, fortunately for Pagán Min himself, the new ruler did not indulge in the customary slaughter of the predecessor, his family and supporters. But Mindon Min did follow the custom of shifting the capital, and by 1861 his vast new palace was completed and Mandalay became the 'centre of the universe' until the British brusquely broke the spell and, in their turn, shifted the seat of power to Rangoon. To this day, though, it seems to me that the Burmans of Mandalay regard their city as the moral, if not the legal, capital of the country.

For the second aspect of traditional Burmese life that the bridge reminds me of, we have to go back to the short and ineffective reign of Pagān Min. There is at least one reason to be grateful to him, for it was he who gave the order that the bridge should be built. Being what we would call the mayor of Amarapura at that time, a certain U Bein assumed the role of contractor for the job. Perhaps contractors for building projects are very much alike in certain ways wherever you find them, and perhaps this has always been so. Certainly in the Mandalay of 1988 there was nothing that disappeared so fast as cement, sand, gravel, lime and sheets of corrugated iron; and certainly the old wooden houses of contractors and men in charge of builders' yards were the dwellings most rapidly replaced by fine new constructions of concrete, brick and tile. Even if he ends up in prison, as one of our neighbours did, the contractor knows that his family is luxuriously housed and that no one is going to pull the house down. Well, U Bein didn't exactly make off with the building materials; having acquired the project funds which were intended to cover the cost of new timber, he used instead pillars and beams taken from the former palace in Ava, abandoned when the capital moved to Amarapura. When Pagān Min found out, he was not amused; and U Bein was charged with fraud. But he couldn't have made a bad job of a timber bridge that is still standing firm after a hundred and forty annual floodings and heatwaves.

Thant and I crossed the bridge, walked along a dusty track through the little village at its southern end and entered the precincts of Kyauqdawgyi Pagoda. I had studied its architecture and mural paintings before; so, while Thant knelt in respect to the Lord Buddha and made an offering of flowers, I went outside and observed the dazzling butterflies that were visiting the bright pink-and-white bougainvillea, which foamed over the pathway like raspberry-rippled ice cream. Having delivered the photographs to a group of delighted young novices, we strolled back through the village and I stopped at a stall I had noticed earlier. Among other foodstuffs on sale were some slender little cooked bodies that turned out to be grilled rats, something which I had never knowingly eaten; so I bought one and we shared it. There wasn't much meat on it – for a good meal you'd need three or four – but it was quite tasty and not all that different from chicken. In fact when, that evening, we took May out to a supposedly good restaurant for a 'welcome-back-from-Rangoon' dinner, the food was so awful that I wished we had treated the grilled rat stall as a Burmese take-away. As was usual after a meal in town, we all went back to my house for an after-dinner coffee and a chat for an hour or so; then I drove Thant and May back to their hostels. If I had known what was being thought and said behind my back, my ears would have been burning.

Nothing happened for a week. That is to say, nothing dramatic. A bomb exploded outside the Czechoslovakian Embassy in Rangoon; there had been a grenade attack on a pagoda festival in Hsipaw by Shan insurgents; and a group of Karen insurgents destroyed a bridge in Bilin. But these events and many others like them were sufficiently distant and sufficiently normal at the time to leave one feeling as if nothing had happened. The head of my department had still held no meeting of the MA examiners, so no MA second-year work could start. Without any class-list, I gave the MA first-years an opening lesson in Phonetics, only to discover afterwards that hardly any MAs had yet reported, and that their seats had been filled by keen undergraduates dying to be taught by Hsaya Gerry. At home, Margaret the cook had been looking down-in-the-mouth all week, and at breakfast on Saturday was almost in tears. I thought this was because I had the day before disapproved of her cutting off the head of the large fish that I had carefully told her not to decapitate. (The head had furthermore disappeared, presumably into the family stockpot out in the servants' quarters.) But it was a far more serious matter than that.

She whimperingly told me that after I had left work on Monday morning, and again on Tuesday afternoon before I had come home from the university, an unknown female had telephoned. When Margaret answered, she was asked if Daw Khin Thant Han was there – she was Daw Khin Thant Han's servant, wasn't she? In spite of Margaret's feeble protestations of 'Nooo, I no Burma servant, I English servant' and so on, the anonymous caller had persisted and, it seemed, upset her very much. Margaret's eyes were clouded with resentment. 'I love madam, I love master, I love Daw Khin Thant Han, I love Daw May,' she wailed. 'But I no happy.'

I said I thought this caller must be just some servant who was jealous because Margaret had a good job and nice new quarters. I didn't believe that, but I smiled encouragingly and told her not to worry about it. I wanted to get back to my toast, but the drama was still to come. Margaret coolly told me that on the previous Sunday evening I had driven home only one of my two guests; that on Monday morning she had seen me bundling a woman into my white jeep before driving off to work; and finally that she had found some long black hairs on my pillow! All this was conveyed in broken but surprisingly fluent English. Her meanings were crystal clear and she seemed convinced that everything she had said was the incontrovertible truth. I felt as if I was taking part in an ancient 'B' movie with the sort of plot in which there are incomprehensible events and accusations, and the nature of the frame-up only emerges in the final twenty minutes of the film.

But at the same time, like the film's innocent protagonist, I realised how serious the whole situation could become. If at that moment a judge were to ask Margaret what had happened, she would no doubt put her little Karen hand on her little Karen Bible and tell him what she had just told me, and no one in a jury would have any reason to disbelieve her. Of course the doorkeepers of May's and Thant's hostels could, if summoned, testify that each lady had returned to her own room that Sunday evening; but in Burma the medium of 'news' was not the accredited report but the credible rumour. I decided to investigate a little.

But cross-examination didn't work. When I started asking her questions, Margaret assumed that I was worried and alarmed that 'the truth' was out, or perhaps she thought I was protesting too much.

'No problem, no problem,' she said soothingly, putting a finger over her lips to show that she could be trusted not to tell anyone; and the more I said there was no truth in her story, the more she said there was no problem. In the end, I took her outside to where my jeep was parked in its usual place under the big *tha-bye-thee*, the so-called 'plum' tree.

'Margaret, on Monday morning my car was here?'

'Yes.'

'And you saw me push someone into the car?'

'Yes. Wear yellow.'

I paused. On Sunday evening, Ma May had been wearing bright yellow, but . . . and then I knew what it was that Margaret had seen. But I continued.

'Which side was I, Margaret, this side or this side?'

'This side,' she answered, pointing to the driver's door. I opened it. I pointed out that the driver's seat was not movable, that it would be silly for someone to get in this side and have to clamber across the gear-lever to the passenger seat. (The jeep had no rear passenger doors.) Margaret said nothing.

'Where were you, Margaret?'

She pointed across to the other side of the garden, where a path led round the garage to her own quarters.

'I come back from market,' she explained.

We walked across. It was quite obvious that the driver's door was not visible from that spot, the car always being parked at an angle. Still Margaret offered no retraction or apology or expression of doubt, so I went upstairs and fetched a large, bright yellow shopping-bag from my study.

'You remember I took fruit to the university on Monday morning?'

I had got the gardener to pick two pomelos and had taken them in the bag as a little treat for my colleagues. I remembered swinging the bag on to the passenger seat before climbing into my jeep, and demonstrated this. For the first time, Margaret smiled; but she said nothing. Did she actually prefer her own explanation?

I wasn't too worried about the melodramatic black hairs. They could well have been Margaret's, though when I suggested this she gave me an arch look as if to say, 'What *are* you implying?' And of course the bit about driving only one guest home was an assumption that followed upon the glimpse of yellow the following morning. But that mystery voice on the phone. Woman. Someone who knew our phone number. Someone who might resent my friendship with Thant and May? Perhaps. Student? Unlikely.

Someone bitter enough to make nasty calls would be an older person, surely.

I had given up speculating and was getting ready to go out when the phone rang. It was Liz's closest colleague, who was checking to see whether I'd had any news from England. Yes, I said, Liz was getting along fine. . . . Yes, thank you, I was fine too. Then, 'And how is your cook – cooking?'

The hairs on my neck twitched.

'Oh, fine, thanks. She's improving quite a bit these days.'

'Well, if you need anything, just ask,' replied the forty-year-old unmarried woman at the other end of the line. I murmured the appropriate formulae of thanks and put the phone down. No, surely not. Not her, of all people? No, of course not. There I was, almost falling into the same trap that Margaret had fallen into: making assumptions on too little evidence. When I considered the whole business later over a glass of beer, I decided that if there had been a mystery caller (I had only Margaret's word for it), Margaret could have simply told me at the time or even chosen to ignore the calls. But she hadn't. Not only that, she had made up and stood by a soap-opera tale of forbidden passion which, if believed by the education authorities, could get May thrown out of her job and me thrown out of the country. What it boiled down to was that Margaret was telling me that she didn't like the way female colleagues visited me in Liz's absence, or took me to various pagodas and monasteries – the mystery voice had apparently mentioned these little trips. It just wasn't Baptist. I was angry, but anger would do me no good whatsoever. Over dinner, I told Margaret that I would be taking Thant to Sagaing the next morning. She pursed her lips, but said nothing.

Although I knew Margaret wasn't telling the truth, it was not until I read Fielding Hall's *The Soul of a People* some months later that I felt my diagnosis of the situation had been correct. I read of something that had happened, perhaps a century before, to the new young wife of a British government officer in an up-country post. He had to go on tour for a fortnight and left her in the care of his servant. When he came back his wife said how very dull it had been, seeing hardly anyone for two whole weeks. The master of the house (the *thakin*) noted this and later had a word with his servant.

'Didn't anyone come to call?' he asked.

'Oh yes,' the servant answered; 'many gentlemen came to call – the officers of the regiment and others. But I told them that the thankin was out, and that the thakinma could not see anyone. I sent them all away.'

. . . for it is the Burmese custom for a wife not to receive in her husband's absence. . . . It would be a grave breach of decorum to receive visitors while her husband is out. (pp. 202-3)

It says a lot for the non-sexist nature of Burmese society (Burmese women were much more 'liberated' than their British counterparts even in Victorian times) that what was sauce for the goose was unquestionably sauce for the gander.

I took Thant to Sagaing as promised. She was expecting to be posted back to Rangoon at any time and wanted to pay a last visit to a monastery towards which her family had some obligation or other. When she had done her duty there, we went to the summit of Sagaing Hill where she prayed in the pagoda called Soon U Pounya-shin. Down in the dusty white heat of the town we had a lunch of noodles and headed for the university; but it was so hot that on the way back I couldn't resist stopping for a glass of *maji-hpyaw-ye*, a muddy-looking but very refreshing drink whose main ingredients, apart from water, are tamarind and jaggery (palm sugar). As I drove along the shimmering, melting roads I looked out for a roadside vendor with a barrow carrying what looks like a mound of fresh green leaves. Yes, there was one, standing in the slight shade of some overhanging branches. Under his sprays of leaves was a covered earthenware bowl containing what looked like flat dark beer that had gone cloudy – not appetising to look at but, with its pinch of salt and squeeze of lime, an excellent pick-me-up.

Liz would be coming back soon. There was no news from her that week, but again she had said that no news would mean good news so I was not worried. Her radiation treatment, she had assured me, was going well. Margaret realised she had overdone things a little and went out of her way to be nice to me, chatting more than usual and asking what I would like to eat. At work, I had succeeded in getting the Head of Department to hold an examiners' meeting, the first for years. (His preferred method had been to collect all the tutors' marks, alter them at will so that every candidate passed, and order a colleague to sign the sheet; he had then handed the countersigned results to the Registrar without consulting his staff any further.) At the end of the meeting we heard that our Rector, Dr Kyaw Sein, had been appointed Minister of Education at the very time when serious student unrest had erupted in Rangoon over the killing of a student. The trouble was serious enough to have us placed on alert: every day, we were to stay on campus until 5 p.m., and small groups of male staff would stay on duty until eleven. By the end of the week the students had been given a message that went something like this: 'There won't be any more tutorials [in Burma these are tests] or practicals for the rest of this term – only a few lectures. We can assure you that you won't be taught anything new, so you might as well go home, though you can stay and learn nothing if your wish. You girls who are staying in the hostels: if you do go, please sign this form to say that you are doing so of your own free will.' This was the official Burmese way of obfuscating the truth – that the government was having to close the universities again. The planking lying in the grass was being made into a stage . . .

That Sunday, Thant went with me to Yankin Hill. It lies beyond Mandalay Hill, nearer to the ridge that marks the edge of the Shan plateau. It was here that Mindon Min planned to build a pagoda even larger than the one that we could just see on the other side of the Irrawaddy at Mingun, that gigantic yet unfinished mass of earthquake-fissured brickwork that was merely the base of Bodawhpaya's projected temple-mountain. Brick was not good enough for Mindon Min. A hill was reduced to hewn blocks of stone and canals were dug and barges built to transport the building material. All this was done by conscripted labour while the King consulted experts, one of whom, a French engineer, estimated that if the original design were to be completed it would take five thousand men about eighty-four years. The aging King was not amused. He had already earned great merit by convening the Fifth Buddhist Synod, which had just ended, and by ordering the engraving of the complete *Tripitaka* on marble slabs; the scriptures eventually covered 729 slabs, each of which was housed in its own miniature pagoda, and every page still stands in the Kuthodaw

Hpaya for all to read. But Mindon had wanted to earn more
kuthō. The stone base of his pagoda, little more than a metre high,
took four years to complete. Soon after that King Mindon died –
or rather, returned to the abode of the *Nats* – and the project was
abandoned.

Neither Thant nor I could see any sign of this forsaken venture.
It was a brilliant morning, burning hot, but at the top of the hill
was a stiff southeasterly breeze in which a pair of kestrels hung
wobbling. They tumbled off the wind with half-folded wings,
almost corkscrewing themselves into the hillside before sweeping
back into the breeze to gain instant height, ready to repeat the
performance. A pair of buzzards sailed in circles high above them,
tiny against the immense pale blue sky. At the foot of the hill
the patchwork paddy fields – bright green, yellow-green, golden,
brown – stretched southwards into the heat-haze and eastwards to
the foot of the mauve-brown hills. It was getting hotter. Driving
back down to Mandalay, the white dust was blinding, the
heat intense.

A student had brought noodles to the house for my lunch, and
now the landlord arrived with some *pauq-see*, Chinese dumplings.
It is one of Burma's most endearing customs that colleagues,
neighbours, students, friends, will bring little presents – often of
food – or suddenly announce that they want to 'treat' you to a
dish of Shan noodles or tea with cake or whatever happens to be
available. I invited Thant to help me eat all this food, then drove
her back to the university. The campus was eerily quiet now that
the students had left. The Institute of Medicine and the Technical
Institute had also been closed down, and Thant told me that a kind
of martial law had been imposed in Rangoon. True to their style,
the government had not officially published the edict but had
announced the restrictions over loudspeakers.

At breakfast time Margaret's face was as long as a fiddle. I had
been entertaining a woman again. At lunch-time it was wreathed
in smiles.

'Good news!' she called out as I came in. 'Madame come home!'
'Good! When, Margaret?'
'Rangoon. Saturday. Twenty-six.'

She had memorised the main facts in Liz's telephoned message.
I said I'd go to Rangoon to meet her, and was rewarded with beams

of approval. Before the day was over, this news was confirmed by the landlord, who had been in touch with the Embassy, by the Embassy itself, and finally by Liz on the line from Manchester.

Five days later I was at Mandalay's little airport, our Tourist Burma friends having made everything easy for me. I had brought a large but lightweight empty trunk and some hand-luggage, and I greeted the familiar faces of the airport staff cheerily. Sternly, the clerk in charge said he would have to measure (British English = weigh) the trunk. No need to, I told him, it was empty. Very seriously he said I would have to pay extra, and muttered something to a tiny, wafer-thin minion. I was about to protest when I realised that this was a bit of straightfaced slapstick humour to liven up a dull day, there being hardly any passengers. The insubstantial little porter had put my trunk on the weighing-machine, standing on it himself to read off the number of *viss*. I looked at the dial, hauled the bony, frail fellow up to the counter and said, as severely as I could, 'This man is overweight. He must pay extra.'

The chief clerk laughed at this turning of the tables, and the porter cackled and patted my arm with a hand that felt like a bird's foot. I later saw him heaving around great lockers and overladen baskets.

The plane was scheduled to land first at Heho, so I was surprised to see Heho airstrip slide past under the port wing. Rather late, the pilot woke up to what he had done and took the plane down steeply in a tight curve so as to approach the landing-strip from the opposite direction. He managed a safe landing – just: the aircraft landed on the port wheel and waddled along the runway decelerating furiously. On the second leg of the flight the pilot overcorrected, determined not to repeat his error. He brought the plane down almost to combine-harvester level while I prayed that there was no such thing as an air pocket at near-zero altitudes. Landing at Mingaladon was like steaming in on a train.

Liz arrived there on the Thai flight as expected and, apart from being tired, was fit and well; but her suitcase was nowhere to be found. By the time we had given it up for lost and notified the airline, we were both tired. For the first time, we were going to stay in the Strand Hotel. Fortunately, it was just for the one night. The dinner (Lobster Newburg) was awful, the service desultory

and sullen; the lights in our room were so dilapidated that I had
to wedge plugs and switches and tilt light-bulbs to just the right
angle to get them to work at all; when I picked up the shower
hand-set and turned the water on, it gushed red and muddy out
of the bathtap – there was no way of getting it to come out of the
shower, nor had there ever been; and the muddy red water wasn't
hot. Worst of all were the mosquitoes. I had travelled and slept
along the banks of Borneo's great rivers without a mosquito net
and with only a sarong between me and the ironwood floorboards
of longhouses and school buildings, but never had I suffered such
torment. Liz had anointed herself with repellent, installed her wax
earplugs and was fast asleep. For the first time in my life, I was
unable to sleep. The alarm clock rang at 4 a.m.. I put a light on,
woke Liz up and got out of bed. The sheets were spattered with
blood and my forehead was like a pincushion. On the wall above
my speckled pillow hung a dozen or more heavy mosquitoes that
were unable to take off. Vengefully, I walloped them with a damp
towel. Now the wall too was spattered with blood and the room
looked like the scene of a frenzied murder.

We were supposed to be at Mingaladon by five-thirty, arrived
at six, watched for two and a half hours as five of the half-dozen
Fokker Friendships (F27s) warmed up, filled up and took off,
and then gazed on despairingly as the remaining aircraft, an older
model, took off. I think the pilot was just reassuring himself that
the old crate could really fly, because it reappeared after about ten
minutes and took a full complement on board. The passengers sat
silent and nervous-looking until the engine note changed and the
nose dipped and I could see the Myitnge River and part of
Amarapura; then the usual chatter and laughter broke out. As
there were no taxis outside the airport we climbed into a horse-cart.
Trotting gently along the dusty track beside the road, then to the
right and on through the university campus where a surprised
colleague waved, northwards towards the palace and eastwards
through the former Civil Lines to our stately home – this was for
Liz a good re-introduction to the pace of Mandalay life.

The final episode in the Case of the Other Woman took place two
months later with the arrival of the anonymous letter. The Ministry
of Education alone received thousands of letters of complaint, all

anonymous, every year. An unhappy police officer called Eric Blair who was serving in Burma in the Twenties knew how rife this practice was, and later built it into his novel *Burmese Days*. In the opening pages, his arch-villain U Po Kyin says:

> A few anonymous letters will work wonders. It is only a question of persisting; accuse, accuse, go on accusing – that is the way with Europeans. One anonymous letter after another, to every European in turn. . . .

It was by this means that the ruin of the Englishman John Florey and his *kalā* friend Dr Veraswami was initiated in Orwell's novel. Fifty-odd years later, in a society in which fear of retribution stifled open criticism, it was the only way of registering a just complaint; and of course it was still ideal for intrigues of various kinds.

Liz, away for a fortnight on a teacher-training duty in Rangoon, returned bearing various goodies from the Embassy shop – and one baddie, an anonymous letter. Over a cup of tea I read through it and said I was fairly sure it had been sent by my Head of Department in retaliation for my involving him in an inquiry into why he had failed to publish the exam results accurately. Liz nodded. She had discussed the letter with a senior colleague in Rangoon who had immediately mentioned the Head of Department without actually accusing him; the official inquiry was common knowledge by now, and the colleague had come to the same conclusion. We couldn't help wondering why he had gone to the trouble of getting someone to post it in London:

London 2nd May 1988

Dear Mrs Abbott,

From Rangoon it is reported that Mr Abbott is getting into trouble with a Mandalay University girl. It would be extremely wise that you find the best way either to stop his notorious affair or get him out of the country before things go too far. It would be regrettable that the local authorities were obliged to take any sort of action.

As you may expect we are not interested in making things too noticeable, therefore this is only a friendly advice, not an official warning.

We decided to ignore the whole thing unless more letters came; unlike Orwell's U Po Kyin, this villain wrote no more.

Some days later I found Margaret in the kitchen once again looking forlorn and crestfallen. In her hands she was twisting something green, but her mind was elsewhere. She turned a long face towards me and I wondered what I'd done wrong this time; but, with the high falling intonation a child would use when pointing at a burst balloon, she said 'Look!' and held up the moss-green slab she had been absent-mindedly kneading. It was an inch thick and semicircular and was – I could now see – one half of a sponge-cake or perhaps a plain cake that hadn't made it to the top.

'I go to market, I buy two *kyat* butter, two *kyat* flour, I make cake for tea, NO GOOD!'

She bent the half-moon shape so that its points touched. When she put if into my hand it sprang back into shape.

'Green!' she said in wonder.

For the sake of solidarity I discussed the type of flour used, the number of eggs, the baking power, the container; but I had no idea what alchemical forces could have produced a tissue of such remarkable colour and resilience. As I squeezed it in my hand I wondered what had happened to the other half. I didn't have to wonder very long.

'I give half to dog,' said Margaret. She paused and managed a rueful smile. 'He no eat.'

9. History Ancient and Modern

Our second April in Burma had begun with scorching heat that bounced off the dazzling dust and cooked you from all angles. I recalled how once, during a sweltering stint down on the plain in Pakistan near Rawalpindi, I had in self-pity parodied The War Song of Dinas Vawr:

> The mountain air was cooler,
> The valley air was warmer,
> The old colonial ruler
> Retired to take the former.

If the weather continued like this it would soon be time for another trip to Maymyó. (The whole paraphernalia of government had moved up into the hills in the old days of British rule, but I would rather prove that it wasn't really necessary to go to such lengths.) Ne Win, 'on tour abroad' as the *Guardian* (Rangoon) put it, had left the country on a plane specially chartered from Swissair. He usually escaped the heat in this way, taking with him a wife and a high-ranking entourage – that is, the people he didn't trust enough to leave behind. It was said that once again Burma had only just enough in the coffers to keep the country staggering on for another fortnight.

It was the week leading up to the Buddhist New Year, which has no fixed date. The exact commencement of the new year is still determined by astrologers, just as it was long before the British ever took Burma. Shway Yoe tells us that it was done 'by the royal astrologers in Mandalay' before Upper Burma was annexed, and of these astrologers he says:

These Brahmin priests were originally brought captives from Manipur,

and have been employed as astrologers ever since . . . They worship
Krishna and twenty-five other deities . . .

At this time of the year their main concern is to calculate, by
using the positions of the constellations, the exact time when the
Lord of the *Nats* will descend to the earth – the event that ushers
in the New Year. They establish whether he is going to stay three
days or four, whether he will arrive on foot or mounted, what he
will be carrying and how he will be dressed. All these details are
important because if, for example, he arrives on foot wearing
shoes and carrying a lantern, there will be long periods of very
hot weather in the coming years; if he is riding on a dragon, on
the other hand, then the rains are going to be exceptionally heavy.
All this is settled a little in advance of the great day, so that people
know what to expect. Then, when the moment arrives, people go
crazy and throw water all over each other with water-pistols, cups,
buckets, hosepipes – anything that will propel water, preferably in
great quantities. *Thin-gyan*, the Water Festival, has begun.

But the approaching New Year festivities were too boisterous for
my taste. I was more at home in the peace and quiet of Mandalay's
shrines and pagodas, and had become interested in the legendary
and historical stories they had to tell. Ma Thant taught me a great
deal, and sometimes I played truant so as to pursue this interest.
On those afternoons when there was no work to do I used to leave
the university campus by the rear gate and, with the airfield on my
left, drive towards a pyramid-shaped roof that gleamed gold above
the trees and buildings ahead. The Mahamuni Pagoda was one of
my favourite haunts. I would park at a rear entrance, leave my
sandals in the jeep, walk into the dark cool passageway and look
at the murals. Among the court scenes were others which showed
nineteenth-century trains (the Rangoon-Mandalay line would be
a hundred years old in a few months' time) and Victorian
horse-drawn carriages with Burmese and British passengers. I
would stroll along the arcade past the astrologers and palmists
towards the massive image of the Mahamuni, the Great Sage. The
figure sits with hands in the position that symbolises his calling the
earth as witness, in the face of temptation, to the blamelessness of
all his existences. Shortly afterwards, he achieved nirvana, having
banished every object of desire; and yet this great gold-covered

image of the Teacher had itself been an object of deadly envy. Little by little I began to piece together the remarkable history of the Mahamuni.

The Lord Buddha passed into nirvana in or about the year 483 BC. His teachings slowly spread throughout the existing Hindu culture, and the Indian emperor Ashoka (260–226 BC) actually adopted Buddhism. Hindu expansion eastwards therefore brought with it a living Buddhism of the original Hinayana form. By the time of Christ, a Hindu state had been established along a coastal fringe south-east of the Ganges delta, and here in the city of Dhanyawati, Buddhism flourished quietly alongside other faiths. In the north-east corner of the city stood a hill called Sirigutta, and on the crown of the hill was placed an image of the Lord Buddha, an image said to be one of the five true likenesses of the Blessed One – two of which were in India and the remaining two in the heavens. Legend has it that the Master himself had visited the city and consented to remain long enough to have his image made by a supernatural sculptor and cast in an alloy of metals selected by the king of that time. The result was a huge statue agreed by all to be an excellent likeness; and the Gaudama had prophesied that although he would enter nirvana at the age of eighty, his image would survive for five thousand years – the length of time that his following would last. More prosaic accounts simply say that a king called Chandrasurya came to the throne in AD 146 and had the great image cast. Perhaps the truth is that, long before this event, there had been *an* image of the Buddha in the hilltop shrine. Whatever the truth of the matter, while the state expanded and the seat of power shifted over the centuries, the great image remained through good times and bad and acquired a magical aura, becoming prized not only as an object of religious veneration but also as a symbol of national continuity among the Arakanese, as they came to be called, and even as the protector of the kingdom.

In the eleventh century the great warrior-king Anāwrahtā, champion of Buddhism in Burma proper, attempted to wrest the image from Arakan. His great-grandson Alaungsithu also coveted the figure. By now Hinduism had faded in Arakan, and it was virtually a Buddhist state. Its chronicle says that divine intervention prevented Anāwrahtā from carrying off the soul of the kingdom, but possibly the sheer size of the statue had something to do with it.

The great image continued to preside over Arakan's fluctuating fortunes.

Meanwhile, other more or less Indianised cultures had begun to flourish further afield in the rice-growing lowlands of Indo-China and, to some extent, Siam. Hinduism and Buddhism prospered there too, and in Cambodia the two religions even blended in a way that would have been impossible on their native Indian soil. By the ninth century the incredible flower of Khmer architecture and sculpture was opening. Three centuries later, Angkor Wat bloomed; and three centuries after that the culture died, never to blossom again. The Khmer kingdom's main philosophy had been the cult of the king-god, whose rituals demanded such massive labours that these alone may have drained the state's human and other resources. It may be that in such a social system Buddhism, a religion of renunciation, had an appeal that other beliefs lacked. There, at any rate, we find the start of another thread in the story of Mahamuni Hpaya, or Arakan Pagoda; for there it was, in 1431, that Thai forces arrived, defeated the Khmer defenders and set off back to their capital Ayudhaya, carrying plundered objects that included thirty large bronze figures, probably temple-guardians.

In these troubled times there was an almost continuous rise and fall of powerful kingdoms, and it was only a hundred and thirty years or so later that Ayudhaya in turn was fighting for her life against invaders led by Bayinnaung, king of Pegu. This Burmese king's forces met fierce resistance and had to retreat, but not before looting extensively. The army went back to Pegu, carrying among other things the old Cambodian statuary, or at least some of it. Far more important were the three white elephants that Bayinnaung had seized. In fact it was to get his hands on at least one of these that he had amassed his huge army of Burmese, Shans and Talaings in the first place, such was the importance attached to the white elephant as a symbol of royalty and invincibility. It was now AD 1564. Five years later, Ralph Fitch, an English merchant visiting Pegu, paid one ducat to see the single survivor of the three beasts, housed in splendour and as pampered as any monarch. Why such reverence for an unremarkable-looking elephant with pinkish-grey skin, reddish bristles and the pink eyes of an albino?

In southern and eastern Asia there is an age-old tradition

glorifying universal power, mastery of the world. In China, the
Emperor – being a Son of Heaven – was quite literally believed
to be the Lord of the World, and the founder of Angkor, King
Jayavarman II, had himself consecrated as universal monarch – a
practice probably derived from the Hindu concept of *chakravarti*,
emperorship of the world. Buddhism had brought with it a brahm-
inical body of knowledge and practices deriving from Hinduism,
and the royal courts maintained a number of Brahmins whose main
role was to determine the best dates and arrangements for important
state ceremonies and activities, by methods involving astrology and
what might today be regarded as witchcraft. The elephant had long
been regarded as a symbol of royalty, and the white elephant was
especially revered, both because it was one of the seven possessions
believed necessary for universal kingship and because it was as a
white elephant that Gaudama Buddha had walked the earth in his
penultimate incarnation. But back to our warring kingdoms.

Bayinnaung remained powerful until his death in 1581, but he
had not been dead twenty years before Pegu fell. In league with the
king of Toungoo, the king of Arakan sent his son with an army to
subdue his powerful and hostile neighbours. The combined forces
were successful; the king of Toungoo took most of the plunder, the
Arakanese prince returning home with a captive princess, some
strange bronze statues and – most important of all, of course – a
white elephant, possibly the one that Fitch had seen thirty years
before. So important to the king of Arakan was the acquisition of this
animal that from then on he called himself *Hsin-byu-shin*: elephant-
white-lord, or 'Lord of the White Elephant'. Another thirty years
passed and in the summer of 1630 a Portuguese friar called
Manrique arrived in Arakan, where a new king still only in his
twenties was known as *Thiri-thu-dhamma*, Defender of the Faith.

By this time the whole of Sirigutta Hill lay within a rectangular
walled enclosure. From the four sides covered staircases ran uphill
through one inner enclosure and then another, and inside this
hilltop enclosure stood the Mahamuni image - and, presumably,
the old Khmer bronzes. The capital had shifted to Mrauk-U (today
Myóhaung, 'the Old City'), twenty-odd miles to the south-east of
the hill as the crow flies.

A century passed, and the once powerful old kingdom of Arakan,
hemmed in by enemies, began also to suffer pangs of internal strife.

Then, stunning a whole population that was prey to superstition, the very earth showed its unease. Earthquakes were considered to be portents of social turmoil, mass slaughter, the overthrow of the kingdom. In the great earthquake of 1762 the land heaved and the sea withdrew, changing land levels and coastlines. Sure enough, the king was deposed by his brother-in-law, who in his turn was killed by one of his officers, who . . . and so it went on until civil war broke out and a warlike Burmese king called Bodawhpaya scented an easy kill. In and around his capital, Amarapura, he assembled an army of four divisions. His three sons each commanded an infantry division; the fourth unit was a seaborne force which was to sail south down the Irrawaddy and then, hugging the coast, northwards up the Bay of Bengal. The land and sea forces co-ordinated well and, facing little resistance, converged upon the capital and took it in December 1784.

The history books tell us that Bodawhpaya's army comprised not only twenty thousand men or more but also two thousand five hundred horses and two hundred or more elephants. The captured arms, including a great gun about nine metres long, were sent back by sea. Half of the infantry were left behind as a garrison in Arakan, and the other half were to bring back to Amarapura the prisoner king and his queens, his family, the court astrologers and soothsayers, anything else of value – and, naturally, the Mahamuni image.

It was a tall order, but it was carried out to the letter. Bodawhpaya welcomed the arrival of the great image with appropriate reverence and had a special building erected for it a little to the north of his capital. There too were placed some bronze figures of obscure origin. In that building the reassembled Mahamuni sat for almost a century until one day the pagoda burned down around it. Of course, the structure was promptly replaced and this was the building where, after yet another century had passed, I liked to go strolling when there wasn't much work to do.

After passing the astrologers and soothsayers I would turn eastwards and join the throng in the main arcade. Like some sunken treasure lying on a sunlit sandy seabed, the Mahamuni sat bathed in light and encrusted with inch-thick gold deposited over the centuries by tides of humanity, beaming upon a continuously changing congregation. The devout, mainly women, sat quietly with their feet tucked respectfully underneath them or turned away from the Master; they knelt in an attitude of prayer, flowers or fresh leaves held between the palms, with fingers spread and held before the brow; they shikoed, bending forward to place on the floor the hands, and then the brow too. Sometimes they would be joined by wide-eyed people from the hills (you could tell from their non–Burman dress) and occasionally by bands of men from far away in the mountains – from Assam, perhaps, or even Tibet.

They were not worshipping an idol; nor were they attempting to save their souls, for according to the faith there are no souls after death. Just as Christians use an earthly figure of Christ on the Cross to represent the humanity of a being who rose above all things earthly, so these worshippers were using this golden image as a focus for their reverential love of a mortal who single-mindedly transcended mortality in a different way, and as a reminder of the profound truths offered by The Great Teacher.

Sometimes I joined them, lowering my large European frame awkwardly into a position that was respectful if not elegant; and no one ever thought this odd. I would watch the calm devotions of the gathering. I would study the face of the image, washed ceremonially every dawn by a saffron-robed *hsayadaw* and therefore completely free of gold leaf, smooth and shining. Strangely – was it a trick of the light? – it looked swollen, as if by toothache. I would watch women rise from their meditations, go to a little counter to buy a packet of gold leaf that they could ill afford, and present it to male attendants whose duty it was to apply the delicate film of gold to the image as instructed. I always found this discordant. Just as Christ would never have forbidden the ordination of women as priests, so (I was sure) the Gaudama would never have forbidden the participation of women in this act of devotion. The only other thing I found discordant was the notice forbidding the taking of photographs of the Mahamuni. I would have understood it if no one was permitted to photograph the venerable old image but, when I went to the pagoda office to see if the rule might be relaxed in my case, I discovered that the apparent prohibition was simply a 'closed shop' being operated by a group of Burmese photographers who didn't want their trade to suffer.

After observing and reflecting for a while, I would find my joints beginning to ache, and would rise from the marble floor and walk outside across the burning hot paving stones to a gallery whose walls were hung with a series of paintings. These showed how Bodawhpaya's returning army set out southwards with the captured golden image on a large raft; how they turned eastwards at Taungup and hauled the great statue over a pass in the Arakan Yoma; how they rafted it up the Irrawaddy to Sagaing, opposite Amarapura; and how the king waded in up to his neck to welcome the Mahamuni with due veneration. The journey had taken more than four months.

Then I would go out into the fierce sun again to a row of suspended bronze bells. Striking my favourite bell three times with the butt of a large wooden stave, its end fibrous with years of use, I would share *kuthō* or merit with my fellow human beings before dodging into the shade again to watch people 'washing' a set of small marble Buddha figures by pouring water over them. There are eight influential planets in Burmese astrology. Each day of the week has its own planetary sign (Wednesday having two to make up the number, one for a.m. and one for p.m.) and every Burman knows the sign under which he or she was born; so there are always eight corresponding Buddha images in the set, each labelled appropriately.

Finally, because my nose so often gave me trouble and because I am not entirely unsuperstitious, I would hop across another stretch of burning pavement to a small gallery containing six bronzes. People with a bodily ailment went there to drive it away by rubbing the corresponding part of the statues. You could tell by the amount of shine on the metal that the most common complaints were stomach troubles and painful joints. There they were: three lions, two warriors and one three-headed elephant – all that was left of the plunder from Angkor Wat after King Thibaw had melted down most of the ancient booty. (He had the bronze recast into cannon for use against the encroaching British.) I would stroke their noses lovingly.

For the 1988 New Year the astrologers worked out that at precisely 16.50:49 seconds on the thirteenth of April the mighty spirit would appear:

dressed in dark-brown raiment . . . riding a buffalo bull, carrying a
bouquet of flowers in one hand and a vessel of cool water in the other.
. . . (*Guardian*, (Rangoon) 11/3/88)

This apparently meant that it was going to be a temperate year
when people would feel as cool as rain and as fresh as flowers. I
have to record that over the *Thing-yan* holiday the heat abated and,
two days after New Year's Day, all the *padauq* trees blossomed.
The umbels of deep yellow flowers hung heavily on two large trees
near our house, and the first thing I saw when I drove out was a
mare with flowers in her hair, standing prettily (and, I thought,
a little self-consciously) between the shafts of a cart that was also
bedecked with yellow blooms. I was reminded of Mölly in *Animal
Farm*. The next thing I noticed was that mothers and daughters,
grandmothers and grand-daughters, girls of all ages from two to
ninety-two had a coiffure finished off with *padauq* flowers in a wide
variety of ways. There were toddlers with little strings of golden
florets looped into their hair on one side of the head; primary
schoolgirls with strings of them wrapped round the base of a pony
tail; some teenagers wore coquettish golden coronets, others floral
bands that half-framed their faces and held the jet-black hair away
from the forehead; sophisticated young ladies wore a small spray
of flowers pinned elegantly above one ear; middle-aged vendors in
the market were behaving more skittishly than usual and flaunting
their flowers by turning their heads rather more, and rather more
frequently, than was necessary; and grinning grannies squatted
bright-eyed in the shade of a bodhi-tree or a balcony, their
silver-streaked heads shawled with large sprays of blossom. I was
enchanted. But by midday many of the sprays were looking dull
and droopy; by evening, there were no such hairdos to be seen; and
by the following morning, even the live blossoms on the trees were
dull and dying. The enchantment had gone. For the Cinderellas of
Mandalay, the ball was over.

It was beginning to look as if the academic year was over, too,
in spite of the fact that it had barely got under way. The full moon
of Kason brought in a cool, rainy May quite unlike the previous
year's furnace; but the new term, due to begin now, was postponed
for a month because the government feared further repercussions
from the incident that had occurred in Rangoon back in March.
The media had reported it as little more than a disreputable

scuffle, in which one student had died of unspecified wounds, followed by a rampage in which student gangs and groups of local residents hurled 'stones, sticks and pointed objects'. But there was much more to it than that. Within a couple of days, Rangoon University's campus had been seething with resentment and the army was much in evidence. A Commission of Inquiry had been set up to establish what had happened and to find out 'who caused the death of a student with gun wound and what kind of gun was used' (*Guardian* (Rangoon), 18/3/88). The government was now admitting that a student had been shot. When I went to meet Liz in Rangoon, people confirmed what was then known all over the country: that many had been killed. Parents were wanting to know what had happened to sons and daughters, perhaps a hundred and twenty or so, who had disappeared without trace. When I got there, forty-two bodies had just been cremated – presumably the army's way of destroying evidence that all or many had been shot.

The first two weeks of May passed. Battleship-grey convoys of cloud would ram the Shan hills and explode in blinding flashes, the shock-waves arriving some seconds later and shaking our timber-framed house so that it rattled like an old railway carriage. The first gust of a rainstorm would arrive, setting the coconut palms swishing and scratching at the kitchen's corrugated-iron roof, and making our lofty and slender areca palm wave about like a busy long-handled feather-duster. It would also bring the kids of the neighbourhood running to where our great mango tree dangled its green but almost fully-grown fruit. Some of the mangoes bounced on the front lawn, but more splashed into the ditch outside the fence or thudded into the grass verge where a poor, bandy-legged old man always tethered his cow and where now a dozen or more boys dashed about filling baskets, staggered off soaked to the skin, came splashing back for more and finally just played in the standing water, the gusts having passed.

The government published not the Inquiry Commission's report but a 'Council of State Release' of the findings. It was now admitted that two students had died of gunshot wounds. The weapon was one of six Remington 12-bore shotguns that had been issued. Very convenient: no bullet to trace back to a particular weapon. Yet where the report mentioned the second fatality it said:

> Maung Soe Naing also succumbed to the [and here there was a blank space] wounds on 15–4–88 while undergoing medical treatment.
> (*Guardian* (Rangoon), 14/5/88)

The blank space was exactly the right length for the word 'bullet'. But only two dead? Where were all the rest? There was a list of totals of those arrested and released at various times, but no matter which interpretation I gave to the ambiguous wording, I couldn't make them tally. It was a fine piece of official obfuscation but I worked out that the minimum unaccounted for was sixty-eight plus 'a few', the maximum a hundred and thirty-two plus 'a few' – and the latter was close to the most reliable estimate I had been given: a hundred and twenty dead or missing. I highlighted the anomalous figures and put the report on the department noticeboard with an instruction: ENGLISH COMPREHENSION. DO THE ARITHMETIC. The next day a senior teacher said didn't I think I should take it down because of erm you know. I said it was just a government publication, so there was no harm.

'But the figures . . .'

'I haven't said the figures are wrong.'

After a couple of days I took it down because it was making some of my colleagues nervous.

The grey skies and rain continued; the *padauq* trees bloomed again, and yet again. Term-time came, but no students turned up. The department had been quiet for so long that the animals had decided the buildings were theirs. One day, after pushing a cow out of the way to get into my office, I was in discussion with a colleague as the cow, unnoticed, put her head through the doorway; we nearly fell off our chairs when her thunderous MOO! reverberated down the narrow, bare room. The next day I all but performed a cartwheel because of what she had left behind in the corridor. Then she brought her calf and the pair of them blocked the passageway in true Burmese fashion. When I pushed, they stood rock-firm, swung their tails and rolled their eyes. They wouldn't move for an Englishman. That same afternoon, coming back to the department, I found the path outside blocked by two fine pigs standing tail to tail across it. They snuffled at the edges of the path and snorted and oinked and made happy burping noises, and grinned behind their mud-covered snouts as I made a detour through the mire. Soon there were (I counted them) two dozen cows grazing outside the staffroom. Once there was a sudden heavy shower and the cow and calf that I had already met came lumbering in out of the rain. They stopped in their favourite place just outside my room and, chilled by the downpour, both animals urinated. I tried to ignore the interminable clatter of cow-piss on concrete, and got on with some lesson preparation. (In the absence of students I was teaching the junior English staff of both campuses, as a staff development exercise.) When I later stepped outside to go to the staffroom my leading foot shot forward and it was only by grabbing at the door (and incidentally crumpling all the papers in my hand) that I prevented myself from wallowing in an incredibly large pool of urine. A wave of the stuff had washed over one foot and I had ruined my notes, so I decided not to go to the staffroom after all.

This was the stuff of real farce; but events in Rangoon were leading to more tragedy. There, the students had been trying to organise a mass *soon-jwe*, a ceremony that may serve any number of purposes, in which offerings (usually of food) are made to monks. The purpose of this *soon-jwe* was to commemorate those students who had been killed in March. Parents, relatives and classmates felt strongly, of course, that the massacre of an unknown number of students, followed by a convenient mass cremation, should not be followed by mass amnesia. But this was precisely what the government wanted. No massacre had occurred. Two unruly students had died of shotgun wounds and a few other people had been hurt in an unseemly riot. Permission to hold a *soon-jwe* was refused. When this regime toppled, as it must sooner or later, the last man would fall into his own blood swearing that a socialist society of affluence was being achieved, that the entire population (except for a few destructive elements in remote areas) was behind the Party, that the People's Army was a benevolent force innocent of atrocities and that of course there had never been a massacre of students in Rangoon. Ancient Burmese history blends readily into legend; for modern Burmese history, new myths have to be created.

The stage was now ready for the great *pweh*, the carnival that ended in carnage.

10. Soldiers Old and New

It was now June, and very hot. Margaret informed us solemnly one morning that U Saw Lader, a leading figure in the local Karen community, had died in his own village in the hills. He had been ill enough for his doctor to recommend that he should leave the heat of the plains, and had been taken there a few weeks before. He was an uncle of my colleague Ma Ma Charity, and I had first met him when I once gave Charity a lift home. Invited in for a few minutes, I had walked into a bombardment of oral and visual information on the conduct of the Second World War in Burma: old photographs in a glass cabinet, more photographs on the walls, a rapid summary of Orde Wingate's greatness and of his tragic death when his Mitchell bomber crashed unaccountably in the hills west of Imphal, oh, and this photograph here. . . . Charity, thinking I might be getting bored with this old soldier talk, had ushered me away.

The next time I had seen him was on the twentieth of December, New Year's Day for the Karen and an important day in their calendar. Margaret had invited me to go and watch the celebrations, which started at nine in the morning with Karen dancing and a speech or two, so we filled the little white jeep with her friends and relatives and duly turned up at a large hall that must have contained Mandalay's entire contingent of Karen. As the only foreigner present (Liz had gone to England for her operation) I was given a front seat. Two young ladies in red-white-and-black national dress were up on the stage gravely intoning a harmonious drone which might have come straight from a medieval monastery, while a dozen boys and girls tripped – sometimes in more than one sense of the word – through their dance routine. The worst blunders were greeted with quiet, good-humoured laughter which seemed to comfort the children rather than embarrass them. Later came a dance of a kind I had seen somewhere else (in Borneo, perhaps?) in which the dancers have to step nimbly between parallel bamboo rails as these stout poles are smacked together to the rhythm of the tune with enough force to chip or crack any interposed ankle. Clack-clack-clack went the bamboos, hop-hop-hop went the ankles, the rhythm speeding up as the dancers warmed to their task. There were two sets of rails, each set resting on three bamboo 'sleepers' and each operated by a pair of girls, and after each 'CLACK' the girls replaced them momentarily on their sleepers so that they were perhaps half a metre apart. Then six stalwart lads came on stage and raised one set by lifting the sleepers on to their shoulders. As they did so, the girls had to rise from their squatting position, still smacking the rails together rhythmically, while the dancers now switched from prancing and hopping to ducking and weaving in order to avoid a scalping, or concussion, or a double karate chop on the jugulars.

Saw Lader had enjoyed that. He told me how he had joined the Burma Rifles in the Thirties and that when the war broke out he was a mere Jemadar. He told me how he had later served under 'Jack' Masters, of whom he had become very fond. Had I read any of his books? Oh yes, of course I had: *The Deceivers*, *The Nightrunners of Bengal*, *Bhowani Junction*, many of them. The old man was distressed when I told him that John Masters had died some years earlier; he praised Jack for his qualities as an officer and friend and then wanted to know what had happened to Fergusson. Who? I asked. (I don't think the old boy realised that I was not eleven years old when the Japanese surrendered.) Good Lord! Hadn't I heard of Brigadier Bernard Fergusson? Hadn't I read *Beyond the Chindwin*, his account of his own part in Wingate's 'backdoor war' in Upper Burma? Or *Return to Burma*, which he wrote after coming back to Burma in 1960? No? Well, he would lend me his copy of the latter volume. And sure enough, a few days later, Ma Charity had turned up at the university with his well-thumbed and underlined copy.

I had managed to return the favour by giving him one of Masters' last novels but, now that he was gone, I wanted to know more about him. His son kindly showed me some of Saw Lader's old documents, and I was able to piece together a little of his wartime experience. The last time I had seen him, just before he went off to his village, he told me that Masters had at some stage recommended him for a Victoria Cross. He may have been a little confused by that time, but the documents showed that he had twice been decorated for gallantry. Throughout his military service, Saw Lader had been known as 'Sunshine' because of the warmth and width of his smile. In April 1944, as a Havildar Major in the Second Burma Rifles, he had been in charge of a road-block when a powerful Japanese patrol appeared. His men were only office personnel and mess staff but, according to the *London Gazette* of 22nd June 1944, his management of the situation was such that the enemy patrol 'was so severely handled that all the troops whom he was covering and the party under his command were enabled to withdraw without casualties, while the enemy dispersed in disorder.' For this action, Sunshine was awarded the Burma Gallantry Medal. He was even better in the jungle proper.

A week or so before that incident, he had been leading a small reconnaissance patrol of a score or so men when it became clear that his party was surrounded by a force of about five hundred Japanese troops. One enemy platoon advanced head-on, evidently intent on capturing his group, but Sunshine and a *naik* (corporal) drove them back with heavy fire. The Japanese then began to advance from the rear, whereupon Sunshine contrived to give the impression that his party was much bigger than it was, and this second attack petered out. Apparently convinced that it was going to take some time to deal with this pocket of resistance, the Japanese began to dig in all round. Saw Lader decided that the time had come to leave, as soon and as silently as possible. The patrol followed Sunshine, crawling stealthily through the jungle until, after an hour on their bellies, they were sure they had passed through the cordon.

Again on a reconnaissance patrol some weeks later, he received Information that three Japanese soldiers were sleeping in a certain house. For intelligence purposes it was important to take prisoners, so with two picked men he went to the house, posted his comrades outside and crept in to find that two of the Japanese soldiers had gone out. While he was overpowering the third, the other two returned but were driven off when the two guards that Sunshine had stationed outside opened fire. For this capture and for numerous other actions, often solo operations, Saw Lader (by

now second Lieutenant Saw Lader, ABRO 886) was awarded the
Military Cross.

Forty-four years later, I thought he was owed more than just
the passing interest of a wandering English teacher. I wrote to
the Ambassador outlining U Saw Lader's service to the Crown
and suggesting that if he wished to send the family a letter
of condolence 'or other token' I would be happy to deliver
it. The funeral was being held in Lader's village down south
in Karen country that was out of bounds to us foreigners; I
decided I'd attend the memorial service, which was to be held in
Mandalay.

While Sunshine had been spending his last days in the hills,
another old soldier had started waving a banner in Rangoon. Long
ago in 1958 the Chamber of Deputies had, at U Nu's suggestion,
put Ne Win in charge of a caretaker government whose task
was to put an end to various civil disorders and to ensure that
insurgency was kept at bay. Ne Win had in turn entrusted the
running of the state-owned sector of industry and commerce to
a very capable right-hand man who soon had the whole sector
running efficiently. The right-hand man was Brigadier Aung Gyi.
When Ne Win seized power ('supreme legislative, executive and
judicial authority') in 1962, Aung Gyi disagreed with Ne Win's
pseudo-socialism and resigned from the Revolutionary Council.
He had later set up a chain of teashops in Rangoon and elsewhere
which gave good value for money and prospered; and now here
he was, thirty years after helping to put his country straight,
openly circulating a letter that expressed grave dissatisfaction
with the government's policies. Copies were being passed around
in Mandalay, so I assumed they were available everywhere. It was
said that he had predicted a change in the national situation as
from the thirteenth of the month. On the fourteenth, students at
Rangoon's Medical Institute No. 2 started wearing black and red to
symbolise death and blood. On the university's campuses, students
were gathering to be addressed by fellow students who were masked
so as to foil the MI personnel known to be thickly-planted in
their midst.

A terrible resentment was simmering. The precise number of
students missing since the March disturbance was not known, but
probably ran to three figures. The *soon-jwe* ceremony that Rangoon

students had attempted to hold in memory of the fallen was said to have broken up when troops appeared on the scene. Parents of missing students had received official letters assuring them that their sons and daughters had been given a proper burial, and that therefore they should not demand a mass *soon-jwe*, though they could of course hold a private one. Now the university campus was once again ringed with soldiers, units of the so-called Pyithu Tatmadaw (People's Army) within whose ranks little of the old gallantry had been permitted to survive. By the end of the week news came by word of mouth that Rangoon University had been closed again; it was supposed that all the other institutions of learning would follow suit.

My use of the word 'so-called' perhaps needs an explanation. In the early days of Ne Win's regime, many Burmese had taken pride in their very own army. The British had largely relied on the services of Indians and ethnic minority groups (Chin, Kachin, Karen and Shan), a policy that Burmans naturally regarded as an affront; and at the end of the Second World War there were four battalions, each of which identified strongly with its own ethnic group. But by now there were five others that were Burman, and these had a short but interesting history behind them.

In 1940 a group of Burmese patriots had left the country and sought military help from the Japanese; their aim was to achieve independence for their country by fighting the British. Calling themselves 'The Thirty Comrades', they moved into Burma with the invading Japanese forces; though trained by and ultimately subject to the Japanese army of occupation, the small group was commanded by General Aung San, one of whose comrades was Brigadier Ne Win. The little 'independence army' soon saw that the Japanese were much harsher overlords than the British had been and Aung San, together with like-minded civilian figures, formed a secret political group called the Anti-Fascist People's Freedom League. When in March 1945 the time seemed ripe to rise up against the occupying forces, it was as the military arm of the AFPFL that Aung San's units went into operation. With the end of the war a few months later, Aung San had the makings of the first independent army Burma had possessed since 1885. Soon after Independence came the assassination of Bogyoke Aung San and, with no charismatic leader to hold the country together, the ethnically-fractured army was subject to disorder – even mutinies and defections to insurgent groups; but in the Fifties General Ne Win as army commander greatly increased the number of battalions, ensuring that each one contained an unexplosive ethnic mix.

When he seized power in 1962, Ne Win changed the role of the army: hitherto it had confined itself to normal defence and security duties, but now it was to take over the very administration of the state as well. In tackling these two tasks over the years, the army had earned itself nothing but shame: the administration of the country was corrupt from top to bottom, the economy was in tatters and the 'beloved' Pyithu Tatmadaw was feared as an army of murder squads. Just a few weeks after his coup, Ne Win had used the People's Army to shoot down demonstrating students in the streets of Rangoon; now here he was, doing so again in 1987; and in the interim his army (*his* army, not the people's) had become notorious for its acts of gratuitous cruelty. Amnesty International had recently published a report on atrocities committed by Burmese troops upon the hill peoples of their own country. The 'noble' Tamadawmen would creep up on innocent women and children harvesting their crops and kill them just for 'fun'; and captives they would torture by rolling a bamboo up and down their shins until the bone was exposed. My phrase 'so-called Pyithu Tatmadaw' needs no further explanation.

To pursue this digression from the events of 1987 a little further into the past, I had noticed that even those British authors who have loved Burma the most have found a strong thread of gratuitous brutality running through her history. Let us assume, for example, that when Thibaw Min came to the throne in 1879 it was necessary for the stability of his realm that he should sanction, however reluctantly, the massacre of seventy or more persons of royal blood, including children. It was, after all, virtually traditional to eliminate potential rivals in this way. Even so, one would expect the deed to be done with the upmost despatch and with the least cruelty. Yet Shway Yoe tells us:

The princesses were subjected to nameless horrors, and the treatment of the children recalled the days when ravaging hordes marched through the land with babes spitted on their pike staffs for standards. The poor old regent of Pegu, governor of Rangoon when the British came in 1852, had his nostrils and gullet crammed with gunpowder, and was thus blown up. But the tale of horrors is not one to enlarge upon. They were conducted by those who became the king's most trusted advisors. All the three days bands of music were playing throughout the palace, and dancers posturing to divert attention from what was going on, and to drown the cries of the victims. (p.456)

Three days! The length of time and the methods used smack of sadism. The victims, some of them not yet dead, were tossed into a huge trench already dug for the purpose. This was filled in and trampled flat by the executioners but, according to a Burmese chronicle:

. . . after a day or two it began gradually to rise, and the King sent all the palace elephants to trample it level again. After some time the trench was opened and the bodies were taken out and removed to the common burial ground and interred there. (Quoted by Scott O'Connor, p.21)

Finally, here is Shway Yoe again, in snippets:

It must be acknowledged that the Burman is a sad bully . . .

The Maha Yazawin (i.e. the Great Chronicle of Kings) delights no less in recounting tales of barbaric diplomacy than in heroics . . .

. . . it is in the relations with the milder-natured tribes, such as the Karens and Chins . . . that the Burman most comes up to the truculence of the Maha Yazawin . . .

The Chins were subjected to such long-continued and systematic ill-treatment . . . that traditions accounting for this oppression actually form a part of the national religion. (from pp.441–3)

Ne Win's Burman-dominated army had, it seemed, simply been following an earlier tradition than the one Sunshine had known. No wonder the Karen, including our cook Margaret, spoke of Burma as a foreign country; and methought the Press protested too much.

To suspect the worst of the Tatmadaw, one only had to read what the leader-writer of the English-language daily, the *Guardian* (Rangoon), had to say about it. With monotonous regularity, the column repeated two messages: firstly, that the traditions of the Tatmadaw were 'noble' – sometimes 'fine'; and secondly that it was necessary to kill those who did not agree with Ne Win's

way of doing things. Not that it was put quite like that,
of course. It was wrong to kill anything, so the Tatmadaw
never killed. It eliminated, annihilated, crushed, but never did
it kill. Furthermore, it never eliminated or otherwise disposed of
people, only 'elements' – elements that were usually 'destructive'
but sometimes 'traitorous' or 'obstructive'. The persistent and
well-substantiated reports of rape and murder never appeared on
the *Guardian*'s pages, of course. Half a dozen column headlines will
convey the official line and suggest the tedium of the propaganda:

1987	28 Sept	The noble traditions of the Tatmadaw
	24 Oct	Noble traditions of Tatmadaw
	20 Nov	Tatmadaw's service to the people
1988	12 Jan	Hand in hand with the people
	22 Apr	Fine traditions of the Tatmadaw
	18 June	The noble task of the Tatmadaw

Another half-dozen now, to show the official attitude towards
anyone opposing the 'correct' views of the BSPP:

1987	3 Dec	Fight against destructive elements
1988	20 Jan	Till total elimination
	21 Mar	Strive to annihilate destructive elements
	14 May	Crush all destructive insurgent elements
	31 May	Fight against destructive elements
	3 Aug	Crush all destructive elements

It wasn't the sort of army that Sunshine could possibly have
served in.

On the morning of Sunday, 19 June, I parked my Union-Jacked
Suzuki jeep on the grass verge of a Mandalay back-street.
Margaret hopped out and led Liz and me down an alley where
a neat handpainted sign said, in English, 'Karen Baptist Church'.
Margaret would have been shocked if she had known that I hadn't
been inside a church, for anything other than attendance at a
wedding, for thirty-odd years. In her worldview all British people
were Christians and went to church; it was just that some of them,
such as the Catterlicks, had rather strange beliefs and religious
practices.

The simple, sturdily-built chapel had a floor that was raised
ten feet or so from the ground. The space beneath it was for
social activities, the church proper being upstairs. Kicking off our

Mandalay slippers we went up to a large, airy rectangular room
furnished with long pews set on clean and well-polished floorboards
of teak. At the far end was a dais set a little to the right of centre to
make room for the choir, whose seats faced inwards. On the dais
stood a lectern equipped with a microphone, and a table bearing a
few bowls of gladioli and roses. Two small stands in front of the
dais were topped with vases of white and yellow chrysanthemums;
and behind the table and lectern, against the wall, stood three
very solid high-backed wooden chairs. The only things that were
out of keeping with the churches I had known as a boy were the
microphone and, set into the wall above the three massive chairs,
a lofty simple cross of rectangular clear glass panels backlit by
coloured lights.

It seems to be a general rule in Southeast Asian places of
worship, whatever the faith, that while a decorum proper to
the occasion must be observed, high formality would be out of
place. This memorial service was no exception: a quiet dignity
was maintained throughout, but no one minded when some lads in
jeans turned up late and strolled down to the front pew, or when
little children ran up and down an aisle chattering happily. Then
two little children walked slowly side by side down the aisle. They
were wearing embroidered tunics that the Karen call *hsiplu* and
were carrying between them a wreath of bougainvillea intertwined
with red roses. The wreath was almost as tall as they were. When
the pastor had received this and placed it in front of his lectern, a
lad in the front row struck up a calypso rhythm, as if to dispel the
first onset of any grief, on his ancient guitar; and the Sunday school
choir sang cheerily, if not always accurately.

For the more traditional-sounding hymns (none of which I knew)
the guitar gave way to the harmonium, at which sat an elderly lady
in horn-rimmed glasses, her grizzled hair swept tightly back in a
bun. Half-hidden by the chrysanthemums, she peered and played
very seriously and occasionally glanced disapprovingly at a little
boy in a yellow shirt who, when he wasn't rolling on the floor and
getting frustrated at the congregation's indifference, was prodding
and slapping other children in the hope of getting some retaliation.
Later the serious-looking lady forsook the staid harmonium for an
electronic synthesiser, leaving the older instrument to a younger
woman; but I don't think she had yet got used to the synthesiser's

greater sensitivity because, when she rested her fingertips on the keyboard, there was a brief but defeaning chord that obliterated the final prayer and made her jump so much that she pulled the electric cable out, so there was then a short hiatus. The refrain of one of the hymns was 'There will be peace in the valley, oh, yes' and, on hearing the word 'peace', a couple of young boys turned round and with cheeky grins gave us the Churchillian victory sign.

The main components of the service were the son's account of his father's achievements and the pastor's own commentary on the life of U Saw Lader; after which, with touching courtesy, the pastor called my colleague Ma Ma Charity to the lectern to summarise in English what had been said in both addresses. A minor ceremony, conducted by an old lady in Karen, then took place. It was the honouring of all those over the age of sixty-five. In this way, we found out that our own nightwatchman was older than he had led us to believe. Young boys and girls came forward with garlands of jasmine and placed them around the necks of the old folk. One old man had a mop of hair that looked whiter than the flowers. Then the children gave each of the elders a little present beautifully wrapped in newspaper.

By now the heat was oppressive and the ladies were flapping their fans to cool their faces. The service ended and we thanked the pastor. People we didn't know came and shook hands with us. Downstairs we found our slippers and were ushered by Margaret to the VIPs' table, where she fussed and clucked and poured tea for us. After some small-talk, it was time to say goodbye and leave. Perhaps Brigadier Fergusson should have the last word on Sunshine:

> It was he who found my adjutant, Duncan Menzies, tied to a tree and dying, having been shot in the stomach by the Japs who had captured him: and he who brought Colonel L.G. Wheeler of the Burma Rifles to give Duncan a lethal dose of morphia and end his suffering. Wheeler did what Duncan asked him, and was himself shot a few seconds later by a Japanese sniper, falling and dying in Sunshine's arms. They had served together for many years. (*Return to Burma*, p.231)

11. *Yaddayā-Kyi*

By the middle of June, rain was still falling regularly and the golden *padauq* flowers had appeared a fourth time. The markets were filling up with small yellow pineapples and large green ones, with jackfruit of both the soft and the crunchy kinds, and with grapes said to have been introduced into Amarapura by Italians more than a century before. But the fruitiest season of the year was waning. I had picked the last of our pomelos and our sweetest mangoes (called *aung din*) were finished; the lychees were no longer coming down from the north and that king of fruits, the durian, no longer came up from Toungoo or – even better – from Moulmein. A tree in the front garden had borne a bumper crop of black, plum-like fruit called *tha-bye-thee*, one taste of which had turned my tongue and mouth into an arid zone, puckering up my face and screwing my eyeballs deeper into their sockets. I took bags full of them to work, where my lady colleagues made short work of them with never a wince. Back home, the overripe out-of-reach fruit began to drip a deep purple stain and then to fall on balcony and drive and vehicle and person alike. When the sun came out and the garden steamed, the festering flesh was suddenly covered with a glistening scab of opalescent flies that erupted in a shrill cloud when anyone approached.

Old wounds were festering in Rangoon, where the students had not forgotten, and were not inclined to forgive, the March killings. Students and sympathisers had attempted to hold mass meetings in the holy precincts of Shwe Dagon Hpaya, Buddhism's most revered shrine, but the security forces (what a misnomer!) had first broken them up and then prevented further large gatherings there. Some women students had addressed crowds on the university campus and told how, during the disturbances in March, they had been raped by members of the security forces while in detention. At least one of these brave young women added that she was pregnant as a result. In some ways the women were more militant than their male classmates, whom they would goad into action with taunts suggesting that they were lacking in masculinity; but both sexes united in dubbing Mandalay University 'The Deaf and Dumb School' because the Mandalay students had remained quiescent for so long. The universities had been closed and now, under Section 144 of the Criminal Procedure Code, a 6 a.m. to 6 p.m. curfew had been imposed; gatherings of any kind were prohibited.

Provincial students sent home from Rangoon by train were anxious that the truth should be known, since the state-controlled media had been indulging in the usual sins of omission and falsification. During their journeys they diligently wrote accounts of what had happened so that they could distribute their reports at the next stop. Also circulating far and wide was the open letter to Number One written by U Aung Gyi, Ne Win's right-hand officer when he had taken over in 1962. No one knew better than Aung Gyi the truth of Acton's dictum that power tends to corrupt, and absolute power corrupts absolutely. This much he had seen with his own eyes; but it had no doubt been true of Man's earliest societies, and I was reminded of an incident that had occurred in April.

But first I should perhaps explain how in the time of the Lord Buddha, a king called Kosala had – in one night – sixteen dreams, strange allegorical visions. When consulted, his prophets advised sacrifices to avert disaster; but the king's chief consort Manlika persuaded him to consult the Buddha himself. He did so, and received interpretations for all sixteen dreams. Pictorial representations of each vision and of its interpretation can be seen in many a pagoda. The visions were prophecies, some of them about the as-then-distant future.

During the early days of April, then, a colleague had, as one of its editors, been vetting contributions to the annual university magazine. One contribution had stimulated quite a lot of comment when passed round in the staffroom, though it was simply an

account of these dreams and their interpretations. I wondered why
so ancient and venerable a story should have aroused such interest.
Eventually, I was shown the manuscript and understood why my
editor friend was reluctant to print it. Here are just five of the
interpretations:

Dream 5:   When unjust kings rule, unscrupulous and wicked men
           will be appointed as judges. Such judges will take bribes from
           both parties.
Dream 8:   When impoverished kings rule, people will have to offer the
           fruits of their labour to the King's treasury as taxes, and will
           be left with nothing to eat.
Dream 12: When unjust and evil kings rule, most people will become
           corrupted. The kings will place these evil persons in high
           positions. Everywhere, the word of wisdom will remain
           unheard and the word of evil will be heeded.
Dream 13: When evil kings rule, everything which requires wise
           and serious consideration will be put aside as matters to be
           treated lightly.
Dream 15: When unjust kings rule, men of high merit will have to
           serve under unworthy men who are in high positions because
           the kings favoured them.

By simply offering such well-known material for publication,
the university lecturer who submitted it was making a political
comment. Bribes, extortion and other forms of corruption in high
places were obviously not new even in the Lord Buddha's time. He
had, as a former prince, a knowledge of such matters which was
considered so pertinent to the Burma of 1988 that my friend the
editor did not dare to print it.

One fundamental message in Aung Gyi's open letter was that
it was vital for the government to face the truth rather than
obscure it or wish it away. To Western ears this may sound
blindingly obvious but he knew that the higher up the ladder
of responsibility a Burman was, the more difficult he found it to
admit that things had gone wrong. Something of the old 'god-king'
tradition had lingered on from the Burmese monarchy. The kings
had been absolute rulers and would therefore have had to bear
absolute responsibility for any failures of policy; but godliness

was incompatible with fallibility, so failures were usually either not admitted or were placed at the door of someone or something else. For example, not long after installing the Mahamuni image in his capital Amarapura, Bodawhpaya launched a full-scale offensive against Siam. He apparently lost his nerve, however. Father Sangermano tells us that:

> . . . he refused all advice, and betook himself to a shameful flight, leaving his elephants, arms, and military stores a prey to the Siamese. Such was his apprehension that he did not think himself safe till he found himself in the vicinity of Rangoon; yet such at the same time was the insanity of his pride that he caused himself to be proclaimed, in all the places through which he passed, as the conqueror of the empire of Siam. (p.72)

On another occasion about fifty years later, Bodawhpaya's grandson Bagyidaw totally underestimated the power of the encroaching British – especially, of course, their Indian contingents – although in his court at Ava he could have taken, and perhaps even did take, informed advice. It is said that on seeing a map that had been prepared for him he objected, 'You have assigned the English too much; the territory of the foreigners is unreasonably large.' The foolish map-maker had ignored the desirable fiction and recorded the undesirable facts. However, when he lost his valiant general Maha Bandoola, who had died a hero's death at Rangoon, Bagyidaw was heard to admit that he felt like a man who had grasped a tiger by the tail: it was unsafe to hold on and unsafe to let go. (Phayre, 1883:250)

Again in 1885 Suhpayalat, Thibaw's queen, is said to have stood with tears in her eyes upon the wooden watch-tower recently built within the walls of Mandalay Palace, watching for the arrival of the British flotilla. Not that anyone had told her of the imminent end of her world as queen; she had climbed the tower although

> . . . she knew only from the talk of the children playing at its foot. She had been quite sure of success, and the Ministers feared to come before her with any tale but one of victory, although the knowledge of defeat was common property in Mandalay. (O'Connor, 1907:98)

Ne Win too had steadfastly refused to acknowledge that he was a failure, that his 'Burmese Way to Socialism' was a charade; virtually the entire population wanted him out of the way, hoping and even praying that he would die soon, but he dealt with those who openly expressed such wishes in the only way he could – by sending in his army of licensed rapists and assassins. He didn't know what to do with the tiger's tail. The philosophy of his Burma Socialist Programme Party had been put together in an apparent attempt to blend some basics of Buddhist belief with Socialist views on the nature of class struggle, and had been published in 1963 as a modest booklet with a grandiose title: *The System of Correlation of Man and his Environment.* Written by a political/military elite in Rangoon, the very first word of its preface 'Our Belief' is a lie ('We, the working people of the national races of the Union of Burma, believe . . .') and the rest of the sentence now carried a terrible unintended irony:

> . . . that man will never be set free from social evils as long as there persist pernicious economic systems which allow covetous men who are devoid of kindness and compassion to impose their designs on the unassuming majority by exploiting human weakness; that only when the pernicious systems characterised by exploitation of man by man and unjust pursuit of wealth are brought to an end and a socialist economic system based on justice is established in the Union of Burma will all the national races be emancipated from the social ills which flow from man's evil influence and rise to a happy stage of social development where affluence and human values flower.

The whole document is seriously flawed, not least in the mismatch between the guiding philosophy and the Party rules. For example, much is made of the Buddhist notion (consistent with modern science) that matter is in a state of continuous flux. Man is 'in a state of ceaseless change and motion' and subject to an inevitable 'flight and flux of mind'; and yet 'once full-fledged membership has been attained, no Party member shall have the right to resign from the Party.' Again, members are assured that they have the right 'to freedom of conscience' but are warned that they must never 'disclose any intra-party discussions outside the Party.' After more than a quarter of a century of the Burmese Way to Socialism, parts of the manifesto had rebounded upon a party whose role was now that of oppressor rather than liberator:

> . . . when the system of economic relations of a given age hampers the advancement of the economic status of the people, . . . the ruling classes and strata defending the status quo oppress and restrict . . . as a result, social antagonisms . . . appear in various forms. These . . . sometimes assume a violent form . . . (pp.17-18)

It was the duty of the Party to so organise the masses 'that they eventually come to have faith in the Party's programme.' Eventually. What a poignant word in such a context. Yet the laughter-loving Burmese people had their own catch-phrase which they used for deflating any such wishful thinking: *La-meh, gya-meh*, which means something like 'It'll come . . . if you wait long enough.'

In circumstances that are embarrassing, frustrating or bewildering most Southeast Asians release tension not by snarling or shouting but by laughing. In some cultures this is just a fairly humourless reflex, but the Burmese have a well-developed sense of the ridiculous and derive a great deal of real pleasure from seeing the funny side of even quite shocking things. In spite of the inquiry into his handling of examinations and in spite of his inability to explain in an audit what had happened to the departmental fund, our HoD had been promoted to the rank of Professor. When the news came through, the staffroom rang with laughter. That was just an in-house joke, but by now the whole country was the laughing stock of its own people. The government's handling of everything was so inept, everything was so topsy-turvy, that political criticism was being more and more openly expressed.

The only truly national exponent of political humour that I knew of was a brave stand-up comedian who called himself Zā-Ganā ('Pliers') because he was – or had been – a student of Dentistry. His humour was simple and allusive but, in such an oppressed society, deliciously daring; his stories, passed on by word of mouth, were rays of sanity in the gathering gloom. There was one typical little tale that used an image ubiquitous in Burma – the clapped-out vehicle – to represent the misguided State apparatus. His forbidden topics sent frissons of nervous delight running through a population riddled with fear – even a joke as simple as this one, freely rendered into idiomatic English:

> There's this ancient patched-up jalopy, full of people, you see, and it's chugging down a busy one-way street in Rangoon. And it's going the wrong way. [Giggles] And it's going backwards. [More giggles of anticipation] So a traffic policeman sees this and stops the car and tells the driver to drive properly.
>
> 'Can't be done,' says the driver. 'This old contraption only seems to go backwards.' [Knowing grins as people cotton on to the imagery]
>
> 'Nonsense,' says the cop. 'Use your gears. Try number one.' [Gasps]
>
> 'Number one's no bloody good.' [Guffaws] 'Been no good for years.' [Hoots]
>
> 'Well, what about number two then?' says the policeman.
>
> 'Number two's useless as well. It's no good. We're stuck in reverse.'

And so on. No doubt there was more innuendo, but the references to Ne Win and to San Yu, the President, were daring enough. I wondered if Zā-Ganā joked about Number Three, Sein Lwin, in the same way. I wouldn't give much for his chances of survival if he did. Sein Lwin had not only been in charge of putting down the student unrest a few weeks earlier; he had, in Ne Win's first months of power, been involved in quelling the student riots of 1962. His nickname was 'The Butcher'.

The once-affluent country, still potentially rich, was now classified as being of 'Least Developed Status' and was plumbing such depths that people found themselves laughing at just about everything. The students knew that university education was of pitifully low quality. The BA (English) had been dubbed the ABC (English), and the BSc (Maths) had become 123 (Maths). Whatever their main subject they all had to study English, and they joked that there was a gold medal for any student who failed that exam. The older generation had long been amused by what Ne Win called 'The Central Organs of Power' – the various State bodies through which he exerted his own power – and now, because he had just taken yet another wife, a woman only in her twenties, the ladies in the staffroom were laughing heartily at the current description of Number One: the leader of the least developed country with the most developed organ.

Just as in English the words 'road', 'rode' and 'rowed' sound exactly alike though they are spelled differently, so in Burmese (but far more so) many a syllable heard on its own is ambiguous. For instance, the flame-of-the-forest tree (*Butea frondosa*) is *sein-pan*; but each spoken syllable in isolation could mean 'immerse in water' and 'penis'. The scope for puns and word play is therefore enormous. One of the more respectable jokes of the day played upon the phrase for boiled sweetcorn, or maize; *pyaungbu-pyouq*. Separately, *pyaung* means 'alter' and *pyouq* can also mean 'dismiss'; *ma . . . bu*, like the French *ne . . . pas*, makes verbs negative. So one topical catch-phrase was:

pyaungbu pyouq	*ma-pyaung-bu*	*ma-pyouq-bu*
The boiled corn-cob	won't change,	won't be ousted

Then, during July, what the Party manifesto had called 'social antagonisms' erupted, civil disturbances all of which appeared to involve acts of racial enmity towards Muslims and which followed such a set pattern that I assumed the troubles were being deliberately fomented by the government's *agents provocateurs* in order to divert public resentment and discontent into a conventional channel. At this time, the troubles were mainly in Taunggyi and Pye (Prome). There were none in Mandalay. Much later, some rumours confirmed my hunch; according to these stories, the government had instigated these riots as a form of *yaddayā*, to ward off major catastrophes. The logic (if that is the right word) behind *yaddayā* is similar to that of some superstitions that I had come across elsewhere: for example, that if you have a minor accident in your new car, you will henceforth be protected from a major one. Months later, back in England, I noticed a form of *yaddayā* pictured in the *Guardian* (London): some self-styled witches had, on a hilltop in Kent, burned a model train in an attempt to prevent Channel tunnel trains being routed through their unspoiled environment.

That form of witchcraft attempts to influence a reality by operating upon an image of that reality – in this case by burning a model train, in another by sticking pins in a doll, and so on; but another kind of image of a reality is its name. The *yaddayā* that Number One was said to be operating at this time almost invariably rested on a linguistic base: on a pun of some sort, in fact. There had been riots not only in Taunggyi and Pye but also in Myedeh; and it was said that the disturbances had been designed to prevent the disasters represented by these phrases:

taung-gyi hpyo	('destroy big mountain')
pye-gyi pyet	('devastate the country')
mye-deh hlan	('overturn the earth')

As with all folklore, it is difficult to tell whether this was indeed what was done, or whether it was simply what people ascribed to Ne Win and his like; but it was believed by many quite well-educated people familiar with their leader's ways.

During September 1987, Number One had started on a series of trips to sacred and venerable places, including Pagān and Sagaing, for the purpose of *yaddayā-kyi* – which I can only express in English as 'the warding-off of evil'. What might a European leader do to ward off further troubles when his (or her) country was in a mess because all government measures had patently failed? Well, in some countries perhaps special prayer meetings might be held in the hope that the community might obtain supranatural assistance. But *yaddayā* is different from this, in that it is not a communal act, or one which a person carries out on behalf of a community. Ne Win was not trying to help his country; Number One was looking after Number One. Considering the plight the country was in, I found this apparent self-centredness offensive; but my colleagues knew that a Buddhist is responsible for his own salvation (to borrow a Christian term) and they appeared to hold no grudges against Number One on this account.

Later, just before leaving Burma, I swapped a few tales with the Ambassador and learned of three more *yaddayā* incidents. The first two were rumours that had reached his ears; the third he could vouch for.

The first was that Ne Win, having been warned of an assassi-nation attempt, had stood in front of a large mirror and had shot at his reflection, 'killing' his own image. The second story was that he had sent for human blood, which had been brought from a hospital, and had trampled it into the ground. The purpose of the first was clearly to protect himself from the assassin's bullet; the second was also presumably to prevent his own blood being shed. The third did not concern Ne Win. There had been several

ferryboat disasters during my two-year stay in Burma and, several
months earlier, the Inland Waterways office had been warned that
there was going to be another disaster on an identified route. The
official in charge had promptly ordered the construction of a model
ferry, and this craft had been ceremonially scuttled in that very
river in order to avert the predicted disaster. Not long afterwards a
ferry did indeed sink on that route, and many lives were lost. You
might think that such an event would be enough to destroy one's
faith in the efficacy of *yaddayā*. Not so. It wasn't a demonstration
of supernatural fallibility or caprice; simply a case of human error.
Some time later, a high-ranking Inland Waterways official was
dining with the British Ambassador and the conversation turned
to the topic of the ferryboat disaster.

'Unfortunately,' the official explained sadly during the meal,
'unfortunately, we made a model of the wrong ferry.'

When we had learnt that Ne Win, now aged seventy-five, had
taken a new young wife – a sixth, I believe – after performing
yaddayā, no official announcement was made; but the rumours
were confident. He had been advised by an astrologer to marry, and
the choice had been the daughter of a well-to-do Arakanese official,
a good-looking woman in her twenties. The Burmese word for
'Arakanese' is pronounced *ya-khine*, and these two syllables sound
similar to two verbs meaning (roughly) 'get' and 'cling to'. It was
said that Ne Win had been influenced by this word-magic even in
his choice of consort.

By this time the astrologers were predicting that the political
'crunch' would come on the eighth day of August. Why then?
Because that would be 8/8/88, the exact date on which an earlier
Burmese kingdom had crumbled. But that had been an '88' in the
Burmese calendar (it was now 1350 BE) and I could not help
wondering what the astrologers thought they were up to, being
influenced as they were by a Christian calendar. Still, there was
another portent whose significance was truly rooted in Burmese
history: Ne Win's own pagoda was almost complete. A couple of
historical episodes will show why this was a cause for concern.

Early in the thirteenth century AD the magnificent ancient
capital, Pagān, was the centre of a powerful kingdom that had
already flourished for two and a half centuries or more. King

Narathihapate was building a pagoda, but the soothsayers were
prophesying that when it was finished the kingdom would be 'shattered into dust'. Sure enough, not long after its completion, Kublai
Khan's hordes swept southwards from China and conquered the
kingdom, putting an end to Burma's most glorious era.

For our second episode we leap-frog five hundred years into the
close of the eighteenth century AD when King Bodawhpaya, ruler
not only of Central Burma but also of Arakan and the peninsular
strip we call Tenasserim, was pursuing several projects. One of
them was the construction of the most massive pagoda the Burmese
(or anyone else, for that matter) had ever seen. But he also had
to maintain a large army in troubled times, and people started to
recall the old prediction about the fall of Pagān. Once again it was
being said that when the pagoda finished the realm would perish.
In the event, because of the worsening economic situation – and,
some would say, because of the prediction – the pagoda was never
finished. Damaged by the 1838 earthquake, the pagoda's remains
are now sometimes unkindly called 'the biggest pile of bricks
on earth'.

A century and a half later, there were almost daily reports
in the Press of 'donations pouring in' for the construction of
the Mahawizayazedi, Ne Win's own pagoda in Rangoon which
stands not far from the incomparable Shwe Dagon Hpaya. In the
latter half of August, these reports stopped and many people in
Mandalay were saying uneasily that the *zedi* was now complete.
Months earlier, many had resented the fact that the *hti* had been
placed on the spire before the pagoda was properly finished;
now the ancient prediction was resurfacing yet again, and the
fortune-tellers of Mandalay Hill were forecasting that some time
soon there would be two months of mayhem. Furthermore, they
were performing *yaddayā* by mixing some lime with powdered
cinnamon and adding water to produce a remarkably blood-like
liquid. They then poured the pseudo-blood into the Irrawaddy to
make it flow.

These three true stories illustrate a remarkable degree of
continuity and cohesion in the fabric of Burmese culture.

With the rioting (especially anti-Muslim violence) spreading and
intensifying, and with Pye now under full Martial Law, the official

account of the mid-March disturbances was published four months after the event (*Guardian*, 21/7/88). Once more the public was being offered a sickening catalogue of childishly transparent lies. After one violent clash seventy-one people had been crammed into a single prison van, and forty-one of them had been dead on arrival. According to the official inquiry an autopsy had been carried out on all the corpses and in every case 'the cause of death was found to be inhalation of tear-gas and also suffocation'. No contusions, no bullet or grape-shot wounds. Then:

> According to the condition of the deaths [sic], the bodies were cremated at the Kyandaw Cemetery beginning after midnight of 19 March.

There was no safe way of demanding why the bodies were so hurriedly cremated. A list of names could have been compiled; parents could have claimed the bodies and given their loved ones suitable last rites. And why wait until now to announce the cremations anyway? Here the disingenuousness was breathtaking:

> The delay . . . is due to the fact that all proper care had to be taken in the interest of law and order and so as to prevent exacerbation of the situation and proliferation of such disturbances.

In other words, we didn't tell you because you would have been even more angry.

By now disaffection with the Party was almost total and was being expressed openly. A cartoon being passed around in Mandalay depicted Number One as a grinning pauper squatting naked behind a row of drums that he was beating. These were labelled STUDENTS, WORKERS, FARMERS and PUBLIC; his drumsticks were labelled ARMY and RIOT POLICE, the hated *loun-htein*; and these were producing the sound of gunfire. A notice announced that this performance was by the CEMETERY VILLAGE HEADMAN'S GROUP. At Ne Win's neck dangled a begging-cup marked FE (foreign exchange) and on the ground before him a beggar's bowl was labelled (in English) BUDGET. It was empty, but a few Japanese yen lay nearby. Behind him pranced his four scantily-clad dancing-girls, clearly identifiable but given initials to make sure: SY was San Yu, President and Vice-Chairman of the Party but also known to be a mere figurehead; SL, Sein Lwin, was Party Joint General Secretary; AK was Party General Secretary Aye

Ko; and finally came Kyaw Tin, another nonentity. A caption said
'Burma Socialist Lanzin party girls doing the blue lizard dance'.
The yes-men were doing their nodding-dance to the tune of a
murderous old pauper.

Meanwhile the old viper was up to something. An Extraordinary
Congress of the Party was held, at which he announced that, as
the recent disturbances showed that people lacked confidence in
the Party, he was requesting Congress to approve the holding
of a referendum to find out how far the disaffection went and
whether a multi-party system would be preferred. Number One
was affecting to be unaware of the fact that the people had already
supplied unanimous answers to these two inquiries. He said that
any referendum should take place 'no later than the end of
September'. It was now the twenty-third of July and, in a country
where it took six months to get a car out of Customs and fifteen
to get one transferred from one owner to another, no one was
fooled. But the public confession of failure was unbelievable: he
felt indirectly responsible for recent 'sad events', he said, and was
getting old anyway; so whatever was decided, he wanted to 'leave
the political arena and turn away from politics'. He added that
five of his colleagues also wished to resign: they included his four
dancing-girls.

It was all too fishy, too stagey. There was the sympathy-seeking
final bow ('This may be the last time I am speaking before a
gathering') which fell very flat; there was the dire warning ('If the
army shoots, it hits – there is no firing into the air to scare') which
let slip his intention to remain in control of the armed forces; and
there was the over-protestation as he passed on to the retired
General Aung Gyi the entire blame for the destruction of the
Students' Union building twenty-six years earlier, an attempt at
exculpation which was so lengthy, so tardy and so futile that it must
have been excruciatingly embarrassing to listen to. The next day,
fifteen delegates discussed his speech. In Party English, 'discuss'
meant 'endorse, support, agree with'. A day was spent endorsing,
supporting and agreeing with things. On the third and last day of
the Congress, Sein Lwin as Joint General Secretary sought the
Hlutdaw members' decisions, so-called. But the very next day
it was as Party Chairman that he addressed the small, powerful
Central Committee. He was also Chairman of the Council of State

and therefore automatically the country's President. By now I had lost track of what was going on.

After the numbness of the shock had worn off, people laughed and called him 'One-Two-Three' because he held the nation's top three posts, but resentment seethed behind the smiles. The Butcher was in charge; the dissident Aung Gyi was in preventive detention; the Press was telling the truth, the half-truth and nothing like the truth and then on the third day of August came the news that during large-scale demonstrations in Rangoon about forty people, many of them students, had been shot dead and that the capital was now under Martial Law. This would allow Sein Lwin free rein. The next day's newspapers carried the proclamation, and announced that schools would remain open. We knew they were closed. Then a headline announced: NO FIREARMS USED IN CONTAINING DISTURBANCES DURING MILITARY ADMINISTRATION PERIOD.

The prices of basic foodstuffs were going up and up; so too was our consumption of frogs, which Margaret considered to be still relatively cheap. At about seven o'clock on the morning of the sixth of August there was an earth tremor – nothing much, but sufficient to persuade Auntie Than Than that the *dies irae* was at hand. She said we should buy rice. We did. After all, there had been a prediction; there had been an earth tremor; the Butcher was in power; and the eighth of the eighth, eighty-eight was almost upon us.

2. 8/8/88

Burma loves fulfilled prophecies. The eve of the big day was
a quiet Sunday, but many hoped that on the following day the
monks – and Mandalay has a huge population of them - would
join the people by taking to the streets, and that some sort
of miracle would happen. The chairman of Mandalay Division
People's Council went to a monastery in town to persuade the
hpongyis not to engage in any provocative behaviour. While he
and his men were talking to the *hsayadaw*, a crowd gathered and
destroyed his pick-up truck. In the evening there was more news
of rioting and shooting south of Mandalay in Yenangyaung and
Pegu. After dinner I went out into the garden. No racket. No
sound of broadcasts. No chatter. Not a palm-frond stirred, and
the stillness was unsettling.

The eighth day began quietly enough. I drove to the home
of one of my 'angels' because she didn't dare to go to work in
her father's military jeep as she normally did, nor did she feel,
as one of my assistant tutors, that she could let me down by
failing to turn up to our staff development classes, which were
going very well. With our assistants, Ma Thant and I gave our
classes and had no sooner finished than a message came from the
main building ordering us to go home immediately since there
were demonstrators on the march not far from the campus. I
drove my nervous angel back through eerily empty streets,
then went straight home. The *hpongyis* did emerge and the
demonstration did gather momentum, but the day was something
of an anti-climax.

I drove out at the usual time next morning. There was a
horse-cart laden with pineapples on its way to Mingala market.

Kids were playing in the streets because the schools had closed
the day before. Ladies with golden flowers in their lacquer-black
hair were gliding along on their bicycles. In Burma, the normal
constantly reasserts itself with a cheerful resilience. Today no
one wanted to attend classes because the All Burma University
Students' Democratic League had called for a one-day nationwide
strike. Given the hot and humid climate, the middle of the day
might seem an odd time to begin an arduous march; but monks
eat only twice a day and have to consume these meals before
noon, so midday was a sensible time for them to set out.

Now that there were no buses, everyone went home before
midday. At Mingala-ze soldiers were dragging barbed-wire barriers
across 73rd Street, and sullen knots of bystanders watched and
muttered.

Past our gate that afternoon marched a long column of people aged
between six and sixty, at the front (as always) some monks, the
sāsanā flag – the banner of the faith – and a portrait of Aung San,
the national hero. Some teenagers saw me watching and called out
the only words they knew, 'Hey, you!' and beckoned, inviting me
to join them. As *yu* can mean 'crazy', which I certainly would have
been had I accepted their invitation, I called back '*Kyanaw ma yu
bú!*' (I'm not crazy). They laughed uproariously, perhaps at my
joke, perhaps at my accent.

Meanwhile the casualties were mounting in Rangoon and
elsewhere. The *loun-htein* were gunning people down quite
indiscriminately, and it seemed to me that Sein Lwin must
make some concessions to popular demands soon. But the butchery
went on. Then came word-of-mouth news of a massacre in
Sagaing, just across the river. Rumour had it that on the
famous 8/8/88 a large number of protesters, led by monks, had
set out for Mandalay only to find that the security forces had
barricaded Ava Bridge – the only bridge across the Irrawaddy
for the whole of its considerable length. The next day, the
thousands had regathered and begun to demonstrate in Sagaing
itself. The whole area, its hills smothered with glistening pagodas
and peaceful monasteries, is considered sacred territory; but
this had not prevented the forces from opening fire on defenceless people and mowing them down. Details were not clear and
consistent at this time, but even the Burmese Broadcasting

Service admitted that thirty-one were dead, so the actual figure
could probably be multiplied by ten. The full truth would
doubtless never be admitted, but it was officially announced
that demonstrations had taken place in forty-one towns across
much of the country, Chin State being the only quiescent
region. What was not conceded was that 22 Battalion in Rangoon
had refused to shoot into a crowd but had merely fired into
the air, and had consequently been transferred out of the
capital; nor did the BBS or the newspapers report that little
girls were going up to soldiers and saying, 'Uncle, when you
came back from the battlefront, we gave you flowers; now
you are shooting at us.'

At this time I was, with the help of my one faithful colleague,
Ma Thant, teaching about fifty of the university's academic staff,
giving them a refresher course in English. They had been
extremely keen to learn, but that morning my class was a little
depleted. I was told later that the absentees were people who had
lost relatives in the Sagaing massacre. By now, the daily pattern
was to hold our two classes and then go home at about eleven
o'clock before the marches and demonstrations started. When I
got home, Liz told me that one of our Australian friends had just
telephoned from Rangoon. He had heard a rumour about a British
teacher helping the student demonstrators in Mandalay, and my
name had been mentioned. As I had been doing nothing of the
sort, it appeared that someone wanted to get me into trouble,
possibly even thrown out of the country; and I had a pretty good
idea who that someone was.

For reliable information people depended on the BBC. Broadcasting House had been painting a gory picture of Rangoon,
where large numbers of people had been defying a curfew and
gunfire had been reported in many quarters. In the evening an
Australian friend telephoned to say that he couldn't get through
to anyone at his Embassy. His latest news was that Rangoon was
a bloodbath. He needed to keep in touch with the capital because
he was responsible for some Australian staff still in Mandalay, so
I gave him the number of a British Embassy friend. The following
morning's BBC news gave some details. Three policemen had
been beheaded in the Rangoon violence, and four medical staff
had been shot dead when they went out to crowds arriving at

Rangoon General Hospital to donate blood for the wounded.
Under Section 144, such a gathering was illegal, so the trigger
could be pulled with impunity. Later that morning I learned
from colleagues on the Mandalay campus that the Sangha Maha
Nayaka (the Supreme Council of *Hsayadaws*) had publicly asked
the people to desist from violence and the government to accede to
the people's wishes as far as possible. This attempt at intercession
was a continuation of an old tradition in which the *sanghā* had
always acted as intermediary between the kings and their subjects
when it seemed advisable for the national welfare. The requests
seemed to be just and reasonable; but the government was far
from just, and the people knew that being reasonable had got
them nowhere.

The next morning, there was no point in attempting to
hold classes; but two members of the English Department staff
turned up (apart from me, that is) and I told them about
the Rangoon rumour that I had been engaged in printing and
distributing leaflets. They knew the rumour wasn't true, but
nothing more was said about it at the time. Later, however,
in the privacy of my room, one of them told me what I had
already guessed: that it was my own Head of Department who
was responsible for the rumour. Two months earlier in Rangoon,
my colleague had heard from a prominent Burmese academic
that my Head had made these charges. I thanked this lecturer
for telling me this, and added that he had only confirmed
my suspicions. What I didn't say was that if the prominent
academic hadn't been a student of mine some twenty years earlier
I might well have been already on my way out of the country as
persona non grata.

That same day it became clear that not only were there no
buses on the streets; there had also been no trains to or from
the capital in the last twenty-four hours; the petrol stations were
closed (presumably so that no one would be tempted to make
petrol bombs); and a detachment of troops had come down from
Maymyó to supplement local forces. No trains meant no mail, no
newspapers and no word-of-mouth reports from people arriving
from Rangoon, so we were now dependent on broadcasts – and,
for reasonably reliable news, that meant the BBC. The BBS was
by this time a laughing stock, the voice of a government that

was consistently refusing to admit more than a grain of the truth and refusing to accept responsibility for the country's parlous condition. For example, Prime Minister U Tun Tin had been expected to make an important speech to the nation. When the time came, he alleged that it was the disturbances that were ruining the economy. The government that for a quarter of a century had been leaching the country of its people's products was now leeching the blood of the people themselves and blaming them for everything. This chronic inability to face the truth and accept the blame made the government appear so ludicrous that an incredulous laugh was the only sane response; and, to their credit, there were still plenty of Burmese who could laugh.

Not only did people rely more and more (and more and more openly) on the BBC, so that the sturdy strains of Lilliburlero filled the balmy Mandalay air at 07.15 hours and at 20.15 hours; they also took to making a communal ear-splitting racket at precisely eight o'clock in the evening, when the main television news was broadcast by the BBS. (Actually, this was not just an expression of contempt for the regime. It was also a cacophony designed to fend off evil, a form of *yaddayā*.) The BBC news was grim: probably more than a thousand civilians, mostly unarmed citizens, killed in Rangoon in this one week; people looting and destroying government warehouses; appropriating guns and ammunition and making petrol bombs; and establishing 'no-go' areas where even the army did not dare to tread. Kawthaung in the south was said to have been taken over by anti-government rebels, the security forces having refused to fight against their fellow countrymen. Later that day, a friend told me he had heard that Pegu and Pakokku had also seceded in this way, though that was only a rumour.

Out of my class of fifty, sixteen stalwarts were waiting for me to teach them the next morning. After the lesson, out of consideration for them, I asked them whether they would like to have a week's break, classes to resume on the following Monday if (as the saying went) the weather was fine. Yes, they nodded. Later, I discovered that they had given their answer out of consideration for me, and would have preferred to go on as usual. However, later still I was told outside the university that

any government servant found working that next Monday would
(or perhaps would not) live to regret it. I was quite sure
that Hsaya Gerry would be exempted from this ultimatum; but
my students were, as lecturers, government servants; so I
thanked goodness for the impulse that made me ask them if they
wanted to opt out for a week. In the event, the classes never
restarted.

After lunch, I drove across town to give a book to our learned
car mechanic, Peter, and to deliver some photographs that I had
taken of a family who lived near the match factory, an area I
wasn't familiar with. Peter thanked me effusively for the book,
but said gravely, 'Go home, my friend. There is going to be bad
trouble today. I will ensure that these photographs are delivered
for you soon, never fear. Go home and stay at home.' (Ah, that
lovely bookish English, redolent of days gone by: 'ensure' . . .
'never fear'!)

I was sure he knew best, so I drove straight down to the teacher
training college, where Liz was sorting out her own belongings.
Having put the packed cardboard boxes in the jeep, I drove home,
Liz following on her bicycle; she had taken to cycling in order to
maintain a low profile. At home, Margaret told us that the wives
and families of the police were cowering in their houses, terrified
of going out of doors. That explained why one of 'Gerry's Angels'
had been absent that morning: the one whose father was a Captain
in the security forces. A wave of humidity had rolled in across the
plains, announcing a shower, the first for a week. The rain cooled
the air and, I hoped, the passions of any hotheads demonstrating
down on 84th Street.

The distant chanting of a crowd drew us out of the house to the
roadside. An orderly procession passed by, led by monks holding
the Buddhist *sāsanā* flag and two red banners. It was a column
of several hundred lustily-chanting citizens. The chant-leader,
carried on a makeshift litter in the centre of the column, was
a woman; she rhythmically shouted a range of slogans such as
'Lower the prices!' . . . 'One party, no good!' (in Burmese, of
course), and these were punctuated with mass choruses of *'Du
ayé, du ayé!'* – roughly, 'We demand our rights!' But they
were fearful of the MI: many of the marchers were masked,
and the woman chant-leader was hooded. When we went back

indoors the telephone started ringing with unusual frequency.
Our Tourist Burma friends were regarding us more and more as
a mini-consular section: a German tourist needed help, could we
supply the home telephone numbers of some German consular
staff in Rangoon? We dug out the Diplomatic List and obliged.
Later, it was Ma Thuzar telling me that there were two British
tourists at the hotel who had used up their limited currency,
sold their T-shirts and other items of clothing, but still needed
money for their air tickets. Could I help? I stuffed some Burmese
currency into a pocket and drove round to the hotel, where a
worried-looking couple brightened up and gave me a UK cheque
in exchange. The streets were eerily empty, but there was no sign
of any trouble.

Back home, over a pre-dinner beer, I began for the first time
to think seriously about what to do if the situation deteriorated
much further. A friend in the Consular Section had telephoned
earlier in the day to find out how things were in Mandalay, and
Liz had joked about sending in a helicopter; but it would be no
easy matter to get ourselves out. There had been no planes into
or out of Mandalay that day, and there might be no more. We
could drive the four hundred miles to Rangoon, but that would
be foolish: the gangs of hungry and angry people who were
waylaying vehicles might take only our money and petrol and
would probably not harm us but, even if we made it as far as the
outskirts of the capital, we might enter a dangerous 'no-go' area
– and there was always the curfew to bear in mind. No, Rangoon
was risky. If the Ava Bridge remained closed, there would be no
possibility of driving north-westwards along the route taken by
the British forty-six years before, as they fled from the advancing
Japanese army; and it was in any case a very long way to India or
Bangladesh. The only other feasible road wound north-eastwards
through the Shan hills: Maymyó, Hsipaw, Lashio . . . China.
This would probably mean going through areas held by insurgent
groups, and such country wasn't a very healthy place to be at the
best of times. Still, it didn't look more than three hundred miles
on my admittedly poor map. There didn't seem to be any town on
the border. The border! The Ministry of Education still had my
passport, had held it for months; it was probably lost. It might

after all be best to lie low and stick it out, whatever 'it' might
be, in a place where we were known and (I think) liked. Or was
I just putting my head in the sand?

After a pensive dinner we listened to the World News, gloomily
wondering why it was the Australian Ambassador that the BBC had
contacted, and not our own. The telephone rang yet again, and
again it was Thuzar; but this time she was jubilant.

'Sein Lwin has stepped down!' she was yelling.

It had just been announced on the local 8 p.m. news. I
found a bottle of Drambuie and five little glasses, and Margaret,
U Chit, U Po Bwin, Liz and I had a tot in celebration. The
hated Sein Lwin had lasted only seventeen days, and the Burmese
people would have the exhilaration of knowing that they had
succeeded in influencing political events. Young men and women
would never again be content with the stultifying serfdom
that they had suffered all their lives. Within thirty minutes
the World Service was reporting the step-down. Good for
the BBC! Then, in the next bulletin, we heard that Her Majesty's
Foreign Office had 'expressed cautious concern' about the current
situation in Burma. My God! Cautious con-bloody-cern indeed!
I took myself off to bed, muttering about cautious massacres.

The next morning a plane passed low over the house and
we heard later that it had dropped leaflets in the town centre.
Demonstrations continued, and people seemed to be gaining in
confidence and pride. The timidest of 'Gerry's Angels' had started
the week visibly frightened and had scurried back to her parents'
house as soon as classes were over; by the end of the week she was
pedalling off alone to join the protest marches, smiling proudly.
A neighbour and her daughter came to visit. The mother in
a round-about way asked me not to take photographs of the
marchers, especially near her house. But the daughter defied
her mother by telling me that she would phone me if there was
another demonstration. She added that just around the corner
there was a notice pinned to a tree. It said in Burmese: WARD
COUNCIL MEMBERS WHO INTERFERE WITH OUR DEMONSTRATIONS
WILL BE BEHEADED.

Perplexed by Burmese politics, I turned to my butterfly collection
– not dead specimens, but photographs of live ones whose species

I was trying to identify. But this task was equally perplexing
in its own way. I thought I had built up a small collection of
twenty-odd species, but now I wasn't sure. The problem was the
phenomenon known as Batesian mimicry. It seems that, over
evolutionary periods of time, certain butterfly species that are
palatable to birds and other enemies have developed different
wing-colourings so as to make themselves look similar to unpalatable species living in the same habitat. This was inconvenient
for amateur lepidopterists like me, to say the least; but some
species had gone one step further. By means of one very simple
masterstroke, they had managed to outwit not only the sharp-
eyed predator but also the well-intentioned student: their females
engaged in mimicry, but the males didn't. This meant that not
only was it difficult to tell whether a butterfly was of species
A or species B, it was also hard to see whether, if it was of
species B, it was male or female – or have I got that wrong?
Take the creature rejoicing in the name Danaid Eggfly (*Hypolimnos
misippus*), for instance: the male is black, with a white oval
patch surrounded by iridescent blue on each wing; the female
looks nothing at all like him, but does closely resemble the
Plain Tiger; but the female Plain Tiger looks much the same
as the male. . . . I put aside my borrowed butterfly manual
and realised that what I had thought were two species was
only one . . . probably. The manual created too many problems
for me; I went back to my contemplation of the political
scene.

Flipping back through my cuttings and jottings, I came across
two pieces of verse that I had written about the political
situation in Burma. The first one was over a year old – it was
dated 'March 1987' – and had been triggered by the sight of a
pair of *chinthe*, the large brick-built lionesque figures that stand
on guard outside pagodas; but it was addressed to the people of
Burma. It ended:

> The tune's deranged. Some ogre wields the wand.
> Where are your gauntlets rusting? Was the gong
> Of anger stolen from the common mind?
> Why was it – like these lions – you sat still,

Snarls petrified, while butchery was planned?
Sit still, aghast that all the notes are wrong?
Your gauntlets will be melted down for gun
To train, and to be trained upon, your sons.

That is rather poor verse, but the thought behind it was
reasonably accurate. The second piece was less than a month
old. In passing, I had seen a young lad – sitting by the road,
strumming on a decrepit guitar and singing one of the moany
love-songs beloved of his generation. A *haiku* came into my head
almost ready-made:

> *Boy with a Guitar*
> Brief fingers still brush
> the rusting strings stretched far enough.
> The breaking-point comes.

Again, not good verse; but the breaking-point had come a
fortnight later, almost to the day, on the eighth day of the
eighth month.

When, in 1861, Mindon Min had made Mandalay his capital, he
created what was virtually a walled and moated city within the
existing urban sprawl, such as it was. Within the enclosed four
square kilometres, his craftsmen had constructed a palace complex
of carved and gilded teak, surrounded with tranquil gardens and
pools. As he approached the building, the visiting dignitary must
have been dazzled by the glitter of glass mosaic and the glow of
gold leaf; and on arrival, passing through the massive doors and
along the shady corridors, he must surely have wondered at the
amount of time and skill and devotion that had been given to the
task of carving every door and window, every post and lintel,
and all the ceilings and eaves in a fashion fit for a king and fit
to receive a layer of gold. These surroundings delighted Mindon
Min for seventeen years until, lying on his couch in one of these
beautiful buildings, he died.

Of his sons, the mild nineteen-year-old Thibaw was in some
ways not the most eligible successor, but it was he who was
proclaimed king. On his orders, the building in which his father
had died was dismantled and re-erected outside the moated

battlements a short distance away, a little to the south-east of Mandalay Hill. For a time, this was where he would go when he wanted to meditate; but after a while he presented it to the *sanghá* for use as a monastery, and a monastery it has remained for more than a century. It was sited close to a building which not only dwarfed it but also outshone it in splendour: Atumashi Kyaung, the 'Incomparable Monastery'. But in 1892 the massive teak superstructure of the Atumashi burned down in what must have been a huge blaze, leaving its little jewel-like neighbour uneclipsed and unharmed.

Meanwhile, the rest of the royal buildings inside the palace were suffering the indignity of British occupation. The palace was now known as Fort Dufferin, after the Governor General of India, an insulting reminder of the fact that Burma was administered as a province of British India; and the former queen's throne-room on the western side of the palace, was now the Upper Burma Club:

> Evening after evening the women come here, a little pale, as English women are in the East; evening after evening the men gather here from the polo ground and the tennis court; the band plays, the markers call the scores at the billiard tables in the Queen's Hall of Audience. On the mirrored walls hang the latest telegrams from Europe; at the foot of the throne, picture papers portray the incidents of some city pageant, some royal procession, some battle of the Empire. Long men lie in the easy-chairs under the swinging fans or sit in the Queen's inner chamber playing at whist and poker. The swish of soda-water bottles, the crack of ice, the click of billiard balls; – of such is the western end of the palace today.
>
> It seems a desecration of a palace to put it to such uses. . . . (Scott O'Connor, 1907, pp. 72–3)

Many British residents were shamefaced about using such a building as a club, and the local people resented it deeply:

> The Burmans, not unnaturally, dislike it, and have made several attempts to fire it, as they have already successfully done with other buildings within the fort. . . . (Talbot Kelly, 1905, p.161)

However, at least Lord Curzon, who had visited the palace as Viceroy of India in 1901, had noticed the dilapidated state of

Mandalay's monastic buildings, and had insisted on the need
to preserve the palace 'as a model – the only one that will
before long survive – of the civil and ceremonial architecture
of the Burman Kings.' As a result of his policy, funds were
set aside for the restoration of many sites in Mandalay, as well
as the palace itself; and a statement of expenditure for the
year 1906-7 shows that the little monastery outside the palace
walls had not been forgotten: 'Special repairs to Shwenandaw
kyaung . . . 724 [rupees]'.

Eventually the Club was housed elsewhere and a church
that had been built inside the fort was removed; the palace was
respectfully treated as an ancient monument – antiquity being
a comparative matter – until the arrival of victorious Japanese
troops in 1942. Although their aircraft had bombed Mandalay,
the palace had suffered little or no damage; and although the
fort was used as a military base for the next three years and
the palace was probably neglected and ill-used, it was still
substantially sound when the British army returned in 1945.
But the Japanese resistance was stubborn and fierce. Mandalay
Hill is not large – you can stroll up its covered stairways in
fifteen minutes – but it took a Gurkha battalion a whole night
to fight its way to the top and another day to clear a way
down the other side, past gun emplacements and underground
bunkers, to the moated fort. The moat was (and still is) two
hundred and twenty-five feet wide; the palace wall twenty-
five feet high, ten feet thick at the base and tapering to a
mere five-foot thickness at the top; and the inner face was
backed with a wide rampart of earth. The hill had been taken
on the eleventh of March after almost three days of fighting. On
the thirteenth the fort was bombed, by the fifteenth it was
surrounded, attacks on the sixteenth, eighteenth and nineteenth
were repulsed and another air strike was planned for the next
morning. That night there was some unusual activity in the
fort: although the British besiegers were unaware of what was
going on at the time, it was later discovered that the Japanese
troops and Burmese collaborators had left the fort, creeping
through a drain system that led from the moat southwards
across the town. Most were captured, but by that time the
air strike had gone ahead; and when the Union Jack was hoisted

again over Fort Dufferin by Major-General Rees, the palace
was no more:

> To our great regret, Theebaw's Palace had been burnt down, whether
> fired by our shelling and bombing, although we had tried to avoid it,
> or by the Japanese to destroy the stores they had in it, I do not know.
> (Slim, p.470)

Of the entire palace complex, therefore, the only surviving
building was the little Shwenandaw monastery; and it was for this
reason that I had become so fond of it, I think, and had learned
to call it Shwe-kyaung-gyi, as everyone else did. On my visits
there I had made friends with a young novice monk by taking
his photograph and giving him copies. Now, one afternoon in
mid-August, I saw him again; this time, he was near the head of
a procession of demonstrators that an excited student had dragged
me out to see as it passed near our house. There he was, just
behind a *hpongyi* and a man carrying the obligatory portrait of
the hero Aung San. The boy gave me an astonished smile, as if to
say 'You again?', and stopped to greet me; but those behind him
bumped into him, and he marched off with a wave and a grin. As
we were walking back the student (whom I shall call Sisi) said,
'Our government is a liar. Everyone knows it is a liar.' I could tell
by the scorn in her voice that, like millions more from all walks
of life, she had found that her government's least forgivable fault
was its treatment of the Burmese people as numbskulls who would
believe any cock-and-bull story they were told. Sisi's mother was
a nervous woman, jittery enough about her daughter's enthusiasm
for demonstrations and about the way Sisi encouraged me to take
photographs of the processions that were now the main features
of daily life.

The Burmese Broadcasting Service had started to inveigh
against the BBC in an attempt to discredit it, but the only result
was that the BBC's Burmese Service was now avidly listened
to. That night, at 8.15, I could hear radios all around the
neighbourhood blaring out the truth as far as the BBC could get
at it. They had been unable to reach the truth about the Sagaing
massacre. According to the official account in the *Guardian*
(Rangoon):

. . . an estimated 5,000 troublemakers attacked the People's Police Force station in Sagaing. The security units had to shoot to defend the station against being over-run by the mob resulting in 31 deaths and 37 wounded. The security units are carrying on with clearing action, it is iearnt.

But rumours put the number of fatalities much higher. In the next few days, quite by chance, I was to find out the truth, or something very near it.

3. Massacre

On Monday, 15th August, the English Department staffroom was almost back to normal after a week of massive demonstrations and the jubilation occasioned by the stepping-down of the hated Sein Lwin. But once the initial *bonhomie* had worn off, it was clear that there was deep resentment of the Sagaing massacre now that the scale of the incident was becoming clearer. Putting together various accounts from various sources, I concluded that there had been perhaps three hundred casualties. It was said that a crowd had approached the town police station; that some missile from the building had hit a girl on the head and killed her on the spot; and that the outraged crowd had converged upon the police station. Automatic weapons had opened fire from several positions, hundreds had fallen and many of the dead and dying had been thrown into the river. Some of the survivors had been transferred to Mandalay General Hospital, but most were in the small, underfunded local hospitals. Any humane regime would have had all the worst casualties taken across the river to Mandalay, but then the scale of the slaughter would have become apparent; so the only bridge was closed. A humane regime would have allowed people to go across to Sagaing to donate blood and to take supplies of food and medicaments, but then people would have seen for themselves the large number of patients and the hideous wounds; so the bridge remained closed, and people who could have been saved were dying.

Various rumours agreed that the order to fire had been given by Kyaw Zwā, the Chairman of the Sagaing Division People's Council, and that the townsfolk had sworn that they would, if they ever got their hands on him, chop him into small pieces and feed these scraps to the dogs of the town. Although this fury was understandable, I found the bloodthirstiness triggered by the bloodshed all the more upsetting because of the time-honoured sacredness of the place – an area that I had become very fond of. And I brooded over the plight of all those wounded survivors.

When I got home, Liz told me that she had heard over the phone that the Australians in Rangoon had managed to penetrate far enough into the government's red tape to have succeeded in presenting the Rangoon Red Cross with medical supplies for the hospitals there, which were trying valiantly to cope with appalling numbers of appalling wounds with totally inadequate resources. I telephoned the British Embassy and asked for medical supplies for Sagaing hospital. No, I said, I didn't know how I was going to get the supplies to the hospital yet, but I would manage. All right, they said, they'd try.

I hadn't long put the phone down when our Tourist Burma friend Thuzar arrived. If the bridge remained sealed off, I asked her, how could I take some medical supplies to Sagaing? What about the small rowing-boats that ferried people across river? I expected some helpful suggestions; but I was up against suspicion.

'Who give you this idea?'

'Nobody. It's my own idea.'

'Liz give you this idea?'

'No,' said Liz. 'It's his idea.'

Long silence.

'You want to take photographs?'

'No, I won't take a camera with me.'

But it was no use. Her attitude spelt out, 'Forget it'.

That afternoon, my friend Ma Thant and I paid a brief visit to Mahamyamuni Hpaya to see if there were still any protest posters there. Because it is very unusual in Mandalay to see a European man walking with a Burmese woman without a chaperone, we were stared at. As we were walking through the precincts of the pagoda, Ma Thant twice burst into fits of giggling: once when a young fellow remarked (in Burmese, of course), 'He looks like James Bond' – all Europeans looking very much alike to the Burmese; and a second time when a woman said to her neighbour in a Burmese stage whisper, 'She looks just like a Burmese woman, doesn't she?'

We found a few posters still pinned up. One said that the Rangoon Students' Union thanked their colleagues and the *hpongyis* and citizens of Mandalay for their support. (Having shown their massive support, the students of Mandalay were now forgiven by their colleagues in Rangoon, who had earlier called them effeminate and Mandalay University 'The Deaf and Dumb School'.) Another handbill alleged that there had been four hundred casualties in Sagaing, many of whom had died, and added that many bodies had been thrown into the Irrawaddy. A third leaflet bore some slogans, two of which said, in free translation: 'Sein Lwin, you may be a dog, but we aren't dogs.' and 'We're not going to take things lying down any more.' But there was nothing more dramatic than this to be seen at the time.

The following afternoon, the British Embassy rang me to say that they had put two trunkloads of medical supplies on the 5.15 p.m. Rangoon–Mandalay train, and that the rest was up to me. I was delighted, and said so. The next morning, I picked up the supplies at the station, drove them home, typed a form of receipt on the inventory, made a few copies and set out for the university. I had been dissuaded from driving straight to Sagaing. My plan now was to get the Rector of my university to telephone the Divisional Medical Office in Sagaing, whose number I had found out the previous evening, and ask if I could deliver the supplies under escort. I had also asked Liz to get her Principal to phone through to anyone who might be able to smooth the way.

The Rector was not present, but the Pro-Rector obligingly telephoned the Sagaing office and put forward the facts. He answered a lot of questions and then, with his hand over the mouthpiece, asked me, 'Is this an official donation?'

I had had time enough to sense the problem: if I said No, I would be asked how on earth I had obtained two trunkloads of expensive medical supplies; and if I said Yes, I would be told that it must go through official channels. I nodded, the conversation came to an end and the Pro-Rector sat looking uncertainly at his desktop.

'They cannot accept it,' he said. 'They are going to telephone us in half an hour.'

'OK,' I said. 'I'll come back later.'

When I went back, the Rector himself was also present.

'There has been a call,' he said. 'The donation cannot be accepted. It must go through the proper channels. Your embassy must contact the Foreign Office and they will instruct the Ministry of Health.'

'So,' I said. 'If the Sagaing Office gets a positive call from the Ministry of Health, it's all right?'

'Yes.'

'Very well. I'll ask the Embassy to do that.'

Back home at lunch-time, I eventually got through to the Embassy, left the problem with them for a while and had lunch. When they phoned back, it was to say that several other embassies had been given the same instructions and had complied, but none of them had got anywhere. The Burmese government's attitude was that there was no problem, so they could not accept the gifts. (According to the government, remember, there had been only thirty-one casualties.) I was, the Embassy man said, on my own.

As I drove back to the university, I was considering the idea of splitting up the consignment into small packets and giving my students a packet each to take over to Sagaing as a personal donation. (The bridge was now open, apparently.) It was while I was sitting in the staffroom considering this possibility that two Military Intelligence men came for me. They sent the Rector across to the English Department to fetch me. They were nondescript characters in ordinary civilian dress – a shirt, *longyi* and Mandalay sandals. They had a good look at me and then, using the Rector as interpreter, asked me several questions the answers to which I knew they already knew. After some further questioning, they demanded to see my car and its contents. Having studied the vehicle and the contents of the trunks, they appeared to lose interest and began to move off. As he turned to follow them, the Rector said over his shoulder, 'So the trunks will have to go back to Rangoon?'

'If the donation is unacceptable,' I answered, 'of course they will have to go back.'

I had no intention of sending the supplies back; but in case anyone was keeping an eye on my activities, I sent the trunks back to Rangoon on the down train. Empty. It was now eight days since the massacre had taken place.

At precisely eight o'clock the following evening, when we had just finished dinner, a cacophony of clanging and banging broke out all around our house. The neighbourhood, and perhaps the whole city, was drowning out the television news programme of the Burmese Broadcasting Service. Its propaganda had become such an insult to the intelligence that the people had coined a new phrase: 'talking like the BBS' meant 'telling lies'. But this communal clangour was not primarily a political comment but a time-honoured means of frightening away evil. The citizens of Mandalay in the Thirties, for example, had done it in order to fend off an outbreak of plague. When I went out into the darkness to hammer with my fists on the corrugated-iron doors of the garage, appreciative comments came from neighbours silhouetted in the nearby windows of dimly-lit rooms.

The next morning, Friday 19th August, Mandalay University silenced once and for all the jeers of those students in Rangoon who had called it, 'The Deaf and Dumb School'. Students and staff alike massed together into a huge, well-organised column of thousands and waited for some signal to start them off. I learned from colleagues that there had been another massacre, this time in Monywa, also in Sagaing Division and also perpetrated on the orders of Kyaw Zwā. Market-place rumour had it that there was a price of a hundred thousand *kyat* on that man's head, payable by the monks of Sagaing. The procession started moving. One poster, held by some students sitting on the roof of a hired bus, said KILLING FIELDS IN BURMA. I watched the column move off, then drove out to the rear route that I used so as to avoid the clogged roads; but even out here among the *padi*-fields I had to pull over for a procession of farmers. Their ancient leader leaned in over the passenger seat, addressed me in a remarkable tongue that was clearly intended to be English yet managed to convey not one shred of meaning and raised his eyebrows, waiting for my reply. On the spur of the moment I decided that a formula of solidarity was needed, and chose the most frequent protest chant:

'*Du ayé!*' I grinned, my fist raised. '*Du ayé!*'

The anxious wrinkles on his forehead migrated south and settled around his cloudy old eyes as he roared with toothless delight, and my eardrums twanged as he thumped my jeep approvingly. He loped off to catch up with his group.

Meanwhile the Party was appointing as its new Chairman a civilian, for a change – Dr Maung Maung. What Burmese politics needed was a massive dose of truth, but I doubted whether a civilian puppet would be able to administer the injection. That evening there was no racket at news-time, for everyone wanted to hear what Maung Maung would say. Predictably, he continued the pretence that the Party had not been rejected almost unanimously by the people. The Party preferred bloodshed to loss of 'face'.

My frustration at being unable to deliver the goods was growing, but then another matter occupied my attention for a day. The young Muslim woman I have called Sisi had asked me to take her to Hpaya-Gyi, the Mahamuni Pagoda, to see 'the photographs'. What these depicted neither she nor I knew at the time, but she had heard tell of them and wanted to see them. Sisi was an enthusiastic supporter of the student protests and of the popular movement for political reform and, since her mother was so worried for her safety, her mother and younger sister came along too. They appeared to know nothing about the pagoda and its contents, so I acted as tourist guide. We started from a quiet rear entrance, and Sisi was a little impatient until we reached the main entrance, with its well-used noticeboard. There were some new stickers on it, but no photographs. She was disappointed, but I was pleased to see one central poster written – correctly, too – in English. About a week beforehand, I had been chatting with some of the university's junior staff about the current situation, and I had concluded, 'Well, we must hope for the best, but be prepared for the worst.'

Now, from the middle of the noticeboard, my words stared back at me.

Sisi went off to consult some *hpongyis* and came back saying that there were some photos 'over there', and she pointed across a stretch of open ground on the northern side of the pagoda. There, we found a group of protest marchers resting in the shade of a few trees. Two of them were holding up poles supporting a banner on which there were large photographs of some of the victims of the

Sagaing massacre. I asked Sisi to enquire whether I could take a photograph – of the banner, not of the protesters. They would have to consult their leader. Someone went to fetch him and after a few seconds he appeared, a stocky, well-muscled, resolute-looking *hpongyi*. Where did I come from? England, I said. In that case, yes. And he hurried back to more important work. When I had taken my photograph, the protesters told Sisi to take me back to Hpaya-Gyi, to an entrance I had never used before. To cross the road we had to weave through a rapidly-assembling procession that consisted, as yet, almost entirely of *hpongyis*, a river of reddish-gold, the robes rippling and the umbrellas eddying as the monks jostled and turned to talk to each other. The sun was at its height, the heat and light intense.

In the entrance, the crowd sheltering from the sun parted to let Sisi and me pass. (We had left her mother and sister behind when we had gone to see the photographs.) As my eyes became accustomed to the shade, I found that there were more posters, hand-made as usual, on the corridor walls. One was a cartoon: Ne Win had a bullock's body and was pulling a cart with a gory corpse on it; following the cart were some dogs with human heads, one of which was Sein Lwin's. I was studying this and wondering why we had been sent here, when someone came up to Sisi and muttered something quietly to her. It seemed that a man, probably a Military Intelligence employee, had followed us across the open ground and the road, and was watching us. At this point an intense-looking young man appeared and asked Sisi if I would be willing to take some photographs to England and give them to the BBC. They were copies of those that I had just seen. He asked so earnestly that it was impossible for me to refuse. I thought he would unobtrusively slip a little packet into my hand but, when I said Yes, he dived into the throng of onlookers gathered in the entrance and swam across what was by now a choppy sea of red-gold robes and umbrellas.

It was at least fifteen minutes later that I caught sight of him wading back across the red sea, holding above his head a rolled sheaf of large photographs. I suddenly felt rather vulnerable and moved into the almost deserted interior part of the corridor. The young man came bustling up, hustled us further along the empty passage, then stopped and called through a metal grille on our left.

The sliding steel gates opened a little and we stepped into a dim side-room, lit only by a little daylight filtering through a dusty, small window. The steel gates were closed and latched behind us. I may not look like a James Bond, but I was certainly beginning to feel like one.

The young man at once squatted and we did likewise. It became clear why we had had to wait so long: the prints had just been made and were still dripping wet. As he spread them out on the woven matting, the steel grille rattled. An overfed, greasy fellow in a straw hat and dark glasses was trying to get in. Refused entrance, he protested arrogantly; told to go away, he merely waited impatiently a few yards away. Our intense-looking young man, perspiring freely, started explaining the content of the pictures to Sisi, who was doing her best to translate this information into English. I tried hard to pay attention, but was distracted by the well-fed outsider, who was once more demanding entry. This time he was pushed angrily away by several young men, and strutted off down the corridor. The worst of the photographs was of a man who had been repeatedly battered in the chest and abdomen with a rifle-butt until, at the moment of death, his eyeballs had started from their sockets. Poor Sisi was getting more than she had bargained for, but she calmly translated as well as she could. There were more shots of people killed in the hail of bullets, and of mass funerals. The young man re-rolled the prints, interleaving them with tissue paper, and I tucked them into my Shan shoulder-bag so that they didn't show. As we pushed our way out into the blinding sunlight at the entrance, the young man slipped away. Sisi's sister was waiting there for us, and I had enough time to urge them to omit any mention of the photographs to their mother, so as to spare her any extra worry. I hadn't liked the look of the man in the straw hat and dark glasses, and scanned the crowd as casually as I could. There was no sign of him; but then, in all the best spy stories, he would by now have been replaced by a colleague in any case. We walked back to my conspicuous white jeep with the Union Jack in the windscreen and I realised what a catastrophic secret agent I would be; this was the only vehicle of its kind in the whole of Mandalay Division, and half the city's population knew who owned it. Sisi's mother appeared, looking relieved but nervous after our long absence, and as I drove them home I chattered about anything and everything except the photographs, which I had concealed behind the back seat.

That afternoon I carefully straightened and dried out the prints, then sealed them in a large envelope ready for despatch to England. I would send them through the Embassy without telling anyone what the envelope contained. Meanwhile, I hid the envelope. That evening an Australian friend rang up to say that a Burmese acquaintance of his who lived and worked in Ywataung, on the outskirts of Sagaing, had been bitten by a rabid dog and needed a rabies vaccine of the type known as 'unactivated human strain'. Such vaccines have to be kept cool, and we had two doses in our refrigerator. I told him he could take these but that, because of the lengthy power-cuts of the previous April/May, I couldn't guarantee that the stuff was effective any more. Still, it was the right sort of vaccine; the poor man needed an immediate shot; and a 'killed' vaccine of this kind, even if no longer effective, would do no actual harm. It was agreed that the patient's doctor would phone me the following morning to arrange to pick it up.

The next morning, doctor and patient arrived at my house and I handed our vaccine over to the doctor. Over a glass of *sepaq-kalin* there was a little polite talk until the doctor asked me how much the patient was to pay.

'It cost me nothing,' I said. 'So you pay nothing.'

For a moment they both looked at me speechless.

'But this . . . this is very precious,' said the doctor.

'So is human life.'

The doctor actually repeated these words softly to himself, as if he needed to remind himself of a simple truth. But I was thinking about my medical supplies.

'Now,' I said briskly. 'There are many people in Sagaing who need medicines . . .'

The patient suddenly became fluent in English. Faltering only occasionally, when he would turn to the doctor for linguistic help, he insisted on telling me everything he knew about the Sagaing massacre. He had actually witnessed it and was fortunate to have escaped unscathed. One witness's account is inevitably incomplete and skewed, if only because everything is seen from only one viewpoint; but where facts are denied and reports suppressed, any account is better than none. Here is his story as I understood it. I have left out only one or two details that might serve to identify my informant, who had seen the Irrawaddy run with blood. Again the *yaddayā* had failed.

The road from Shwebo (to the north) meets the road from Monywa (to the east) at Ohndaw, about fourteen miles outside Sagaing, before continuing into the town itself. There had been a farmer's conference of some kind at Ohndaw, the farmers being mainly wheat and cotton growers because Sagaing Division is too dry in most places for rice cultivation. Many of these farmers had gone down into Sagaing, so on the ninth day of August 1988 the downtown area was unusually crowded. Here as elsewhere, political demonstrations had been growing in frequency and scale, and resentment might have been running high after the apparently unprovoked shooting of an unarmed man the previous day, an act which so angered the crowd that they had demolished the wheat-flour trading office where the shooting took place. At three o'clock, said the rabies patient, a single shot rang out, seemingly as a signal; for immediately, automatic and single-shot rifle fire sliced into the crowded streets from a dozen vantage-points. These positions included: down by the river, the residence of Sagaing Division People's Council Chairman himself, Kyaw Zwā; the residence of the Deputy Divisional Superintendent of Police; a hall next to the football ground; the Party Unit building, where one Han Htay was in charge; and, of all places, the division's Judicial Affairs Committee building where U Myo Aung resided.

(At this point, I cross-examined the patient – with the doctor's assistance – but could come to no other conclusion than that the massacre had been quite carefully planned. These armed men were already in position on roofs, in upper storeys and even, if my informant was not mistaken, in trees. But back to the account.)

When the firing stopped, the streets were littered with the wounded, the dying and the dead. An unknown number, dead and living, were dragged to the river and thrown in. Some were finished off with rifle butts. Some were taken to the mortuary, which was too small, so rows of corpses were laid in an outside compound. A certain number were dragged to the barbed wire that surrounded the police station compound. The security forces cut through the wire and dragged these bodies through the gap, distributing them about the compound and thus making it look as if the police had fired at an invading mob in self-defence. (I assume that 'official' photographs were then taken for the historical record.) The bridge was closed, the telephone link with Monywa cut. The patient thought that as many as three hundred might have died.

That was one version of one massacre; and in Mandalay we were getting word-of-mouth reports of another in Monywa soon after the Sagaing slaughter, and also at the hands of the ruthless Kyaw Zwā, who was said to have bayoneted the babies left behind by dead or fleeing Communist fighters, when in his younger days, he had been in charge of operations up in the hills.

When at last I was able to steer the conversation round to the problem of distributing my medical supplies, the two grateful men assured me that I should leave the matter in their hands for the moment. There was a *hsayadaw* who would have no difficulty in ensuring that the goods reached their proper destination. They would be in touch the next day, they said. But that was the day of the most massive demonstration Mandalay had yet seen (the BBC said a hundred thousand, I would have put it at a quarter of a million) and it was Wednesday before the Venerable *Hsayadaw* could pick up the supplies.

He was due to arrive at my house at nine in the morning, but the morning passed. Lunch-time came and went. Our cook Margaret cleared away the plates and then said, 'This morning I see yellow car go past house. Four time go past.'

She thought that the MI were on to me and was nervous. I too had begun to think that something had gone wrong; but I told myself that, with all the huge demonstrations to take care of, the *sanghā* were probably extremely busy. This was probably the case, for at 5 p.m. the *hsayadaw* and another doctor arrived in a small pick-up vehicle. The *hsayadaw* supervised as the doctor and I checked off and packed the syringes and anaesthetics and solutions and dressings. All this was loaded on to the pick-up and driven away to Sagaing and, apart from the *hsayadaw*'s receipt and my diary, I was now 'clean', having sent off the photographs the previous day. A drink was in order.

There are two postscripts to the Sagaing story. The first was the visit, two days later, of the rabies patient, another doctor and a third man. No, I regretted that I hadn't been able to locate any more vaccine, though I had tried; no, I no longer had the supplies because the *hsayadaw* had collected them; but yes, I would write a note to him asking him to spare some supplies for this doctor. I wrote the note and gave the doctor a few left-over gauze dressings. My visitors began to speak more freely. The doctor was on the run from the police because he knew too much about the massacre. He confirmed that it had started on the stroke of 3 p.m. when the shutters and windows opened and the gun-barrels appeared. He described one exit wound which had burst open the face of his young niece and another which had spilled the entrails of a young man. The number of people who had been shot in the back, or in the back of the head, had been high. He still had about a hundred patients in Sagaing, many of them still carrying a bullet which could not safely be removed in the existing conditions and with the equipment at his disposal. After the first wave of victims had arrived, his staff had resorted to pulling down the dusty curtains and tearing them into strips for use as bandages.

With the doctor standing by me, I telephoned the Embassy and asked for medical supplies, from any source. The message was noted for onward transmission, and then I was advised that 'in view of the current . . . etc' my wife and I should have a bag packed in readiness for departure to Rangoon. I put the phone down and told the doctor that with no planes or trains in operation I didn't think the chances of getting any more supplies were good. He accepted this as part of life's inscrutable pattern. The third man then confirmed that a photographer had been ordered by the police to photograph the scene at the police station after the bodies had been dragged through the breach in the barbed wire. The doctor added that police officers had actually trodden on the bodies in order to squeeze the wounds so as to make blood flow on the ground for the sake of verisimilitude. He had never experienced such brutality in all his life, he said. And he shuddered to think how much greater the carnage would have been if the machine-gun that one soldier was using had not jammed.

The second postscript? After we had been evacuated from Burma and set down in Bangkok, we waited to see if we would ever be allowed to return. I allowed three weeks to pass without making any public mention of the Sagaing mass murder. Then another of

Ne Win's proxy killers, Saw Maung, took over; and I knew that we would not be sent back. I contacted a *Times* reporter and told him the story, and when he mentioned photographs I told him to approach the BBC. He found out that the photographs I had sent from Mandalay had been destroyed by the BBC because there was no supporting text to go with them. To cap it all, *The Times* didn't even report me accurately. I had been careful to remind their correspondent that I was giving him details that had been reported to me; the article said that I had seen the massacre with my own eyes. It was this version which a year later found its way into Bertil Lintner's book *Outrage*, and if they ever make a film of the book I shall no doubt be depicted as a reluctant hero dodging a hail of bullets and surviving to tell the tale, for Burmese history does seem to insist on shading into legend.

14. Departures

'Ah!' breathed Ma Thant, 'I haven't seen that for a long, long time.'

She was looking wistfully at the emblem on a leaflet that had been handed out: the 'fighting peacock' which had been the symbol of student solidarity all those years ago, before Ne Win had the Students' Union building blown up in 1962. It was now Monday, 22nd August, and a huge demonstration, to include outlying communities, was scheduled to take place. A handful of old hopefuls had turned up to see if I was going to teach, but most were getting ready to march. No, there wouldn't be any classes today.

Ma Thant had borrowed a wide-brimmed bonnet because after the previous march her nose had peeled. But my most diminutive Angel would not be coming. In spite of her twenty-three years her mother had forbidden her to take part. She managed to answer my wave as we went past her house, but her cheeks glistened with tears of frustration. Thant disappeared into a throng of thousands that stretched in a solid column from the steps of the main building out along 73rd Street for as far as the eye could see – almost all the students and staff of the university, plus friendly contingents from Rangoon's university and its Institute of Technology. As they moved off I waved goodbye and again drove home via my muddy back route.

Later in the morning Liz and I walked round our neighbourhood and down to 30th Street. It was glorious. Mandalay's grid of lanes and streets had become a vast zigzag of veins carrying the life of the city in ever-broadening streams towards its heart – not the city centre, but Hpaya-Gyi and The Great Image. Monks in their reds and golds; Buddhist nuns in shell-pink and orange robes, each with

a chestnut-brown folded cloth placed over the shaven head against
the sun; *padi*-farmers in their broad conical hats; side-car drivers
pedalling old ladies slowly along free of charge; women with babies;
young men proudly carrying homemade placards and banners; all
chanting a demand for basic human rights in a most disciplined and
good-humoured way. More than a quarter of a million people were
on the march, many of whom would have to bed down in Mandalay
for the night before returning to their outlying villages. Those taking
part would never forget the occasion, but one tearful young lady
would perhaps never completely forgive her mother for denying her
the experience.

It was the following Friday that saw the most impressive demonstration of all. There was no point in trying to use my jeep
that morning because the roads were jammed with phalanx after
phalanx of joyous, chanting people. Every school in the city had
turned out, and there was a troupe of Chins, a Muslim group,
a band of Hindus, a Christian parade (Baptist, Catterlick, the
lot), the University column, a Tourist Burma team in which our
friend Thuzar marched jauntily, squads of farmers ('peasants' in
Party English), a contingent of policemen(!), groups representing
all manner of trades and professions, in all a euphoric multitude
shepherded by the monks of the city in a – a what? Not a
demonstration, for the word smacks of aggressiveness; it was a
parade, a carnival.

Well, if they could walk, so could we. We zigzagged through the
back-streets so as to come out on the main road that runs northwards
alongside the palace moat almost to the foot of Mandalay Hill. The
whole two-kilometre stretch of tree-lined road was a sea of green
and white, with banners like colourful sails billowing above. *WE
ARE IN THE HELL OF NE WIN* said one of them. The road
was packed with schoolchildren and their teachers. The air was
full of treble voices chanting slogans, and bright with slanting
sunshine; and shy smiles blossomed into laughter as I joined in the
responses.

'*Sandá, sandá!*' the cheer-leaders would chant.

'*Pyá! Pyá!*' I would respond, along with their fellow marchers.

'*Thabeiq, thabeiq!*' they yelled.

'*Hmauq! Hmauq!*' I shouted as I marched alongside.

(I never once broke the terms of my contract by taking part in any political activity, but I came very close to it on several occasions like this one.)

When the column turned westwards at the corner of the moat Liz and I climbed the hill and, together with other onlookers, watched from a rocky knoll the demonstrators assembling at the rendezvous area far below us, each school contingent looking like a long white millipede with green legs. I was just working out that the average age of the crowd must have been about seventeen, when suddenly everyone ran away. I was squatting under a small thorny tree, and a snake had slithered down the trunk. It sped past my leg, heading downhill, and the other onlookers came back. I was reminded of how I had been left standing when the wall of the classroom had fallen in. My fate would be what I had merited by my behaviour in previous lives; no Buddhist would think of trying to interfere with the predestined.

By one o'clock the rally was dismantling itself tidily, the columns heading homewards in the same good humour but with less energy. At the foot of the hill Liz and I got separated and I couldn't find her. I headed for home too, taking a short cut through the welcome coolness of the Kyauqdawgyi Hpaya, where a man hurried up to me and asked, 'You are Christopher Guinness?'

With my satchel slung from one shoulder, I probably did look like a reporter with a tape-recorder, perhaps even the famous BBC correspondent who had become well-loved for his persistent reports on events in Burma. I explained that I was only a teacher. Then, half-way home, a group of bystanders waved excitedly and one called out, 'Christopher Gunnit?'

Again I shook my head apologetically. It was not long before a rumour was going round that the BBC's Chris Gunness was in town, joining the protesters on the march.

The next day Margaret brought me an envelope, delivered by hand, in which there were two letters. The first was from Sisi's mother:

Hello Gerry and Liz,

   Do congratulate me! You know yesterday I took part in the procession from our TTC group. First I and my son watched the processions in front of the hospital at 10.30. About 11.30, the TTC group came and my friends from Eng. Dept shouted to me to come along.

In this way I was among them and felt v. happy to be able to
do so.

It's v. systematic, the Hpongyis guarded us all the way. Nothing
disorder was permitted to do. There were many posters, banners. A
certain Hpongyi was giving speech at one corner. Sometimes, there
were 2 or 3 lines of demonstrations on the roads. At such times, there
were welcoming shouts, cheerings and clappings to each other. There
were feedings all the way. You know, the whole thing was video-taped.
We met a car with some Hpongyis and a man recording on video
tapes twice, 2 different groups (I doubt if my sentence is correct)
on the 26th St. and near Hpayagyi. My daughters said so too. Their
university group was v. big, they said. Today my son is participating
with his school.

Yesterday I reached home at 5pm and Sisi and Lele at 5.30. I
guessed yesterday demonstration had ⅔ of the population of Mdy
at least. Because wherever I looked from my place, to the east, to
the west, I saw the processions coming. I saw v. old people too.
Nearly all the members of the houses took part in their respective
groups. Yesterday, I got feet sore before I reached A Road and I
had to manage hard. One of my knees got hurt too. I'm walking a
limp today.

Yours, etc

(I saw a photo-copy of Time Magazine cover stuck on the wall beside
84th St. 2.8.88 issue, I think. There are news too.)

Sisi had taken the opportunity of slipping her own note into the
envelope before delivering it:

Good morning sir!

How will you do if MI come to you and ask about your photos
sir. I am quite worry about that. So, I told you not to return
altogether at first. If they (MI) saw you went back alone, they'll
think you were a tourist and they'll no longer try to follow you and
investigate you.

But now, MI will see that we all went back in your car and they
became knew that we came there together. And so they'll know you are
not a tourist. And they may investigate who you are, from where you are,
and the place you live.

My thoughts are right sir! How will you do if they come to you sir.
Mother told us if MI co

Sisi had indeed tried to persuade me to drive back alone from Hpaya-gyi after getting the photographs but, had I done so, I would never have been able to explain to her mother why I had ditched the family in a congested area on a sweltering day and miles from home. Poor Sisi was now, I could see, alarmed. I was touched to see that she had crossed out the final unfinished sentence, preferring not to go into what the MI might do to me if they came for me. The poor girl was naturally afraid that I might tell the MI who it was that had accompanied me to Hpaya-Gyi on the Day of the Photographs, but she had tried to concentrate on expressing her concern for my safety. It was strange how the timorous mother and the enthusiastic daughter had reversed their roles.

Life in Mandalay had taken on a dreamlike quality. Enormous columns of people of all ages were taking to the streets daily in an impressively orderly way, each contingent shepherded by teachers or *hpongyi* or both, and on every face a smile for the Englishman leaning out of his white jeep or standing by the roadside. There was an almost palpable sense of corporate well-being, so that sometimes the whole street seemed to glow with euphoria. The sudden hope of overthrowing an evil regime, of rearing up like a whipped horse to cast its cruel rider into the dust, had released phenomenal energy and given a direction to traditional Burmese resourcefulness. We had seen people making cardboard on frames set up in their gardens, where the pulp would dry thoroughly in the fierce sunlight; others had set about weaving rectangles of split bamboo as frames on which to mount the cardboard. Some painted their slogans in Burmese, but others took the trouble to use English in the hope that some foreign camera would record the messages for the outside world: WE NEED DEMOCRACY . . . WE DENOUNCE RAPIST GOVERNMENT MASSACRE . . . SOCIALIST PARTY – GET OUT!

Administratively the city was in a sort of limbo. The Party had lost its hold completely at street and ward levels. The Party office near our house, which once had blared propaganda at all hours, had remained closed and shuttered for some days now, the security forces had disappeared and even the traffic police now vanished. One-way streets immediately became two-way thoroughfares, of course; but if any Party commander was biding his time in the hope that anarchy would turn into mayhem, he was disappointed. In fact, the city was not in a state of anarchy; a hierocracy was in operation. The monks were controlling the traffic at busy intersections in town; they were manning some of the petrol-pumps; they were dealing with crime by hauling the culprits off to the pagodas and incarcerating them there; and it was the monks, or rather the *hsayadaw* in each area, who had set up neighbourhood security boards to prevent lawlessness – especially theft and looting. The whole city was being taken care of by these boards, each chaired by a *hpongyi*. They ensured that round-the-clock vigilance was maintained by requiring every able-bodied male in the neighbourhood to take his turn at guard duty. This monasterial administration was working well as a holding operation, but one couldn't help wondering how long it could last.

The Burmese people had magnificently rejected the BSPP and its architect Ne Win, and had repeatedly confirmed a desire for liberal, democratic, multi-party government. (I had reservations about having *many* parties, which might simply encourage factionalism in a complex society like Burma, and I tried to persuade people that all they needed – at least for the time being – was one opposition party, so that in the Hlutdaw the verb 'discuss' could reacquire its true meaning.) The response of the state-controlled Press was to step up the 'anti-multi' propaganda. The *Guardian*'s headlines ran: DEMAND FOR MULTI-PARTY SYSTEM AND DANGER TO THE COUNTRY (Wednesday, 17th August.) Here, those demanding the system were accused of having 'no political objective and programme, no policy laid down' – hardly surprising in a country where parties other than the BSPP had been banned by law for so long.

REPUGNANT PRACTICES OF ELECTIONS OF MULTI-PARTY SYSTEM (Thursday, 18th August). In the bad old days when Burma had had such a system, said the writer, canvassing for votes 'had been done by outright lying and cheating, making of hollow promises, coercion and bloodshed'. One's immediate reaction was: 'So what's new?'

MULTI-PARTY SYSTEM WANTED BY INSURGENTS (Monday, 22nd August). This was an attempt to persuade people that they were playing straight into the enemy's hands, and was pure 'Animal Farm': it was Squealer saying 'Jones will come back!' And the very next day brought the Burma version of 'Comrade Napoleon is always right':

BOGYOKE AUNG SAN'S VIEW OF PARLIAMENTARY SYSTEM AND ONE-PARTY SYSTEM. According to this article the beloved Aung San had in 1940 written:

> There should be only one State, one government, one party, one leader. There should be no opposition party as in the parliamentary system.

I had no way of knowing whether the quote was accurate and, if it was, whether Aung San had still the same view in 1948; but I very much doubted the latter.

I took the Embassy's message seriously enough to take some empty cartons to the university the next morning and pack up my own books and notes. Things were being made to look more and more anarchic. The highly-populated Insein prison had (been?) burned down, and there had been many casualties; and other prisons were releasing all detainees, the criminal as well as the political ones. I say 'made to' look so, because I saw all this as a central policy designed to contribute to the destabilisation of the country to a point at which massive and bloody military action would appear to be justified. There were food shortages in Rangoon where, in some districts, looting was going on; this was said by many to have been actively encouraged by army personnel. Aung San's daughter Suu Kyi had addressed half a million peaceful protesters at the Shwedagon Hpaya, thus entering a dangerous political arena.

I also took to the university some photocopies of articles and newspaper cuttings from the foreign press. These were for the news exhibition* set up by the students, a display of reports and comment from Thai, British and American journals and newspapers, enlivened with the students' own cartoons. There was even one contribution from Spain: a Spanish friend had sent me the front page of *El País*, dominated by the famous photograph of a male student kissing the boot of a fully-armed soldier as he begged the line of soldiers, bayonets drawn, to join the ranks of the peaceful protesters. Visitors to the exhibition, which was open to the public, found this picture very moving. As the exhibits grew in number, so did the number of visitors. I have never seen more startling proof of the power of motivation in language-learning. People of all ages

---

* See the Sagaing massacre exhibit in the Appendix, p. 217

were expending prodigious amounts of energy in their painfully slow reading of journalistic English; friends or strangers were asked to help by explaining or translating a word or caption; and people who could hardly rub together two words of English were accosting me:

'No human rights have.' (The phrase 'human rights' was known to all.)

'We, . . . we democracy!'

'Burma bad, but . . .'

To this lad I said, 'But we shall win.'

'Aah!' He nodded gratefully and walked off saying, 'We shall win we shall win we . . .'

I privately thought that things would get a lot worse before the people won, for disturbing pieces of news were arriving thick and fast from various sources. Trouble was coming closer. From an Australian friend I learned that an oil-mill adjacent to his office had been ransacked by soldiers, who had loaded every drum of cooking-oil on to trucks and driven off, presumably to the fort. Convoys of both petrol and rice had been seen, by other friends, also heading towards the fort. A bren-gun carrier and two armoured cars had been observed coming in on the main road from Meikhtila, and arms and ammunition were said to be arriving in Mandalay by plane. I now remembered that a fortnight earlier a colleague had described to me how she had been kept awake all night as soldiers outside Bank No. 1 had loaded some trucks. That cargo must have been chests of banknotes, also destined for the moated palace stronghold; after all, unpaid soldiers would soon become disaffected and mutinous. Rice, cooking-oil, money, petrol, arms and ammunition: it looked to me as if Mandalay Palace was to be used as a fortress from which the army would be able to break out, given the slightest excuse – or perhaps, as in Sagaing, needing no pretext whatsoever. The emptying of prisons was also disquieting. After the release of prisoners from the gaols of Insein, Bassein and Sittwe, there was now a steady stream of detainees (arrested demonstrators and criminals alike) leaving the prison within the palace walls. Well-organised as ever, the monks were checking them out as they crossed the moat bridge, keeping records of who they were and where they lived, and even arranging for many to be delivered home – one way of checking the bona fides of those released. It was no coincidence that prisoners had 'escaped' from a nearby gaol on the road to Maymyó; someone was deliberately brewing mayhem.

Who? Ne Win was rumoured to have left the country, been refused entry to Thailand, tried India and failed, and finally left Burma via the seaside resort of Ngapali. I didn't believe this but, if it was true that he had fled the country, perhaps Sein Lwin (of whom nothing whatsoever had been heard since he stepped down) was waiting to achieve the target of victims that he was said to have set himself: ten thousand. He was already more than halfway there. According to our house-agent friend Auntie Than Than, the bestial Kyaw Zwā was holed up with his troops somewhere near Monywa, a large and prosperous town which, like Mandalay, was now run by the monks. Also disturbing was the fact that the domestic news broadcasts, still mouthpieces of the regime, were openly admitting that Monywa was no longer under government control. I reasoned that a regime so unused to telling an unwelcome truth would tell the truth about a situation only if it secretly welcomed that situation; and I could think of no reason, other than a bloodthirsty one, why Ne Win should welcome the current state of affairs.

It was now beginning to make a little more sense to leave Burma for a while. I spent most of that Sunday (28th August) packing books and notes on the assumption that they would no longer be needed even if law and order were to return the following day. We were due to leave at the end of our two-year contract in a few weeks in any case. The next morning sixteen expatriates, mostly Australian, flew to Rangoon and by nightfall were snug in their Bangkok hotels. That left four foreigners in town: Liz and myself, and two research students – one a British girl and the other a young American fellow. I helped Ma Thant to move her things back into her tiny billet on the campus and then we headed straight for Hpaya Gyi, the Mahamuni Pagoda, for I had at last found an excellent use for all the money I had secretly earned by marking university exam papers – at the stingy official rate, about a hundred and twenty pounds sterling: we were going to present it to the demonstration fund, whose committee headquarters were located near the northern entrance of the pagoda. The lads manning the desk were visibly astonished to see me approach, and clearly delighted at the sum I donated, and literally dumbfounded. It wasn't until I had collected my receipt and had stood up to leave that there was some whispering and nudging and one young man craned forward with a bright smile of gratitude.

'Thanks a lot!' he drawled in an accent straight out of a cowboy film.

We were still resisting the Embassy's increasing pressure on us to leave, for the simple reason that it made no sense to go from a relatively peaceful Mandalay to a strife-torn Rangoon. Now we heard that we would be flown out to Bangkok; we no longer had a logical excuse for staying, so we agreed that we would leave on the Thursday morning plane. I got the last of my papers from my room in the university and showed Liz the exhibition of news and views there. She photographed the Sagaing exhibit so that I could check its map and text against the oral account I had been given. We drove across town to tell the British research student that we were leaving and that the Embassy advised her to do likewise. Back home, I got the gardener to dig a hole where our compost-heap was, so that we could bury three plastic jerrycans full of precious petrol, which would no doubt be in short supply when (if?) we were able to return. As the university's main building was closed, Liz arranged with her Principal the provision of an official letter authorising us to travel to Rangoon.

The next morning, we found groups of soldiers posted in and around the little airport. The airport manager's shed appeared to be closed, its corrugated-iron doors shut and guarded by two armed soldiers, but one of the soldiers opened a door for us. Yes, the manager said, he expected a flight on Thursday. No, there were no problems: BAC had enough aircraft fuel to last eleven days. He would make a provisional booking and we should come the next day with the fare and the authorising letter. (Tickets were never issued more than a day in advance, even at the best of times.) Outside the airport in the shade of a tree, a crowd of two or three dozen people waving currency notes in the air were clamouring for one of the small sheets of paper that were on sale. These were forms of application for an air ticket, forms normally issued free of charge but now transformed by the military build-up and the known shortage of fuel into a saleable commodity. As usual, we rich foreigners had not been required to pay for ours.

Back home we found that the twin-tub washing machine's spinner had jammed. I knew nothing whatsoever about these machines but after a sweaty half-hour of trial-and-error diagnosis I managed to get it going again. Then Liz found that her car battery was dry and dead. I put an airconditioner on, collected the distilled water that dripped from it, topped the battery up and put it on charge. Meanwhile, U Kyit the gardener had excelled himself. He proudly showed me the brick-lined pit that he had made, in which nestled three five-gallon plastic jerrycans, all full of petrol; he then covered the pit with slats of wood and covered these with a pile of dead leaves and kitchen waste. I fully expected soldiers to come requisitioning fuel so, to avert suspicion and to distract them from my little depot, I left the rest of our petrol in the garage.

The army units were still largely inside the palace and had still not taken up positions on Mandalay Hill, which surprised me. Another thing that surprised me was that no one seemed to have thought of blowing up the four road-bridges that crossed the palace moat – something that could be done quite easily and without loss of life. There were two other exits, admittedly: a wooden footbridge and the railway line, which ran north–south through the palace enclosure, close to its western wall; but these too could easily be demolished at night without bloodshed.

That evening Sisi came to the house to warn me that the army would, according to rumour, be occupying the university campus and other demonstration centres in the next few hours. I decided that after dinner I would go and persuade Ma Thant to move out again to her aunt's house. During dinner the heavens opened and the roar of the downpour was unbroken for more than an hour. As it began to ease off, I set out in my little jeep. The roads on the way to the university, 30th and 73rd Streets, were flooded with a foot or so of water; when I tried to make speed I simply succeeded in throwing a great curtain of filthy spray all over the windscreen, so I had to be content with chugging, like a tug along a canal, through waters that reflected the dazzling lightning. The army had a reputation for raping and killing defenceless women. I was hoping that they had not already moved in, that I would not be turned back at bayonet point at the gates.

The headlights showed, through a bright arras of rain, that the iron gates were shut. My heart sank. But then I saw some figures moving. I inched the jeep forward. They were students, soaked to the skin, their hair plastered flat, guarding the gate. One of them splashed forward and I wound my window down. In my halting Burmese I identified myself.

'I English language teacher. Ten minutes, back come will,' I shouted.

'*Ya-ba-deh, hsaya.*' And the gates swung open.

Ma Thant listened to what I had to say and without a word went to pack a bag. Gerry's brightest 'angel', who had been chatting to Thant, came over to chat to me. Her dismay when she heard I was leaving was heartrending. I was already feeling annoyed at having to leave; now I felt thoroughly guilty. I was sitting in a bamboo chair just inside the billet; Gerry's angel was looking sadly at nothing in particular; the rain was draping a glittering bead curtain outside the black doorway; from beyond there came the deep twanging of amorous frogs; and suddenly I regretted my compliance with the Embassy's wishes. I wanted to stay.

Thant was back within five minutes. I dropped her off at her aunt's house. With a word of sincere gratitude, she hitched her *longyi* up a little and waded up the path to the house. The rain was stopping at last.

The following morning we picked up the letter of authorisation to travel and went to the airport to get our tickets. Six army petrol tankers preceded us and continued southwards as I turned into the airport's parking area. This time, soldiers were standing grim-faced and with fixed bayonets at every gate and doorway, but everything here and in town was quiet and we arrived home with our tickets, ready to decide how to spend our last twenty-four hours in Mandalay until we were able to come back. Almost immediately the telephone rang. It was the Embassy. In view of the general strike planned for the next day, tomorrow's plane might never reach Mandalay . . . so would we please catch today's plane? Today's? But that is due to leave in about two hour's time! Yes, but would we please try to get on it? OK, we would try. The university being shut, I left Liz to telephone her college to find out if they could lend us their van, and would they check to see whether there was indeed a plane today, and whether our tickets could be exchanged or something.

While these inquiries were being made, I hastily carted into our store-room the twenty-seven small cartons that I had packed with books and notes and a few other belongings. Then, running

with sweat, I parked the jeep in the garage and locked the doors.
The study upstairs was full of Embassy equipment – photocopier,
typewriter, duplicator – so I locked that up and retained the key
along with the store-room key and one for the garage. Telephone.
Liz answered. Yes, there was a flight at 13.30, the manager would
give us two seats and the TTC van would come for us at 12.30. An
hour early? Yes, because there were still big protest marches going
on and it might be difficult to get past the columns of people. I
looked at my watch. It was now 11.30. An hour to pack and see to
any last-minute arrangements.

Staff pay – this month's and for a month in advance – had
already been issued by Liz. Packing, then. How long would we
be away? No idea. Might be sent back to England, therefore
raincoat, two sweaters, long-sleeved shirts, two ties, stout shoes.
Might just languish in Bangkok, therefore cotton short-sleeved
shirts, light cotton trousers, pair of flip-flops. Camera. Brief-case:
cheque-books, various official Burmese cards and documents,
Embassy letter explaining that my passport was 'with the Embassy
for official purposes' (but I knew, and so did the Embassy, that it
had long been lost in the dim recesses of Burmese bureaucracy).
Anything else? Bloody hell, I'd nearly forgotten my diary! Five
instalments in envelopes. UK stamps for sending them off to
England by diplomatic bag – I daren't risk getting caught with them.
Reading-glasses. No more room, so selected professional notes and
correspondence must go into carrier bag along with our last bottle
of Mandalay beer.

Beer. Time for a quick one? Yes, there's a can of Tiger in the
fridge. Deep swig. Run upstairs, shower and change into respectable
clothing, leaving sweat-sodden shorts where they fall. Hurry down
and put luggage in the hall. Ma Thuzar has arrived and is hugging Liz
and weeping. '*Pyan la-meh, pyan la-meh*,' I say. 'We'll come back.'
Bu this only makes her weep all the more. Another swig. Aah, just
what the doctor loud hooting outside front door load cases on TTC
minibus tell driver to pull van forward reverse Liz's car under portico
open bonnet and lock car up leaving gardener to remove battery for
storage. Goodbye Margaret, U Kyit, U Po Bwin, goodbye Thuzar,
pyan la-meh . . .

As soon as the minibus turned the first corner, we could see
groups of demonstrators on the move, blocking the roads. The

driver zigzagged his way down to 30th Street and I asked him to turn left into 71st, stopping him outside the house of Ma Thant's aunt. Question: How do you say goodbye in a very great hurry to a very dear friend? Answer: Very badly. A breathless explanation, a tiny present, and the key to my university office. 'I'll be back.' Again that wish that sounded like a promise.

On the road again, we met more demonstrations, went down more side-streets that were deeply rutted but unfrequented except for a few young children and occasional cows, geese, piglets. Coming out on to the airport road, we saw soldiers here and there with fixed bayonets – long, sharp, double-edged knives, not at all like the British bayonet of my National Service days, which was like a short fat knitting-needle (because, I had been informed, the knife-shaped ones tended to get stuck between ribs, vertebrae and so on, thus leaving the assailant defenceless until he could wrench it out). At the airport we walked past the bayonet-tipped rifles and into the manager's office. He converted our tickets so that they were valid for the next flight. At the check-in desk, the clerk's passenger list had two blank slots at numbers nine and ten, which he filled with our names. Somewhere there were two ticket-holding would-be travellers who were, or were going to be, very disappointed and angry.

Of course, the plane was late. That was normal. Or perhaps there wasn't going to be any plane this time – a thought which I confess cheered me up a little. We ate Margaret's hastily-packed sandwiches and washed them down with our last Mandalay beer, which tasted of caustic soda. We went into the spartan departure lounge with its concrete floor and slatted benches under wobbling, rusted ceiling fans. Two Burmese men came and sat near us and we began to chat amiably. After a few minutes the one who did all the talking knew who we were, where we came from, where we worked, where we were going and why. I was used to Burmese inquisitiveness and was going to return the compliment, but the conversation inevitably turned to the current unrest. I described in some detail how if I were a student leader I would immobilise the palace garrison by blowing up the bridges and railway line at night. He listened attentively, then sat in silence, nodding thoughtfully. This was my cue.

'And you. Are you travelling to Rangoon too?'

'No, I work here. Security.'

The air temperature seemed to drop quite suddenly, my breathing appeared to have stopped and it was very quiet. It felt like ages before he added proudly. 'Anti-hijack. And we have had no hijacks for forty years.'

The air warmed up again. I took a great gulp of it and went to the window to see the long-awaited F27 arriving from somewhere up in the wild northern hills.

Falling away behind me now were the sacred places that I had grown to love: the golden pyramid of Hpaya Gyi and, like perfect white stalagmites, the pagodas of the ancient capitals of Amarapura, Ava, Sagaing . . .

The air in Rangoon was heavy with moisture, the sky slate-grey. Mosses and algae glowed greenly on walls that flaked and roofs that sagged. Large areas of the city were quite literally disintegrating, and provided an apt setting for the breakdown of the fabric of government which was taking place. The inhabitants were taking care of themselves, setting up rosters for security duties and administering summary justice. They had erected a system of barricades: the inhabitants of each street had blocked both ends with fences of woven bamboo backed with sandbags or whatever suitable materials came to hand. In the centre was a gap wide enough to allow a car to enter or leave; and just inside this barricade lay the means of closing the gap – more panels and reinforcing materials or, in one case at least, a huge sewer pipe which could be swivelled across the open space and wedged in position with large stones. These barriers were unmistakable proof that the people placed no trust whatsoever in the security forces; nor could a neighbourhood trust outsiders of any kind, since it was well known (I had seen it for myself) that plenty of Military Intelligence employees operated in plain clothes. All able-bodied men in the barricaded street would do their fair share of guard duty, and ad hoc street committees were not slow to deal with those suspected of working for the MI, of looting or of being bent on sabotaging the people's solidarity in any way. There were plenty of these hired thugs, paid by Ne Win's cronies to create mayhem, and not just a few of them met their end at the hands of enraged fellow citizens, for street justice included capital punishment. One evening an American marine had been on his way home by car and found the road blocked by a crowd. These people had insisted that he should come with them to see and to tell others what happened to enemies of the people. When he arrived one of the 'accused', probably an MI agent, was lying headless in the street and several others awaited a similar fate nearby. It was being said that after an execution some people were indulging in cannibalism in that they were eating the liver of the dead man and thus, according to an old belief, acquiring his strength and other powers. As this was reported in the *Guardian* (Rangoon), I was inclined to doubt whether it was true; but pent-up fury can take barbaric forms.

If such stories were true, they were far from typical of public behaviour. The vast majority of people remained resolutely hopeful and ineffably good-humoured. If there was savagery, the blame was to be laid at the door of Ne Win who, despite the rumours, was almost certainly still in Rangoon, ensconced spiderlike at the hub of a vast web of evil intrigue. I thought, and still think, that he was not merely engineering the downfall of the national uprising but was also punitively orchestrating the crushing of a people's spirit. (In the former he was successful; in the latter he was not.) In view of his obsession with his own health and survival, I guessed that he was psychopathic enough to abhor the thought of a nation surviving to rejoice in his passing. He had certainly cried havoc and let slip the dogs of civil war. Was he also, in his dotage, viewing himself as a kingly figure more sinned against than sinning? To twist King Lear's cry of tender anguish to one of vicious petulance, was he inwardly screaming

Why should a horse, a dog, a rat have life,
And me no life at all?

If I was right it was all very Shakespearean, this causal link between the atrophy of the royal body and the breakdown of the body politic.

The following morning there was a great deal to get done if, as planned, we were to fly out to Bangkok that afternoon. It was the day of the great General Strike and the Thai plane might not come, but we had to assume it would. It was now 9 a.m. Before 1 p.m. the Embassy would have to supply me with a new passport, procure re-entry visas for both of us and obtain our flight tickets. Meanwhile we had to pick up some mail from the German friend of a German friend who had been unable to take it to Mandalay as planned; we had to leave labelled house keys and car keys in safe keeping at the Embassy; there was the dissertation of a Burmese student to leave there too; there were my diary instalments to send off to England . . . and I'd even remembered to bring back the British Council library book on the butterflies of India, mustn't forget that. Incredibly, and to the Embassy's great credit, all flight and passport arrangements had been completed by one o'clock; but the plane didn't come, because the air traffic controllers had joined the general strike. In fact most of the population seemed to be out in the streets yet again, marching in orderly and cheerful fashion; and driving across the city was a problem. Thank goodness for an Embassy driver!

Next morning, word went out that there was definitely going to be a flight to Bangkok, but no one knew when. We were to be on standby as from 08.00 hours. We had heard nothing by midday, when the Ambassador kindly invited us, along with our Rangoon-based colleagues in English teaching, to lunch and a chat at the Residence. Then more waiting. Word came at last that the flight would depart at about 5.30 p.m. and we set out for Mingaladon in the Embassy LandRover.

People had continued marching through the sporadic showers, but now they were heading for home. The authorities had warned people that they must vacate all public premises that they had occupied, or face the unspecified consequences. Most people seemed to have complied. From the very beginning, bystanders everywhere had encouraged the demonstrators in the traditional manner, by running out with cool water or other refreshment. Government thugs had killed a few marchers by offering poisoned water. Monks had caught at least three of these agents, forced them to drink their own water and watched them die excruciatingly of cyanide poisoning. The marchers were now carrying their own refreshments. There were few on the roads by now. At intervals there were army trucks, full of heavily-armed soldiers, parked unobtrusively just off the main roads. Troops had also taken up strategic positions elsewhere, including Kanbe TTC, where we had been treated to our first display of educational unreality.

The airport road was almost empty. In Mingaladon there were far fewer people than usual, and many of them were departing Europeans. As I passed the Security Office I peered in; three short, dark soldiers were loading magazines with snub-nosed bullets and

placing them next to a pile of already-loaded sub-machine guns. Ne
Win's guns would speak louder than the people for a while, yet the
people would win. But when?

It would have to be over the Old Man's dead body. In Rangoon
I had seen a copy of a brief document that was circulating publicly.
Dated 23rd August – just a week before – it was headed 'Top
Secret' and appeared to be the minutes of a meeting held in
Number One's lakeside residence in Rangoon. ('Top Secret,
Bottom Open', to quote a contemporary Burmese aphorism.) Ne
Win himself was in the Chair and those present included Sein
'Butcher' Lwin, President Maung Maung, General Saw Maung –
a Ne Win loyalist and confederate of The Butcher – and three of
the Old Man's daughters, one of whom (Sanda Win) was said to
be the venom in the fangs of the MI. According to the minutes
the purpose of the meeting was to coordinate actions specifically
designed to create a lack of common trust, sow disorder and foster
lawlessness. Rumours were to be put about that Ne Win had fled the
country; division was to be engineered within the opposition's ranks,
among the general public, the students and the monks; and 'covert
actions' (unspecified) were to be undertaken by the armed forces as
underground activities conducive to a state of anarchy. While all this
was going on, apparent concessions could be made to the public's
demands, even to the point of promising multi-party elections, but
such measures were to be simply the prelude to a decisive military
coup. The meeting closed, as so many Party meetings did, with the
chanting of slogans, including 'Chairman Ne Win will live for more
than a hundred years!'

I had no way of knowing whether the document was genuine.
Authentic or not, it rang terribly true. It fitted the picture I had built
up of an unrepentant old man, petulantly unwilling to relinquish
power and afraid of dying; a man hell-bent on two courses of action
– to fabricate a situation which would give him an excuse to assert
his supremacy, and to punish his people for their rejection of him.
These tasks were simply two sides of the same bayonet.

15. Waiting

In Bangkok, we waited to see whether we would be able to
go back to Mandalay. I was miserable. I had first arrived there
as a young teacher of English in 1959, long before it had been
converted into a concrete metropolis full of luxury hotels and huge
department stores that faced each other across giant race-tracks
hazed with pollution. I recognised that I was suffering not only
from culture-shock but also from time-warp.

In Mandalay the traffic, mainly bicycles, proceeded at a stately
fifteen miles an hour for most of the time; here the almost unbroken
column of sleek automobiles and airconditioned coaches screamed
through the concrete-and-glass canyons at three times the pace and
with ten times more decibels. In Mandalay there were two 'large'
hotels, each of two storeys; here they were set thickly on the ground
and soared overhead, and more were being built all the time. Mandalay vehicles dated mostly from the Fifties and early Sixties, some
of the jeeps and buses being even older; here all the vehicles looked
new. In Mandalay when, as you often did, you gave someone a little
present of food, you asked if you could have the plastic bag back;
here, the *rubbish* was disposed of in large plastic bags.

The Bangkok of thirty years earlier had merited its sobriquet,
'The Venice of the East', being enlaced with canals or *klong* of
various sizes which acted as quiet streets and market-places as well
as providing free (if noisome) public bathing and toilet facilities.
Now there was hardly a *klong* to be seen, and there was just the
one Floating Market – preserved because it was a tourist attraction.
The Pattaya of my youth was a stretch of lonely and beautiful
beach, accessible by rough jungle track; now, it was a Thai Miami
or Acapulco.

In 1960 it had taken me thirty-six hours by train to reach Chiengmai, the locomotive stopping every so often to pick up fuel as well as passengers. On arrival, you found a Railway Hotel consisting of a few bungalows on stilts and an apparently sleepy town not unlike those of the Mid-West as depicted on cowboy films. I say 'apparently' sleepy because on certain nights when the streets were strangely empty, the clop of plodding hooves announced that the harvest of the hills was passing through. A few hours' walk over the mountain from Doi Suthep, just outside the town, you came to a Meo village where you were stoned as you approached. Cowering at the edge of the forest, you noticed the village aqueduct: the chute, starting at a source somewhere up the mountain, was of overlapping runnels made from bamboos split in half lengthwise and with the nodes removed; the height of the bamboo stilts supporting it ensured that the chute wound down the slopes at a gentle angle, allowing very little of the cool, clean water to spill. You could see the village of a dozen small dwellings thatched with leaves and arranged around a central communal quernstone and, on the slopes beyond the village, the patchwork of poppy fields being harvested.

Now, luxury trains and broad highways sped the tourist to a great, bustling city whence there were daily trips to tourist-traps: hill-tribe villages. This was all inevitable, no doubt, but I was sad to find that the Thai people were losing what their Burmese neighbours still retained – a sort of effortless grace and graciousness in the negotiations of daily life, welcoming and greeting, helping, buying and selling, and so on. But perhaps this was true only of the city folk; I hoped it would not be an inevitable consequence of so-called 'development' that the Burmese would lose that calm natural grace. One thing the Thai had not lost, I was glad to see, was their intriguing use of the English language. In the old days, one of my favourite signs in English had been on Silom Road. Hanging above the pavement was a painted board bearing the delightfully ambiguous text: YOU ARE WELCOME TO THE STARLIGHT CLUB.

Now, on a short bus trip through town, there were anonymous-looking clinics that made alarmingly ambitious claims such as VD AND EVERYTHING and PEKING CURE: GENERAL AND HAEMOR-RHOIDS. But the winner was the sports shop (not a clinic) that offered: ATHLETIC BALLS. Liz wouldn't let me get off the bus to investigate, which I suppose was just as well; a man sporting (yes, that's the word) a pair of those would no doubt only end up going to some anonymous-looking clinic for his VD and everything, and maybe even for a Peking Cure if he overdid things.

We were on our way to Wat Phra Keo, the Temple of the Emerald Buddha, which I felt obliged to show Liz because it is such a remarkable architectural complex. Neither of us could summon up any great interest. True, it was a day of unusual heat and humidity, but the brilliance of the temple seemed shallow, its spiritual purpose grossly commercialised, its precincts overpopulated with unhappy-looking tourists (like me) all armed to the teeth (like me) with sure-fire automatic cameras and menacing sawn-off zoom lenses. We trudged around, as tourists do if only to get their money's worth, and left. What we needed, we decided, was some peace and quiet; we arranged to go to Hua Hin for five days.

Hua Hin had been a sleepy fishing-village in the Sixties, a place where if you rose early you could follow the cattle as they were led through the shallows; you watched their hooves wading through the clear water, retrieved the shellfish they kicked up and took home a bucketful for boiling or frying. After dark, you could walk out along the same stretch of beach, but this time well above the water's edge. You were armed with a good flashlight and a capacious bucket, and you took with you some of the local youngsters. As you strolled along you swung the torch from side to side so that its beam made an arc just a few yards ahead of you. The foraging crabs were startled by the swinging beam of light and, sometimes dozens at a time, would stand on tiptoes and scamper at full pelt down the banked sands towards the sea. They never ran the other way. Your young helpers would bound forward to cut off their chosen quarry before the creatures reached the water, pounce with a yelp and, more often than not, return triumphant to drop the captive into your bucket, which was soon full. Next morning, the granny or auntie of the house where you were staying would produce a delicious breakfast for the whole family: deep-fried fresh whole spider-crabs to be crunched, claws and all.

Of course, Hua Hin was no longer quite the idyllic place I remembered but it did have cheap clean hotels and cheap tasty

seafood, and its pace of life was closer to that of Mandalay. I
tried to telephone Ma Thant, but the operator said that Burma
was not responding. From now on, we would have little more than
Thailand's English-language newspapers to keep us in touch with
what was happening in Burma, and their reporters hardly ever
mentioned Mandalay.

The demonstrators in Rangoon were maintaining their momentum. Student leaders, along with other opposition leaders such as
Aung San Suu Kyi and General Tin Oo, were giving the BSPP an
ultimatum: if the government did not resign, the massive strike
(scheduled to take place the coming Thursday) would not end
until the government had fallen. Meanwhile, soldiers were digging
trenches around the Ministry of Defence – an activity that I found
humorously symbolic at the time – and were also digging in around
other military positions. Government-paid killers were still looting
and slaughtering in an effort to discredit and destabilise the
campaign for democracy. A former Major called Zaw Htaung led
a band of forty thugs in the looting of a biscuit factory, knowing
that the local vigilance committee was bound to appear on the
scene. He had promised his men a substantial bounty for the head
of every monk or student leader they killed. When the committee
and other residents duly turned up, a score of them were killed in
the resulting violence, but eventually almost all the gangsters were
caught and taken to the *hsayadaw* of a nearby monastery, who
promptly ordained them into the monkhood. Presumably they were
given the choice of becoming *hpongyi* or being handed over to the
enraged citizens. If Number One was orchestrating disorder so as
to have an excuse to use bullet and bayonet, the *sanghā* was doing
its best to deny his officers that excuse.

Thursday came – again it was the eighth of the month –
and Rangoon came to a standstill as planned, with perhaps a
million people demonstrating on the streets, still with something
of that exhilarating carnival mood that we had experienced in
Mandalay. The marching contingents included a recently-formed
'Housewives' Union', whose members clanged their pots and
pans as they processed, about two hundred blind folk calling
themselves 'The Union of the Blind', and even a group of
parading transvestites. As well as the monks, there were also some
Christian groups. The Burmese Broadcasting Service, still rigidly

state-controlled, actually admitted that some soldiers had also deserted their posts to join the demonstrators; but it then added the laughable excuse that they were 'mentally ill due to drunkenness and malaria'. This was typical of official announcements designed to explain away the unpalatable truth: it demanded such a degree of credulity that it constituted an insult to the intelligence. I believe it was this underestimation of ordinary people which, more than anything else – more than institutionalised corruption, chronic shortages, inflation or demonetisation – had goaded the populace into the massive but peaceful protests that were still going on.

And still the army did not move. Probably there was no need to because, although there was plenty of opposition to the BSPP, there was still no coherent Opposition. What was needed was an interim government acceptable to all, especially the students and the *sanghā*, with a sensible plan of political reform and economic action. Until such a group appeared, time would be on the side of the BSPP establishment. A Mandalay University colleague had once said to me, 'Put two Burmese together, and you've got an argument.' I hadn't found this true of daily life in Burma, but it was beginning to appear true of Burmese politics. The following day U Nu, Burma's Grand Old Man who had forsaken politics for the study of the Buddhist scriptures, announced that he still considered himself the legitimate Prime Minister and that he had set up a twenty-five member 'parallel government' with named Ministers. This move must have been too high-handed, for it was immediately rejected by the student leaders; and Aung San Suu Kyi expressed astonishment, calling the plan 'preposterous'.

Meanwhile in Mandalay (and how I wished I was still there!) people continued to pour through the streets in tens of thousands. They pleaded with the troops inside the palace to come out and join them. Police units had already joined the cheering crowds, who gave them garlands of flowers in gratitude. There were even rumours that the whole of North-Western Command might defect. This was my last tantalising glimpse of what was going on in Mandalay.

Down in Rangoon, some two hundred uniformed air force men had left Base 502, about fourteen miles north of the city centre and joined student leaders on the university campus. Though they were only privates and low-ranking personnel they constituted the first visible large-scale defection of armed forces, and they were wildly cheered as they marched inside a protective cordon of students. There were reports that the army had orders to shoot these defectors if they attempted to pass a certain point on Prome Road and, when the contingent reached this spot, civilian citizens fell to their knees and begged the soldiers not to shoot. After a tense delay, the soldiers gave way and allowed the group to pass.

In the downtown area soldiers were removing mattresses from the once luxurious but now decrepit Strand Hotel and taking them to the parliament building, which squatted in the centre of a barricaded 'no-demonstration' zone. The Party diehards were obviously expecting that the coming Emergency Congress would be an embattled affair. Elsewhere there were dangerous outbreaks of honesty: the employees' union of the Ministry of Planning and Finance issued a statement that Ministry officials had been forced by the Party 'to draw up false propagandistic reports' so as to hide the truth about the country's economic problems; the Ministry of Foreign Affairs employees' union, deciding to stay on strike for at least another four days, announced that twenty-two of the twenty-nine Burmese embassies around the world had expressed their solidarity with the protesters; and the bank workers' union had closed all the banks, accusing the armed forces of intimidating staff and illegally withdrawing large sums of money. With all this truth flying about, more than two hundred diplomats and dependants were getting ready to leave for Bangkok that evening.

The next day, Saturday 10th September, the Party held its Congress – two days ahead of schedule. Chairman Maung Maung told those assembled that the Party's weakness was that 'it was born as a ruling party and grew up as one', reminded them that absolute power corrupts absolutely, and said that the time had come for free and fair multi-party elections. Many protesters cheered the announcement of these words, but there was really no point in cheering a regime whose resignation you were calling for. Perhaps Burma's biggest handicap by now was that such a large proportion of the population was, in political matters, naïve. Remembering that Ne Win had been virtually in sole command for twenty-six years and assuming that youngsters could hardly develop political awareness before the age of fourteen, one realised that only the over-forties could possibly have any memory – let alone experience – of what democracy meant in practice, of how a multi-party system could be made to work; and most Burmese were under forty. Their slogans and banners demanded 'democracy' and 'a multi-party system' yet, when asked, they could characterise the two concepts only negatively: democracy was something that Ne Win's regime had not practised and competing parties were things that had not been permitted. People were very confident about what they were rejecting and why they were rejecting it; but they were uncertain about the nature of what they were advocating and ignorant of how to set about constructing it. The more thoughtful protesters, including the student leaders, dismissed Maung Maung's pronouncements. They didn't want this government to make concessions yet still be in a position to govern; they wanted it to resign. No regime which in effect said that it was advocating its own downfall but which refused simply to resign, no government of that sort could be trusted.

It really was beginning to look as if you couldn't put two Burmese politicians together without producing dissension: three of U Nu's shadow ministers had already publicly detached themselves from his proposed cabinet. U Nu had not only failed to consult the Bar Association of Burma and the student leaders; it also appeared that he had omitted to inform these three that they were to form part of his cabinet. Or perhaps they had been consulted but were now dissociating themselves because of disagreement over some policy matter. By now, Burma's official newspapers – hitherto rigidly controlled by the state – were giving increasing coverage to opposition news and views, and unofficial news-sheets were proliferating. (Suddenly, there was no paper shortage, I noted.) Documents were circulating which purported to be the genuine minutes of High Command meetings, and at least one of these had turned out to be highly accurate in its prediction of events, whether it was genuine or not. The Chief of Staff of the armed forces, General Saw Maung, was now appealing to the public to cooperate with the military in order to get the proposed general elections under way. But the party had been talking in terms of holding them in a couple of months' time whereas, as Aung San Suu Kyi had observed, it would take a couple of years to make all the necessary arrangements for a bona fide election.

We had now spent a fortnight in the care of the British Embassy in Bangkok. I had been nursing dark misgivings, and these had now composed themselves in the form of a chill premonition. I saw a Burma of the near future, seedy and dismal, its people sullen and abject. An inwardly sneering Ne Win was trying to appear avuncular as he patiently addressed the nation, speaking as one might to a sobbing child that one has had to smack. He was teaching them a lesson, explaining that it had been the Party – the people's own party, after all – which had (at his suggestion) made the way clear for private enterprise; but the ungrateful people had not come forward to support the economy in this way. The Party had then bowed to the people's demands by releasing all detainees; but the people had seen for themselves the consequent destruction and looting and killing. The Party had called for a multi-party system; but this too the people had rejected. The Party had even, in the person of the Chief of Staff himself, begged the people to cooperate with their beloved Tatmadaw – the people's own army, after all – in preparing for general elections; but still the people had not listened. 'All this,' Number One was saying, 'all this is true and can be proved. Even certain foreign and imperialistic media cannot deny it . . .'. The terrible thing about this premonition was that it was true, in a twisted sort of way.

I didn't want to believe that the Burmese people would end up in such a position, but I was convinced that it was Ne Win's intention that they should. A man who could allow his country's economy to bleed dry for a quarter of a century while he stockpiled dollars in Switzerland; a man who could steal the best jewels from the annual Gems Emporium, some of them no doubt destined for his chain of jewellery stores in West Germany; a man who could abandon his country for six weeks every year during the hottest weather, chartering a flight to Europe in order to luxuriate there among his friends, and of course his potential enemies; a man who could countenance the wholesale slaughter of tribespeople in the hills and university students on the plains; a man who could abandon (or at any rate appear to abandon) his nation by suddenly stepping down in such an irresponsible, almost indifferent way; a man who could forsake both common sense and the noble truths of Buddhism for the black arts of *yaddayā*; such a man was surely capable of a megalomanic

sadism that would require the submission and degradation of
a people that rose up against him. Yes, he was teaching them a
lesson.

When Liz and I went off to Khao Yai National Park for a few
days, there still being no instructions for us from the Embassy,
I lost touch with what was happening in Burma because there
were no newspapers or radios in the motel-style accommodation.
But there were clouds of beautiful butterflies, so I spent some
time adding to my collection of photographed specimens. The
park's other distinctive feature was its leeches. They seemed to
be everywhere: not only on the sunless and steamy jungle paths
where you expect them, but also on open patches of mown grass
and up in cultivated bushes, where the butterflies I was stalking
hung like orchids or vibrated like bright tuning-forks or glowed
against the light like stained glass windows. The third morning
was grey and humid. I was pursuing a huge black specimen as
it fluttered into some bushes. I had never seen a member of this
species motionless before, but this one settled on a sheltered leaf,
draped its black forewings over the white-blazoned hind wings
and sat stock-still. This butterfly knew that it was about to rain.
I took a quick photograph and trotted back to our room with the
sighing sound of a steady downpour following me. For almost all
the rest of our stay, the rain kept the butterflies hidden and
me indoors. I peeled off my wet shoes and socks, removed
a leech from an ankle and settled down to read *Labyrinths*,
a collection of disturbing short stories and essays by Jorge
Luis Borges. What I did not know was that, while I was
reading this book, the carnival was coming to a grisly end in
Rangoon.

One of the Borges' essays, 'The Wall and the Books', is about the
Emperor Shih Huang Ti, who united various kingdoms, ordered
the building of the Great Wall of China and decreed that all
books written hitherto be burned. Borges says that he burned
the books 'because his opposition invoked them to praise the
emperors of olden times'. Hm. My colleagues in Mandalay had
occasionally come across a book or document that triggered
memories of the good old days before Ne Win, even before
Independence. I read on.

Shih Huang Ti, according to the historians, forbade that death
be mentioned and sought the elixir of immortality and secluded
himself . . .

That sounded familiar, as did the emperor's 'magic barriers
designed to halt death.' Borges goes on to say that it is not known
whether the book-burning preceded or followed the wall-building.
Depending on which order we choose, he says, we can derive either

the image of a king who began by destroying and then resigned himself
to preserving, or that of a disillusioned king who destroyed what he had
previously defended.

Both of these conjectural images reminded me of Ne Win. He
had not literally built a wall to exclude the barbarian hordes, but he
had partially satisfied his xenophobia by erecting an administrative
barrier around his realm and thus minimised foreign influences
for twenty-six years. (When people are able freely to compare
their own lot with that of others, they are able to evaluate,
complain, challenge. Ne Win's isolationism was, consciously or
unconsciously, a mechanism for preventing any challenge to his
own authority.)

Number One had not actually ordered a burning of books
in an attempt to abolish history, but he had tried to interfere
with the past in cases where he thought his supremacy might
be challenged. One trivial example of this was that he had seen
to the destruction of all photographs in which he had appeared
to be subordinate to Sunshine Lader – except one that Lader had
himself shown me. A more momentous example, one which had
tragic consequences: on the death of the illustrious U Thant, who
had been Secretary-General of the United Nations, Ne Win had
refused to allow the return of the body to Burma so that funeral rites
could be performed there, and many of those who protested were
murdered. So far as I know, Number One had not forbidden any
mention of death; but he had certainly become preoccupied with
fending off his own demise by means of *yaddayā* and I had detected
a suggestion that, in performing these primitive rituals, he viewed
himself as an emperor. In olden times when a monarch died it was
not appropriate to say that he had merely 'died'; it was necessary
to use the language of the court and say that he had 'departed for
the abode of the *Nats*'. There is a village in central Burma whose

name resembles that phrase, and there (rumour had it) Ne Win
had gone to perform *yaddayā* so that it could be said that he had
already visited the abode of the *Nats*, the logic being that you can't
die twice. If he had indeed done this, he had equated himself with
the kings of old. Furthermore, if he hadn't actually sought the elixir
of immortality as Shih Huang Ti had done, he had sought the elixir
of youth which, if it existed, would probably be better: rumour had
it that he had tried not only various medicines and the stimulus of
a young and pretty wife, but also transfusions of a negro youth's
blood, black people being viewed as more vigorous than others by
those ignorant enough to take *yaddayā* seriously. It was only now
that I remembered that Ne Win was himself ethnically Chinese. He
had adopted his Burmese name (which means 'sun-shine' – which
in turn rang bells in my mind) only in the early 1940s, until which
time his name had been Shu (or perhaps Xu?) Maung.

I went back to Borges:

> Perhaps the Emperor . . . called himself Huang Ti so as to *be* in
> some way Huang Ti, the legendary emperor who invented writing and
> the compass.

Did that young man up in the Burmese hills so long ago
call himself Ne Win so as to be in some ways powerful as the
rays of the sun? Was he now deliberately destroying 'what he had
previously defended'? It looked as if that sun was setting blood-red
as he plunged Burma into a night of chaos. But was he hoping that,
if the medicines or the pretty wife or the black man's blood or the
yaddayā worked, he could rise again and in a new dawn earn the
glory that he was said to crave? These speculations were, I knew,
becoming far too fanciful; but then there was no knowing what
devious and ruthless fantasies were being rehearsed in an embattled
mind that was as doomed and as deadly as a dying king cobra.

We got back to Bangkok on the evening of the nineteenth of
September to find that General Saw Maung had put a bloody end
to the Burmese people's aspirations – for the time being, at least.
Of the dawn of a new era there was no sign. There was no point in
waiting any longer.

The *pweh* was over.

Postscript

Almost a year has passed since our arrival back in Manchester one frosty morning, but my little white jeep is still on the high seas, half my mind is still in Mandalay and Ne Win is still working his sinister Punch and Judy show in Rangoon. My HoD retired, the colleague who edited the university magazine became a *hpongyi* and the others have soldiered on, organising self-help training-sessions day after day. Those known to have been active in the demonstrations are being posted to other towns in an attempt to destroy the jubilant solidarity that I had been privileged to see. Of my dear friend Ma Thant and of Gerry's Angels I have heard nothing for some time.

Along with thousands of other despairing young people, Ma Thuzar left her beloved Burma; she is studying in California. The young dentist–comedian Zā Ganā was not so fortunate. He was arrested soon after Saw Maung's pitiless clampdown. His only crime had been to make people laugh at the transparent manoeuvres of the military blockheads manipulating political affairs from behind the scenes – especially, of course, Number One's subterfuges. It is reported that the MI's interrogators hung Zā Ganā upside-down and made him go through his routine of satirical jokes, and that he was so badly beaten up that he was hardly recognisable. He had lost, no doubt as the result of a little light-hearted military satire, most of his teeth. And still Ne Win goes on punishing his people. Today's paper (*The Guardian*, 21/10/89) tells me that according to the government's own announcement a hundred people have been sentenced to death in the past three months alone. I shudder to think what the true figure would be. Because it has nothing to gain financially from doing so, the British government has publicly expressed no concern, cautious or otherwise, about such matters.

After the heartbreaking slaughter of tens of thousands in Rangoon and other towns in 1988 came the sickening experience of watching events unfold in Beijing, in the sure knowledge that what had happened in Burma (and had already been forgotten) was about to happen again in China. It was all so chillingly similar.

There was the same festival atmosphere as first the university students, then the workers and even the security forces joined in the demonstrations that demanded just a bit of democracy – a concept as foreign to Chinese youngsters as it is to their Burmese neighbours. There was the same absence of violence, the good humour as demonstrators chatted to 'the People's Army'; the long period of inaction on the part of the government as the protests spread to all parts of the country; then the same brutal assault that silenced the reasoning and pleading, not just at a distance with anonymous bullets but also at close quarters with bayonets and, this time, even tank tracks. Because the foreign devils were in Beijing with their cameras the world was able to see and to shudder at the events in Tien-an-men Square; ten times as many had fallen in Burma.

Then there was the same fervent desire on the part of the people that the outsider should photograph, record, tell the world what had really happened; because they knew there was within the Party that same compulsion to reinterpret the events, hiding any facts that could be hidden, distorting any that could not be denied outright and fabricating evidence that would seem to justify the military action. The official lies showed the same contempt of the average person's intelligence: only 'a minority of ruffians' were to blame, who were waging a bloody rebellion; only twenty-three students died in Tien-an-men Square; and so on. There was the same reliance on foreign broadcasts for the truth, the same military disposal of bodies without funeral rites; and there were the same frontal exit wounds.

The geriatric Chinese government called the protesters 'scum' and the 'scum' called the old men 'fascists', the word used in many of Mandalay's posters to describe Ne Win and his clique. The scum (roughly one human being in five) had been brought up to believe that Communism and Fascism stood at opposite ends of a line in positions labelled 'Left' and 'Right', and that the two were as different as night and day. If ever the peoples of Burma and China really believed this, they have learned the hard way that the straight line is a false metaphor. They know that the line should be made into a circular dial by bending its two extremes upwards to meet at a totalitarian midnight, and that the difference between their socialism and fascism may be only as big as the difference between a minute to midnight and a minute past. Sunday may change to Monday, one year become another; but the darkness is the same.

Manchester, 21 October 1989

Appendix

A further account of the massacre in Sagaing

In the students' own 'news room' inside Mandalay University there was an exhibit giving an account of the massacre and a map of the town centre where the butchery occurred. Names of some of those committing the atrocities were also given. Having photographed this exhibit, I got it translated by Burmese friends in Britain. Here it is.

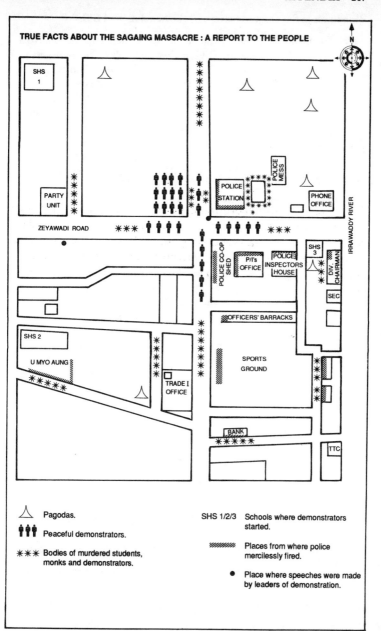

TRUE FACTS ABOUT THE SAGAING MASSACRE : A REPORT TO THE PEOPLE

SHS 1

PARTY UNIT

ZEYAWADI ROAD

POLICE STATION

POLICE MESS

PHONE OFFICE

IRRAWADDY RIVER

POLICE CO-OP SHED

P/I's OFFICE

POLICE INSPECTORS HOUSE

SHS 3

DIV. CHAIRMAN

SEC

OFFICERS' BARRACKS

SHS 2

U MYO AUNG

TRADE I OFFICE

SPORTS GROUND

BANK

TTC

△ Pagodas.

👤👤👤 Peaceful demonstrators.

✳✳✳ Bodies of murdered students, monks and demonstrators.

SHS 1/2/3 Schools where demonstrators started.

▨ Places from where police mercilessly fired.

● Place where speeches were made by leaders of demonstration.

Bloodbath in Sagaing: Massacre by the henchmen of B.S.P.P.

8/8/88 (08.00 hours)   Demonstrations started at State High School No.1. Sagaing Division People's Police Force ruthlessly manhandled and captured leader U Tin Win and some student leaders. When the demonstrators asked the PPF to release them the Police started shooting and as a result two students got shot and one of them died of the injuries.

9/8/88   Student leaders and monks led a peaceful demonstration through the town and made their headquarters at SHS 2. They again demanded the release of U Tin Win and the student leaders.

(14.40 hours)   Because the Police said that they were going to release the leaders of the demonstration, most of the people of Sagaing went to greet them. Without any form of warning the authorities mercilessly shot into the groups of people. The pattern of shooting was not to disperse the the crowds, but with intent to kill. They were shooting from all places around the town as shown in the map. During that massacre altogether 218 people died including children, monks and students who were unarmed, and an additional 100 people were injured. The authorities were shooting from trenches, on top of trees and from houses. They not only shot people down from the front but from behind as well. It is very clear from the events that it was premeditated murder. To make matters worse they further killed the injured who were lying down, and tried to get rid of the bodies. Some of the bodies were taken in to the Police Station compound to make it look as if the demonstrators were attacking the Police Station. The person solely responsible for the above events is Sagaing Division People's Council Chairman Kyaw Zwa. This report is to let people know how evil and cruel the B.S.P.P. are. These are all true facts and no form of exaggeration is included in the report.

DOWN WITH THE B.S.P.P. Our revolution must succeed.

Upper Burma Students' Union
Mandalay University
Mandalay

Bibliography

This is a personal list of books that helped me to understand Burma. Other useful titles can be found in the bibliographies of Bunge (1983) and Gottberg (1984), listed below.

Archaeology Department, Ministry of Culture, *Pictorial guide to Pagan*. Rangoon: Ministry of Culture, 1963.

Boudignon, Françoise. *A letter from Burma*. Rangoon: UNICEF, 1984.

Bunge, Frederica M. (ed), *Burma: a country study*. Washington, D.C.: Department of the Army, 1983.

Burma Socialist Programme Party, *The system of correlation of Man and his environment*. Rangoon: BSPP, Sarpay Beikman Press, 1963.

Collis, Maurice, *The land of the great image*. London: Faber & Faber, 1946.

Collis, Maurice, *The grand peregrination*. London: Faber & Faber, 1949.

Collis, Maurice, *Into hidden Burma*. London: Faber & Faber, 1953.

Cornyn, William, *Outline of Burmese grammar*. Baltimore, Md.: Linguistic Society of America, 1944.

Courtauld, Caroline, *In search of Burma*. London: Frederick Muller Ltd, 1984.

Courtauld, Caroline, *A guide to Burma – Asia's secret treasure trove*. Bangkok: Asia Books Co., 1988.

Cox, Hiram, *Journal of a residence in the Burmahn Empire*, etc. London: John Warren and G. & W.B. Whittaker, 1821.

Curle, Richard, *Into the East: notes on Burma and Malaya*. London: Macmillan & Co. Ltd, 1923.

Edwardes, M, *Ralph Fitch: Elizabethan in the Indies*. London: Faber & Faber, 1972.

Fergusson, B., *Beyond the Chindwin*. London: Collins, 1945.

Fergusson, Bernard, *The wild green earth*. London: Collins, 1946.

Fergusson, Bernard, *Return to Burma*. London: Collins, 1962.

Ferrars, Max and Ferrars, Bertha, *Burma*. London: Sampson Low, Marston and Company, 1900.

Fielding Hall, H., *The soul of a people*. London: Macmillan & Co., 1898.

Foucar, E.C.V., *They reigned in Mandalay*. London: Dennis Dobson Ltd, 1946.

Foucar, E.C.V., *I lived in Burma*. London: Dennis Dobson Ltd, 1956.

Fraser, J.F., *Quaint subjects of the King*. London: Cassell & Co. Ltd., 1909.

Gottberg, John (ed), *Burma* (Insight Guides series). Hong Kong: Apa Productions (HK) Ltd, 1984.

Harcourt Robinson, C., *Burmese vignettes*. London: Luzac & Co. Ltd, 1949.

Hearsey, May, *Land of chindits and rubies*. London: Mrs M.A. Leverston-Allen, 1982.

Hunt, Gordon, *The forgotten land*. London: Geoffrey Bles, 1967.

Huxley, Aldous, *Jesting Pilate: the diary of a journey*. London: Chatto & Windus Ltd, 1926.

Kingdon Ward, F., *Burma's icy mountains*. London: Jonathan Cape, 1949.

Klein, Wilhelm, *Burma the golden*. Hong Kong: Apa Productions Ltd, 1982.

LeMay, Reginald, *The culture of South-East Asia*. London: George Allen & Unwin Ltd, 1954.

Lewis, N., *Golden earth*. London: Jonathan Cape, 1952.

Lu Pe Win, *Historic sites and monuments of Mandalay and environs*. Rangoon: UBSCP, 1960.

Lu Pe Win, *Pagodas of Pagan*. Rangoon: BSCP, 1966.

Ma Mya Sein, *Burma*. London: Oxford University Press, 1944.

Mannin, Ethel, *Land of the crested Lion*. London: Jarrolds Ltd, 1955.

Masters, John, *The road past Mandalay: a personal narrative*. London: Michael Joseph, 1961.

Maugham, Somerset, *The gentleman in the parlour: a record of a journey from Rangoon to Haiphong*. New York: Doubleday, Doran, 1930.

Maung Htin Aung, *Folk elements in Burmese Buddhism*. London, New York: Oxford University Press, 1962.

Mead, Margaret (ed), *Cultural patterns and technical change*. Paris: UNESCO, 1955.

Orwell, George, *Burmese days*. London: Victor Gollancz, 1935.

Pe Maung Tin & G.H. Luce, *The glass palace chronicle of the kings of Burma*. London: Oxford University Press, 1923.

Phayre, Lt. Gen. Sir Arthur P., *History of Burma*. New York: Kelley, 1883 (reprinted 1969).

Raven-Hart, Major R., *Canoe to Mandalay*. London: Frederick Muller Ltd, 1939.

Richards, C.J., *The Burman – an appreciation*. (Burma Pamphlet No.7) London: Longmans, Green & Co. Ltd., 1945.

Rodriguez, Helen, *Helen of Burma*. London & Glasgow: Collins, 1983.

Sangermano, Father V., *A description of the Burmese Empire*. (trans. Tandy, W.) Westminster: Archibald Constable, 1893.

Scott, Sir J.G., *Burma and beyond*. London: Grayson & Grayson Ltd, 1932.

Scott O'Connor, V.C., *Mandalay and other cities of the past in Burma*. London: Hutchinson & Co., 1907.

Seagrave, G.S., *Burma surgeon*. London: Victor Gollancz, 1944.

Shway Yoe (Sir J.G. Scott), *The Burman: his life and notions*. London: Macmillan, 1882.

Slim, Field Marshal Sir William, *Defeat into victory*. London: Cassell, 1956.

Sykes, C., *Orde Wingate*. London: Collins, 1959.

Talbot Kelly, R., *Burma*. London: A & C Black, 1905.

Tennyson Jesse F., *The lacquer lady*. London: Heinemann, 1929.

Tennyson Jesse F., *The story of Burma*. London: Macmillan & Co Ltd, 1946.

Theroux, Paul, *The great railway bazaar*. London: Hamish Hamilton, 1975.

Toke Galé, *Burmese timber elephant*. Rangoon: Trade Corporation (9), 1974.

Wheeler, Tony, *Burma: a travel survival kit*. South Yarra, Victoria: Lonely Planet Publications, 1985.

Williams, J.H., *Elephant Bill*. London: Rupert Hart-Davis, 1950.

Williams, J.H., *Bandoola*. London: Rupert Hart-Davis, 1953.

Williams, Susan, *Elephant boy*. London: William Kimber, 1963.

Winston, W.R., *Four years in Upper Burma*. London: C.H. Kelly, 1892.